W9-DFN-904

The Labor Economies of Japan and the United States

Robert Evans, Jr.
foreword by
Solomon B. Levine

The Praeger Special Studies program—utilizing the most modern and efficient book production techniques and a selective worldwide distribution network—makes available to the academic, government, and business communities significant, timely research in U.S. and international economic, social, and political development.

The Labor Economies of Japan and the United States

PRAEGER SPECIAL STUDIES IN INTERNATIONAL ECONOMICS AND DEVELOPMENT

Praeger Publishers New York Washington London

PRAEGER PUBLISHERS
111 Fourth Avenue, New York, N.Y. 10003, U.S.A.
5, Cromwell Place, London S.W.7, England

Published in the United States of America in 1971
by Praeger Publishers, Inc.

Library of Congress Catalog Card Number: 77-153834

Printed in the United States of America

FOREWORD

In recent years, social scientists as well as other scholars have been increasingly concerned about the narrowness and ethnocentricity of their disciplines in understanding and explaining human behavior in diverse national contexts. This concern has given rise to numerous urgings that scholars broaden their investigations beyond the confines of their own national borders, especially for the purpose of testing the validity of theoretical concepts and analytical approaches through inter-country comparisons. Undoubtedly, these urgings reflect the viewpoint that the world of scholarship should truly be global, that hope for peace in international relations lies in large measure upon the free flow of ideas and common understanding across national boundaries, and that the nations of the world are becoming increasingly interlocked economically and politically.

Many scholars throughout the world have responded to these deeply-felt needs, and international comparative analysis, particularly in the social sciences, has become a major new thrust within universities and scholarly communities everywhere. Unfortunately, many of the attempts to carry our comparative studies on a cross-national basis have only revealed the large difficulties and the considerable time involved in their undertaking. Too often, either the results produced have tended to focus almost exclusively upon one country or another without going beyond implicit comparisons, or they have tended toward superficial treatments lacking analytical depth and sophistication and bordering on misinterpretation. While some of these works have been path-breaking and enormously rich and insightful, they remain but the beginnings of the development of comparative method in the field of international studies.

In this light, Professor Evans' study is a rare event. It is among the very few inter-country comparisons that have come forth with explicit focus on analyzing the differences and similarities in certain important aspects of economic and social life between two major nations of the Western and non-Western worlds. While the study may generate academic disagreements over its methodological approach, findings, and conclusions, nonetheless it stands out as a singular model for the in-depth type of international comparative analysis that has long been overdue in the discipline of economics and the social sciences generally.

Lying behind the book is the careful preparation and thoughtful consideration for the research problems Professor Evans investigated. As has been the case in other scholarly works by the author, he did not take his task lightly. At least two years were spent in preparing for data gathering in Japan, including substantial and intensive study of the Japanese language and of the history, economy, and culture of Japan. A full year was required solely for gathering data in Japan and, as a highly important component in cross-national research, in discussing and collaborating with colleagues in the Japanese scholarly community. Another two years were devoted to preparing the analysis, rechecking data, and further work with scholars in Japan and elsewhere.

Throughout this process, Professor Evans has maintained an admirable perspective. Not only does the study focus on an important set of questions of vital concern to the economies of both the United States and Japan, but the questions are not treated within narrow disciplinary confines. While the application of economic analysis is a chief focus of the study, Professor Evans has been markedly conscious of the influence of history, law, culture, social structure and other non-economic aspects of human behavior in both nations. This intermixture reflects his long-held concern with viewing economic activity within its total social context, especially when dealing with the development, evolution, and operation of markets for labor, the human factor of production.

This remarkable blend of both disciplinary and inter-disciplinary considerations is reflected, I am sure, in the balanced conclusions. Professor Evans reaches in comparing the labor economies of Japan and the United States. He is not led to conclude on the one hand that the two nations, the first and third most productive economies in the world today, have little or nothing in common with one another, nor to the opposite pole that economic growth and industrialization have been producing two increasingly convergent societies. Rather, he sees persistent similarities and differences--"a similarity interlaced with differences," as he puts it--which not only help Americans to gain important insights of Japan and Japanese of America, but also to gain insights of themselves compared to any other nation. As Professor Evans points up, depending upon which aspect of economic life one wishes to focus upon, the differences or similarities may become more pronounced, but their relative strength rests on viewing any given aspect within a total framework of a nation that encompasses its social structures, institutions, and functional processes. The book succeeds in conveying this perspective.

Professor Evans' study is a source of personal pleasure for me. It was the good fortune of the Keio-Illinois Research and Exchange Program in Industrial Relations, of which I have been an active member, to learn of Professor Evans' interest in extending his work on labor market behavior to Japan. Thanks to the support of the Ford Foundation, which largely financed the Program, Keio University and the University of Illinois were able to sponsor Professor Evans' preparation and work in the field, as one of several studies undertaken by American and Japanese labor scholars individually and in collaboration with one another. Thanks to his deep sense of commitment to the study and to the analytical and conceptual skills he eagerly applied in this work, Professor Evans' book has notably advanced the efforts long needed in the field of cross-national comparative study.

Solomon B. Levine

PREFACE

This work had its origin in a casual conversation with a friend, Hanami Tadashi,[*] professor of Law at Sophia University in Tokyo. We were discussing the U. S. Departments of Commerce and Labor and Japanese Ministries of Labor and International Trade and Industry's joint publication, Nichi-Bei Ryōkoku no Chingin Jijō (Wages in Japan and the United States). Like many government documents, it contained an abundance of facts but little analysis. In the course of the conversation, I undertook to write a book that would analyze many of the aspects covered in the government document. I hope this book accomplishes that purpose.

The last decade has seen an increasing interest in comparative labor studies and in the degree to which universal principles apply to industrial relations in different countries. In order to further our understanding of the dynamics of industrial relations systems, it will be necessary to undertake and complete a number of comparative studies. These will have a variety of forms, including the extensive comparison of the systems of two countries, the form of this work. Thus, my aim is to make a contribution to comparative labor studies by examining the performance of selected aspects of the labor economies of Japan and the United States.

The subject matter represents a mixture of many factors. The emphasis has been upon the traditional concerns of the labor economist: wages, mobility, etc. This is in part because the more institutional aspects of the Japanese industrial relations system have been the focus of several recent books which have also given some consideration to comparative factors. A more important reason for the emphasis on the economic dimensions is my own interest in these areas and a conviction that the essence of an industrial relations system lies in the economic relationships. In the economic area the choice of subject matter has been shaped largely by those concerns which have been central to the labor economies of both countries and for which adequate data and studies exist.

[*] Japanese names follow conventional Japanese usage, with the surname first. The same order is used in the citation of Japanese-language materials, but author names of all English language materials follow the Western order.

Japan is often seen by foreign scholars and visitors as "different" and thus set apart. I do not wish to diminish the rich cultural heritage, the calm beauty, the language (with which I daily struggle), all of which combine to form the uniqueness that is Japan. Yet it is my feeling that, in general, and especially for labor economics, the differences between Japan and the United States are more apparent than real. Shūshin Koyō (lifetime employment) is said to characterize Japanese employment practices, yet millions of employees are not so engaged. In the United States one speaks of a lifetime of job mobility, yet for millions, and increasingly so, lifetime employment is available to the individual who wishes it. This conviction that the dynamics of the respective economies are increasingly similar despite surface dissimilarities represents one attitude which underlies the book. I trust that the reader will agree.

My special debts are almost too numerous to name. The primary one is to Professor Solomon B. Levine (University of Wisconsin), who first encouraged my interest in Japan, assisted in arranging for me to participate in the Keio University-University of Illinois Exchange Program, and throughout the intervening years has provided helpful comments and support. In Japan my chief debt is to Professor Sano Yōko, whose work on Shuntō is extensively cited. She also provided guidance for my research and assisted with day-to-day problems during my year in Japan. Chapter 5 draws heavily upon earlier work done in connection with Professor George Delehanty at Northwestern University. Professors Bernard Karsh (University of Illinois), Henry Rosovsky (Harvard), Kozo Yamamura (Boston College), and Charles A. Myers (M.I.T.) have offered helpful comments. In Japan the staffs of the Sangyō Kenkyuū Sho, (Institute of Labor and Management Studies, in Japanese commonly referred to as Sanken) under the direction of Minemura Teruo, and the Japan Institute of Labor, under the direction of Nakayama Ichiro, were of great assistance. At the Japan Institute of Labor these included Professors Shirai Taishirō, Matsuda Yasuhiko, and Hanami Tadashi. At Sanken they were Professors Tsujimura Kōtarō, Obi Keiichiro, Ozaki Iwao, Nishikawa Shunsaku, Nihei Yasumitsu, Kuroda Masahiro, Izeki Tashikai, Torri Yasuhiko, and Shimada Haruo. The staffs of a number of companies which support Sanken graciously answered questions and provided tours of their facilities.

Part of this material was presented at the Industrial Relations Seminar at M.I.T. and at meetings of the Japan Economic Seminar under the direction of Professors Henry

Rosovsky (Harvard), Hugh Patrick (Yale), and James Nakamura (Columbia). The comments of those attending were appreciated.

The bulk of the work associated with the preparation of the material was made possible by a two-year association with the Keio University-University of Illinois Exchange Program, including one year as a visiting professor in the Sangyō Kenkyū Sho at Keio University. Much of the writing was supported by a summer grant from the East Asian Research Center at Harvard University. I am indebted to all three institutions, but they should not be held accountable for any of the views expressed here.

My gratitude to my wife Lois and my children--Karen, Robert, Janet, Thomas, Linda, and Laura--is extensive. Their enjoyment of our year in Japan added to the pleasure of this work and made the many hours more worthwhile.

CONTENTS

Chapter		Page

Chapter Page

LIST OF TABLES

Table		Page
14	Male Job Tenure, United States, 1968	83
15	Wages in Japan and the United States, 1948-69	103
16	Consumer Prices, Japan and the United States, 1948-69	106
17	Labor Productivity, Japan and the United States, 1948-69	109
18	Labor Force and Labor Force Participation Rates, Japan and the United States, 1948-69	112
19	Unemployment and Quit Rates, Japan and the United States, 1948-69	113
20	Shuntō Statistics, Japan, 1956-70	128
21	Skilled/Unskilled Wage Differentials, United States, 1914-69	162
22	Skilled/Unskilled Wage Differentials, Nonelectrical Machinery Industry, United States, 1945-68	163
23	Size-of-Firm Wage Differentials, Japan, 1909-67	171
24	Manufacturing Statistics, Japan, 1919-39	173
25	Wage Ratios, Japan, 1919-38	174
26	Iron and Shipbuilding Wage Ratios, Japan, 1898-1936	177
27	Indexes of Selected Wage Differentials, Japan, 1927, 1933, 1936	181
28	Representative Manufacturing Wage Differentials, Japan, 1968	183
29	Dispersion of Monthly Wages in Manufacturing, Japan, 1958 and 1965	186

Table		Page
30	Selected Wage Differentials, Japan, 1954-69	187
31	Size-of-Establishment Wage Differentials in Manufacturing, United States and Japan	192
32	Low-Wage Manufacturing Industries, United States, 1963 and 1969	209
33	Low-Wage Manufacturing Industries, United States, 1958 and 1963	211
34	Low-Wage Manufacturing Industries, Japan, 1963 and 1967	215
35	Cross-Sectional Characteristics of Low-Wage and Nonlow-Wage Industries, Japan, 1963 and 1967	218
36	Three-Digit Industries Which Escaped the Low-Wage Trap, 1954-63, 1963-67	239

The Labor Economies of Japan and the United States

CHAPTER

1

THE LABOR MARKET'S INSTITUTIONAL CONTEXT

INTRODUCTION

The U.S. labor movement grew up in the shadow of European labor, especially that of Great Britain, and its activities, wages, strengths, and failures were constantly being compared, often unfavorably, with what had been accomplished in Europe. Thus the comparative analysis of labor and labor economies has a long tradition, but it was probably not until 1960, with the publication of Industrialism and Industrial Man by Clark Kerr and associates,[1] and a number of related books and articles which have followed, that international comparative analysis became a central concern to the American labor scholar. This recent increase of interest in comparative studies among labor scholars reflects several factors, the most basic of which is a desire to develop a theory to explain the universal and particularistic characteristics of national systems of industrial relations. What are the factors which lead some patterns to re-create themselves regardless of national boundaries and others to give rise to unique, culture-bound solutions? Coal mines are dirty, dangerous, and isolated everywhere. Does this give them an impact upon industrial relations which is the same in Pennsylvania as in Kyūshū? The ability to answer that specific question and, more generally, to have a theoretical understanding of the answer would be greatly prized. The evolution of such a theory will follow various paths. Some will involve tracing a single aspect, such as labor protest or strikes across a number of countries.[2] Others will concentrate upon a more extensive comparison among a smaller number of countries. This study is an attempt to provide an intense bi-country study of selected aspects of labor economies which may then be valuable either in the development of such a theory or in its testing.

Beyond knowledge for its own sake and the neatness of a sophisticated theoretical understanding of the world, an intercountry analysis has a practical usefulness for discussions of labor policy in the United States. Labor policy discussions divide into two types: debate over appropriate goals--such as the freedom of unions to organize without management coercion--and evaluations of various institutional arrangements or policy variables are designed to achieve a given policy goal. These evaluations of policy variables or institutions are very difficult, partly because the federalization of labor policy has made it impossible to alter laws and administrative arrangements in only a few states in order to observe their impact. The states can no longer serve as social laboratories, but in a limited way it is possible to substitute the experience of another country. If one observes that quite diverse institutional arrangements in two countries seem to coexist with relatively similar patterns of wage differentials, then one may be less confident concerning the ease with which wage differentials may be influenced by institutional or governmental policy changes. The results of this inquiry should be of value in such determinations.

Why draw a comparison between Japan and the United States when their institutions, cultures, and levels of economic development are so divergent? In part the choice was prompted by the fascination for all things American which the Japanese have had since Admiral Perry ended her self-imposed isolation in 1854. In 1969 the gross national product of Japan was the third largest in the world. Her shipyards built more than half the free world's new ship tonnage. The products of her automobile industry (Toyotas, Datsuns, etc.) are becoming as commonplace upon our streets as the products of her camera and audio industries have become in our homes. In accomplishing all this Japan has become the only non-Western nation to achieve sustained and successful economic growth. Politically she has gone in the lifetime of most adults from being a hated enemy to being a trusted friend. For these and a thousand other reasons, the working of her economy, the minds of her people, and their style and way of life have been of intense interest to the foreigner.

Students of labor have been no exception. A knowledge of some aspects of Japanese industrial relations--primarily unionism, collective bargaining, the legal aspects of union management relationships, and employment practices--has recently been made available to readers of English in several books and a number of articles. Yet other aspects of her labor economy--aggregate wages, wage differentials, manpower problems, etc.--have been left largely to articles tucked away in various journals. Hence, one subsidiary object of this book is to present these aspects of Japan's labor economy in an analytical context.

Japan's labor economy could have been studied by itself. Yet because Japan is the only non-Western country to achieve sustained growth, the question is often raised of the extent to which its method of development represents an alternative and perhaps superior guide for developing nations of today to the experience of either the United States or the Soviet Union. For example, it was discussed frequently at the Japan Labor Institute's Second International Conference in 1967. This question is perhaps best answered in terms of a comparative analysis, for only in such a context can the uniqueness of the Japanese labor experience be fruitfully understood. An added impetus to the comparison comes from what seems to be an undue emphasis by some scholars upon the differences between Japan and other countries, especially in the area of industrial relations. Last, it is the labor economies of these two countries, the United States and Japan, which have been the professional interest of the author and in which he can make a contribution.

It would be natural to begin such an inquiry with a universal theory of labor markets, but such a theory does not exist. One alternative would be the use of neoclassical wage and employment theories. Yet helpful as these might be, their essence is in statements of equilibrium conditions. Consequently, these theories imply little if anything about dynamic paths toward equilibrium or the institutional forms in which the specifics of the equilibrium state are worked out. A second alternative would be to adopt some version of the convergence thesis, the idea that the process of industrialism generates an inherent logic of its own, a logic which in time brings all economies to a general similarity. The most widely discussed version of the convergence thesis is still the one set forth by Clark Kerr and his colleagues.[3]

Two hypotheses may be drawn from the approach of Kerr and his associates: (1) that as industrialism proceeds, the setting of rules in the labor market becomes so complex that more and more groups must be given a voice in their determination, and (2) that the rules become less particularistic by area, industry, occupation, etc., and more universal in character.[4] There is nothing in the concepts of greater democratization of rule-setting and particularistic rules becoming more universal that necessarily implies that the roles of the rule-setters would be the same in different economies or that the universal rules toward which the particularistic ones would evolve would be the same in two different economies.

Therefore, no convenient or useful theory of social change is available. The lack of such a theory forces us back upon an ad hoc system of trying to bring together the major similarities and differences.[5] Most of the explanatory mechanisms for the principal differences and similarities, as well as for minor and allied ones, which will be suggested in the following chapters may be identified as belonging to one of three broad classes of factors: technology, history and culture, and the stage of economic development. The association of the characteristics of the economies with these causal factors will be central to the analysis which follows.

The role of technology is complex and varied. A particular technology will largely dictate the ratio of men to machines for a given level of output. It will strongly influence the optimum sizes of plants or firms. New technology will require new skills and may even modify the traditional pattern of employee skill acquisition. These impingements of technology upon the labor market will result in altered patterns of wages, levels of employment, and perhaps even in the dynamics of equilibrium adjustment and in the encouragement of retardation of employee organization.

It is simple enough to stress the importance of history and culture in the definition of a country's industrial relations system, but it is more difficult to identify the essence of the history or culture which has played the critical role. Nor is it only a nation's own history which is important, for clearly post-Marxian union history must reflect a pattern different from that of 18th-century union stirrings in England and the United States. Perhaps the most difficult aspect in understanding the role of history and culture is to distinguish between differences in form which are highly influenced and those in substance which may or may not be equally affected. Certainly the latter is of a particular importance in a comparison between a Western and a non-Western country.

In the abstract the stage of economic development is

probably the most easily understood of the three. The manner in which it is handled is less obvious. The Japan of 1900, only 40 years out of seclusion and with a railroad network only just beginning, cannot be compared directly with the United States, which by 1900 had a fully developed railroad network. Then which year in U. S. history does one use? As will be seen, simple rules are not sufficient, and individual judgment must be used for each situation.

The principal applications of these three--technology, history and culture, and level of economic development--lies in the chapters dealing with labor supply and mobility, aggregate wage movements, wage differentials, and low-wage industries. Yet it is not possible adequately to understand and appreciate the meaning of various levels and movements of wages, etc., without some knowledge of their institutional setting.

In1968 many unions in the United States were discussing early retirement for their members, and workers for whom early retirement was already available were increasingly choosing to retire before reaching the customary age of 65. Yet in the same year in Japan 74 percent of retirement-age workers were still employed, 54 percent of them by the firm from which they retired.[6] In the United States a year-end bonus is both rare and often limited to a plump turkey for Christmas dinner. Bonuses in 1968 constituted only 1.0 percent of total employee compensation. In place of the plump turkey the Japanese worker's bonus might be equal to as much as six months' wages. The average yearly bonus in 1969 was equal to three months' wages. Consequently, the summer and winter bonuses are eagerly awaited by workers, their families, and the owners of large department stores.

These examples suggest that there are wide differences in the employment characteristics in Japan and in the United States. Nor is it only in employment practices that the differences between U.S. and Japanese ways seem very great. As Bernard Karsh[7] has pointed out, even concepts like "freedom of association," "the right to strike," and "collective bargaining" appear to mean substantially different things to Americans and to Japanese.

A complete understanding of the reality and meaning of these differences would involve extensive familiarity with the many political, social, economic, and moral contexts of the labor markets--in other words, a knowledge and appreciation of each country's industrial relations system. In that way one could understand why a concept such as "freedom of association" means different things in the two countries.

Yet for most comparative analyses of labor markets it is neither possible nor necessary to achieve a complete understanding of the industrial relations system. The minimum requirement is an appropriate knowledge of those contexts and institutions which significantly affect the operations of the labor markets or whose linguistic terms give a distinct flavor to a country's industrial relations system. In the free world economies, the employment relationship is the minimum institutional context which must be understood prior to a comparative examination of the major wage and employment patterns. This is because the role of the state typically involves only the most limited control over other institutional arrangements--for example, the allocation of employees to employers or workers to specific occupations. In addition, the determination of the terms and conditions of employment is typically left almost entirely to private parties, often with no real guidelines provided by the central government.

The employment relationship has two major aspects which must be understood: the interaction between an individual and his employer, and the more structured relationship between employers and their organized (unionized) employees. Consequently this chapter will be concerned largely with the degree of similarity or dissimilarity between individual employment relationships in Japan and the United States and the different experience of unionism in the two countries.

UNION DEVELOPMENT AND GROWTH

In recent years there have been several attempts to develop a conceptual framework for the analysis of labor movements which are set in different cultures and time periods. These have been useful in giving labels to the leadership groups and to providing classifications of alternative strategies which they might follow. They have also shown that the various elements of a strategy will hang together in a consistent manner. Yet, as Adolph Sturmthal notes, these frameworks do not indicate how the choice of strategies is determined in any given country.[8] Consequently, there is really no basis upon which to judge which type of leadership group and strategy will evolve in a particular country, and thus it is inappropriate to use these frameworks as a model against which union development in Japan and America can be judged. Lacking a general model, an alternative would be to select one country as "most typical" and then examine other countries in terms of the representative country's experience. This, too, is undesirable because there is no basis upon which to choose a "most typical" country.[9]

In the absence of a more elegant model for union development, we are forced back upon the view that (1) there are various social, psychological, political, and economic factors associated with union growth and (2) the particular pattern of any country will depend upon the interactions of these variables. From this it follows that attention should be given to key situations and events. Thus the basic development of the labor movements in Japan and the United States can be traced out by a concentration on the events and variables of several key situations.

Unions in the United States

An overview of union growth in the United States may be obtained in the context of nine special periods.[10] These are (1) the years from about 1825 to 1835, (2) the two decades before and after the beginning of the Civil War, (3) the era of the Knights of Labor, (4) the success and failure of the American Federation of Labor from 1886 to 1914, (5) World War I, (6) the 1920's, (7) the Wagner Act and the Congress of Industrial Organizations, (8) World War II, and (9) postwar decline and stagnation. The relevant statistical data on the course of unionism for selected years are given in Table 1. It is evident from the table that, with the exception of a very short period peak in 1886, the union movement did not become a significant part of the nonagricultural labor force until about 1920, when it counted some 16 percent of the workers as members. The figures in Table 1 also suggest the operation of cyclical elements because, until 1930, high points of union organization, such as 1864, 1886, and 1920, were followed by sharp declines in membership--they did not serve as plateaus from which new organizing drives were launched. An additional point of interest is that the high-water mark of unionism, as measured by the proportion of the labor force which was organized, was reached in 1945, when 35.5 percent of the nonagricultural labor force was organized. Since 1945, and especially since 1954, the growth in the labor force has outpaced gains in union membership.

The initial efforts toward unionism in the 1820's contained three aspects which are particularly germane. First, the

TABLE 1

Union Membership in the United States, Selected Years

Year	No. of Members (thousands)	Percent of Nonagricultural Workers
1864	200	4.4*
1880	200	2.3
1886	800	17.1*
1890	372	2.7
1900	867	4.8
1910	2,141	8.4
1920	5,048	16.3
1930	3,401	11.6
1940	8,717	26.9
1945	14,322	35.5
1950	14,267	31.5
1954	17,022	34.7
1960	17,049	31.4
1966	17,940	28.4
1968	18,916	27.9

*Estimate.

Note: Canadian members of American unions are included before 1930 but are excluded after that.

Sources: 1880-1920: Lloyd Ulman, "American Trade Unionism--Past and Present," in Seymour E. Harris, ed., *American Economic History* (New York: McGraw Hill, 1961), pp. 393, 421. 1930-68: United States Bureau of Labor Statistics, *Handbook of Labor Statistics, 1970*, p. 339.

unions were largely local in character, their members and concerns limited to a single urban center. Second, the members of the unions were not, for the most part, factory employees but skilled indigenous craftsmen. Third, the unions had close relations with middle-class elements, and many of their demands were not directly related to the work place.

The next period of significant unionism covers roughly the years from 1850 to the sharp recession of 1877-78. During these years may be found the beginnings of at least a few national unions which are still in existence: the Typographical Workers in 1852, the Stonecutters in 1853, the Iron Molders in 1855, the Machinists in 1859, etc. The origins of most of these were local and many, like the Iron Molders, began as largely social organizations. These years were not easy ones for the unions. Lost strikes, depressed times, and the Civil War all took their toll. A greater source of weakness, however, was the lack of effective leadership and of funds. Illustrative of the latter is the colorful notice in *Fincher's Trade Review*:

> Expelled for the non-payment of dues . . . Fred Hinman . . . contemptible scoundrel who did not pay his dues . . . left town without paying his board, his child's funeral expenses and failed to return a borrowed overcoat.

In the post-Civil War years there were several attempts to form a truly national union or at best a national labor organization which would represent the various trade organizations. These efforts met little success, though they yielded the short-lived National Labor Union and the Industrial Congress. It was not until the middle of the 1880's that a truly national union emerged in the United States. The rise and decline of the Noble and Holy Order of the Knights of Labor is one of those comet-like events which add a degree of spice to the slower-moving currents of normal history. In 1881 the Knights may have had as many as 20,000 members. Then, through the use of selective boycotts and a few key strikes, the most notable being against the Wabash Railroad in 1885, success and membership skyrocketed, leading to a gain of some 500,000-600,000 members in a single year.[11]

Even in success, however, the seeds of failure were spreading. The national craft unions (such as the printers and carpenters) wanted to have trade locals within the Knights.

The dissatisfaction of the craft unions with the Knights' policies and the personal divisions between the leaders of the two groups increased, and in 1886, when the membership of the Knights declined following the loss of a strike against Jay Gould's railroads, the craft unions withdrew from the Knights.

After the national craft unions withdrew from the Knights, they came together to form the American Federation of Labor. With the advent of the AFL, the American labor movement began to trace a continuous history. There would be new downturns in membership, more repression from employers assisted by laws and the courts, but never again would unions completely disappear.

The rise in union membership was slow but fairly steady after the founding of the AFL, especially in 1900-05, during which time (1902) the mine workers succeeded in organizing in the anthracite fields. Despite a growing membership, the union movement faced two great obstacles, the "isms" on the left and the failure to organize in the great manufacturing industries. This failure to organize in manufacturing was intensified by technological change.

The political far left, in the form of Communism, socialism, syndicalism, and anarchism played a noisy, colorful, at times violent, but essentially minor role in American union history. The largest and most colorful group was the Industrial Workers of the World, or Wobblies, an outgrowth of the Western Federation of Miners. In spite of some success in the great Lawrence textile strike of 1912 and among agricultural workers in the West, the Wobblies secured little in the way of lasting improvements for their membership. The union's association with violence, which some of its leaders advocated, and extremist socialism and its opposition to World War I resulted in its leaders' being persecuted. It would seem that Wobblie propaganda and the use of sabotage were too extreme for the Americans of that era. The IWW left its name in song and story, but little in the way of a lasting impact upon the American labor movement, for even at its peak membership the union's role was largely a symbolic one.

The importance of World War I for the activities and position of U.S. labor cannot be stressed too strongly. It was not just that union membership more than doubled, going from 2.1 million in 1910 to 5 million in 1920 and from 8.4 percent of the nonagricultural labor force to 16.3 percent, or that Congress passed the Clayton Anti-Trust Act, which seemed to promise that unions would now have freedom from excessive legal restraint. The most important event was the legitimization of labor which resulted from President Wilson's inclusion of Gompers and other labor leaders as important members of the wartime establishment.

To the union leaders the advent of the 1920's must have appeared bright and promising, because periods of prosperity had always added new members to their ranks. But the bubble burst and, in the midst of unparalleled prosperity, the unions lost close to half of their membership. Employment in highly unionized industries such as shipbuilding was drastically cut back in the conversion from war to peace. The return to "normalcy" also meant a resurgence of strong anti-unionism among employers and the continuance of a legal system which maintained its supremacy of property rights over other types of rights. Even once-powerful unions were caught up in the repressive times. The Ladies Garment Workers dropped from 105,400 members in 1920 to 32,300 in 1929. The Mine, Mill, and Smelter Workers Union (heir to the old Western Federation of Miners) disintegrated, as did the Seamens Union, which had 105,000 members in 1920. The 1927 convention of the Miners was attended by half a dozen men, and the Seamen's convention was attended by nine members.

Perhaps an even more important reason for the decline was that the boom of the 1920's was in the mass-production industries, where the pure craft unionism of the AFL had always been least effective. The crash came to the stock market in 1929 and to the economy in 1932, but to unions it had come in 1921 and every other year in the decade.

If union fortunes in 1930 were a dramatic reversal from those of 1920, then 1940 was witness to an even more dramatic reversal from 1930. A dying institution had been transformed. The number of union members more than doubled in 10 years, going from 3.4 million in 1930 to 8.7 million in 1940. Union members as a proportion of nonagricultural workers rose from 11.6 percent to 26.9 percent during the same period. The principal source of this remarkable growth was the passage of Section 7a of the National Industrial Recovery Act and legislation of an intermediate nature which culminated in the Wagner Act of 1935. The new spirit, energy, and philosophy which the Committee for Industrial Organization, now known as the Congress of Industrial Organizations, brought to the organization of unions and the rivalry for new members were important factors in the spread of unionism.

During World War II, as had been the case in World War I, the labor movement was invited into the highest councils of government. Compared with World War I, the role and the importance of the labor movement in the councils of government were much enhanced. A not unnatural by-product of this was a major growth in membership, close to 6 million in five years. This was the largest numerical increase in membership in American history. The end of the war found unions in an enviable position. They had achieved new highs in union membership absolutely and as a percentage of the nonagricultural labor force, bargaining relationships newly established in 1940 had matured, and the idea of unionism was increasingly accepted as legitimate by managers.

Glowing as the vista of the postwar period may have seemed, its promise has remained largely unfulfilled. In the main these years have been ones of plateaus in the number of members and a decline of membership as a proportion of nonagricultural employment. There were, of course, exceptions to the general trend. The Teamsters Union, under energetic, dynamic, and at times less than honest leadership, consolidated its hold over the trucking industry and in some parts of the country extended into a number of other industries as well. The Building Trades, as a group, also prospered. Government support for unions did not lessen appreciably, but its character may be said to have shifted from that of active support to mere protection of labor from its worse enemies. The first break came with the passage of the Taft-Hartley Law in 1947, despite the determined opposition of the union movement. Additional regulatory legislation in the form of the Landrum-Griffin Act followed in 1959. In a manner reminiscent of the 1920's, the growing sectors of the economy were not in the areas which have traditionally been union strongholds. The union drive for more members was also blunted by a lack of serious effort, a symptom of what some friends of unionism have called its old age. For all of these reasons and more, the union movement has been largely stable, neither expanding nor contracting significantly during the postwar years.

The Essence of U.S. Unionism

The most fundamental characteristic of American unionism has been that truly rapid and extensive union growth, especially in industrial and government employment, has taken place only during periods when the relevant governmental unit, usually the federal government, has taken a favorable and encouraging position with respect to union membership.

This encouragement has been manifest chiefly in government prevention of employer opposition to unions and their members.

A second fundamental characteristic has been that the most successful style of unionism has been the one which concentrated upon basic bread-and-butter issues--in other words, business unionism. The social and humanitarian concerns of the unions of the 1820's and the Knights of Labor failed while the business unionism of the pure craft unions succeeded. The radicalism of the IWW did not survive the 1920's, but the AFL did. Nor can the temporary alliance of the CIO with more radical elements in the 1930's be taken as proof of the contrary, for the success of the CIO was in an appeal to all skill classes within the employing unit. It was not in either radical or political demands or formulations. This is made evident by the organizational success of those AFL unions which embraced the plantwide units of the CIO without getting involved with the social goals which the CIO also embraced.

A third characteristic has been the lack of a meaningful radical unionism. Socialism, Communism, and syndicalism, three ideological forces which have markedly affected the labor movements of almost every other country in the world, have been limited in the United States to the scares under Harding and the fight after World War II against the Communist domination of certain unions within the CIO. And even these "Communist" CIO unions displayed few outward signs that they had been influenced by the ideological beliefs of their officers.

A fourth major characteristic has been the extent to which control has been lodged with national offices. While the craft unions of 100 and more years ago insisted upon local autonomy, this gradually evolved into greater centralized control, a movement which reached its apogee in unions like the Steel Workers and the Auto Workers, in which almost all of the control has been held by the national officers. In recent years there has been some relaxation of central control and locals have been permitted to strike over local issues. The skilled craftsmen in the auto companies have been allowed a degree of veto power over national decisions which concern them. Yet this downward delegation of authority has not really shifted the locus of power from the national executives.

Unions in Japan

The course of Japanese unionism may be divided into about seven periods: (1) the years between the Meiji Restoration in 1868 and 1894, (2) the period bounded by the Sino-Japanese War (1894-95) and World War I, (3) World War I itself, (4) the years of depressed growth, 1920-35, (5) the decade of the military, 1935-45, (6) the American occupation period, and (7) the years since the peace treaty freed the Japanese government from Allied direction.[12] The broad sweep of Japanese union growth may be seen in Table 2. It indicates a slow but steady growth into the middle 1930's, followed by decline and dissolution. Yet at no time during these years were unions a significant force. This is shown by the small proportion of the nonagricultural labor force which was organized. After the Pacific War, unions seemingly sprang full-grown, expanded rapidly until 1949, and then grew hardly at all for 11 years. Then between 1960 and 1965 the number of union members again increased at a rapid rate, fast enough to reverse the previous downward trend in the proportion of the labor force which was organized. Modest gains continued to be recorded to the present.

The Prewar Years

In the period from the end of the Tokugawa years (1868) to the Sino-Japanese War (1894-95) there were few if any trade unions. There were a few guilds, mainly of artisans and craftsmen, which were the direct descendants of the guilds of the Tokugawa era. In addition there were some spontaneous and unorganized groups of industrial workers who engaged in strikes in some mines and in a few textile factories. Besides unions there were also a few minor political parties, such as Tōyō Shakaitō (Oriental Socialist party) and Shakaitō (Rickshaw party), which also registered a protest of the emerging industrial conditions. Like the early unions in the United States, these organizations lacked a firm foundation and were most often associated with specific, localized events.

During the 10 years between the Sino-Japanese and Russo-Japanese wars, there were significant increases in the size of Japan's industrial sector. Coupled with this growth were the tiny stirrings of a union movement. In 1897 Katayama Sen established Rōdō Kumiai Kiseikai (Society for the Promotion of Trade Unions). This group assisted in the formation of unions in the steel industry, railways, shipyards, and printing

TABLE 2

Union Membership in Japan, Selected Years

Year	No. of Unions	Membership (thousands)	Percent of Nonagricultural Labor Force	Rate of Organization[a]	
1921	300	103.4	.8	--	
1930	712	354.3	2.3	--	
1936	973	420.6	3.0	--	
1939	517	365.8	2.1	--	
1944	0	0.0	0.0	0.0	
1946	17,266	4,925.6	30.5[b]	41.5	
1949	34,688	6,655.5	35.0[b]	55.8	
1955	32,012	6,285.9	24.9	35.6	37.8[c]
1960	41,561	7,661.6	24.6	32.2	33.8[c]
1965	52,879	10,146.9	28.0	34.8	36.1[c]
1969	58,812	11,248.6	27.4	35.2	

[a] The rate of organization is the number of union members in the June survey divided by the number of employees in the June labor force survey.

[b] Estimate.

[c] The *Survey of Manpower*, which provides the denominator, was changed in 1967, resulting in a lower rate of organization. These are the rates on a basis comparable with the earlier data.

Sources: Prewar: Suehiro Izutaro, *Nippon Rōdō Undō Shi* (Tokyo: Chūō Kōronshu, 1954), p. 73, as reported in Iwao F. Ayusawa, *A History of Labor in Modern Japan* (Honolulu: East-West Center Press, 1966), p. 154; Kazushi Ohkawa, *The Growth Rate of the Japanese Economy* (Tokyo: Kinokunya, 1957), pp. 245-46. Postwar: The basic source is the Ministry of Labor's annual *Rōdō Kumiai Kihon Chōsa* [Basic survey of trade unions].

establishments. The most successful of these was probably the Iron Workers. That union was established in December, 1898, and had 42 locals and 5,400 members by the fall of 1900. Unfortunately for the unions, all of their activities did not fare very well. There were various reasons for their failure. The unions lacked experienced leadership and funds. They did not generate a great deal of enthusiasm among the workers. Also, the defeat in the Diet of the proposed factory legislation of 1898 caused many workers to lose interest in the idea of unions. (Factory legislation finally passed in 1911, to become effective in 1916.) There was also the serious problem of legal suppression under the Public Peace Police Act of 1900.

In 1912 the Yūaikai (Friendly Love Society) was established under the leadership of Suzuki Bunji. Its orientation was largely toward the provision of mutual benefits and the extension of labor education. In 1921 its name was changed to Nihon Rōdō Sōdōmei (Japan Labor Federation). By 1921 there were some 300 unions and 100,000 members, though, as can be seen in Table 2, this represented less than 1 percent of the nonagricultural labor force.

By 1929 the number of unions had doubled and union membership had tripled. Pre-Pacific War peak in the number of unions, 993, was reached in 1935. The peak in membership, 420,584 members, came in 1936. Yet given the increase in the nonagricultural labor force in the early 1930's, these gains represented only modest improvements in the proportion of the work force that was organized. Despite seeming progress in membership and in status, other factors did not bode well for the unions. One serious problem was the increasingly fractional nature of the Japanese union movement. It began in May, 1925, when Sōdōmei split because its right wing attempted to oust the Communists from the organization. By 1927 there were three major labor groups: Sōdōmei on the right, Nihon Rōdō Kumiai Dōmei (League of Japanese Trade Unions) in the center, and Nihon Rōdō Kumiai Hyōgikai (Japanese Council of Labor Unions) on the left. From one major, central labor organization in January, 1925, the Japanese union movement passed through some 14 or 15 different amalgamations during the next 15 years. They included Sangyō Hōkoku Kai (Industrial Patriotic Society), usually known as Sampō, a government labor front which was set up in 1938, to be followed in 1940 by a government order outlawing all unions.

A second difficulty was the inability of the unions to obtain meaningful contracts. This was due largely to management's extreme distaste for dealing with unions, the inexperience of union leaders, and the general weakness of the organizations. Sōdōmei had only 49 agreements by 1930 and 117 by 1937. Both difficulties, the splits and the inability to obtain contracts and to organize, stemmed largely from the same basic source, the attitude of the government toward labor unions.

The basic approach of the government toward the unions was a carrot-and-stick policy. In the mid-1920's it granted universal suffrage (for men only, in 1925). The last of the "carrots" came in 1925, when the Social Bureau of the Home Ministry drafted a bill to legalize unions. Pressure on the Diet from the military and others altered the bill to such an extent that even right-wing unions opposed it, and it was defeated in the Diet.[13] Yet the government also produced the heavy stick of the Chian Iji Hō-an (Maintenance of Public Peace Bill), which was designed to suppress elements advocating changes in the political character of the Empire or denying the validity and appropriateness of the system of private property.

Following the Manchurian incident in 1931 the government came increasingly under the de facto control of military and industrial interests which were opposed to the idea of trade unionism and especially to those sectors within it which advocated left-wing political ideals. Despite the fact that unions and membership increased at least until 1935-36 and that in the years 1938-40 the Diet passed other social legislation long demanded by proletarian parties and unions, the unions were unable effectively to oppose the trend toward a militaristic domination of politics and the resulting limitations on their freedoms. By 1940 there were only 49 unions, the same number as in 1914, and by 1944 even the three unions and 155 members of 1943 had been reduced to zero.

After the Pacific War

Under the urging and direction of the Allied Occupation, the basic Japanese trade union laws were drastically altered. On September 30, 1945, Sampō was dissolved and on October 10 the former leaders of Sōdōmei met to reorganize. The reorganization followed on November 3, but not before the first large-scale strike had occurred. This strike, a 50-day one at the Yomiuri newspaper, also introduced to the world a Japanese contribution to trade union tactics, Seisan Kanri. The term means production control, but the modern American term "a work-in" gives a more accurate impression of what actually took place.

Once freedom to organize was assured, union membership grew rapidly, as can be seen from Table 2. The eight unions and 4,026 members of October, 1945, became 1,516 unions and 901,075 members in January, 1946, and 12,923 unions and 3,813,665 members in July, 1946. In the United States during the 1930's, union membership had leaped forward under the motto, "President Roosevelt wants you to join." Union membership now leaped forward in Japan under the conducive atmosphere generated by General MacArthur's favorable views. In many cases all of the employees of a company, save the president, would join the union, an occurrence that was made possible by the nature of the enterprise union which became the dominant form of postwar unionism.[14] One reason for the enterprise nature of the postwar organization was the fact that the wartime Sampō basic unit at each plant provided a model for postwar organization. Growth was slow after 1946, when almost 5 million members were listed on the rolls. There were over 6 million members in both 1948 and 1949, but 6 million members on a continuous basis was not reached before 1955. Despite the moderate and continuous increase in membership after 1955, the more rapid growth of the labor force resulted in a steady downward course in the rate of union organization from the high of 55.5 percent in 1949 until it reached a low of 33 percent in 1959. The organization rate has rebounded slightly since 1959, having been between 35 and 36 percent all during the 1960's.

The slow growth in membership after 1949-50 reflects the interplay of a number of factors. During the Occupation, Communists and left-wing socialists played an important role in the rebirth of the labor movement. This was because their leaders constituted a disproportionate share of the men who had prior experience in the leadership of trade union activities. It also reflected the Occupation's special favor to persons who had opposed the Japanese government during the military period. It should be noted, however, that most of the men who came forward to lead unions at the enterprise level were new leaders, men who had had no experience with prewar unionism.

Then in the years after 1946, the increasing divisions between the United States and the Soviet Union caused the Occupation authorities to take a dimmer and dimmer view of Communists within the Japanese labor movement. The left-wing-oriented union leaders' position with the Occupation was not enhanced by their roles in urging a general strike and strikes of governmental employees in order to change the political complexion of the Japanese government. The end result of this estrangement between the Occupation and the Communists was an order for the dismissal from public posts of 24 members of the Central Committee of the Japanese Communist party. This move was followed by large-scale dismissals of Communists from other jobs, and on July 30, 1950, the government ordered the dissolution of Zen Rōren (National Liaison Council of Japanese Trade Unions), which initially had represented 4.5 million union members of all political ideals but which by 1949 had become dominated by Communists and had fewer than 800,000 members.

The move against the Communist unions was one example of a retarding force in postwar unionism, a return to the factionalism of the prewar years. Initially efforts were made to reach accommodation among various groups and to form a single, large central labor federation. Eventually failure was acknowledged, and in August, 1946, Nihon Rōdō Kumiai Sōdōmei (Japanese Federation of Labor) and Zen Nihon Sangyōbetsu Rōdō Kumiai Kaigi (National Congress of Industrial Unions) were established. Sanbetsu on the left and the revived Sōdōmei on the right supported and guided their respective political parties, the Communist and the Social Democratic.

Following the bitter opposition of the Occupation authorities and the Japanese government to extreme left-wing activities--an opposition which had led to the demise of Sanbetsu--a new attempt to find a semblance of unity led to the formation of Nihon Rōdō Kumiai Sō-Hyōgi Kai (General Council of Japanese Trade Unions) on July 12, 1950. Sōhyō essentially represented the anti-Communist or non-Communist unions. Its models seemed to be American and the goals which it stressed were democracy within unions, opposition to Communism, and an intention to concentrate upon economic activity. An emphasis upon these goals was short-lived, and in July, 1952, at the third convention, they were unrecognizable.

No simple set of explanations will explain Sōhyō's change in attitude. Seemingly the most powerful factor was Secretary-General Takano Minoru's attempt to reassert the labor movement's political influence once the peace treaty was signed. This attempt involved unrestrained political action directed both at the conservative government's general policies on war, peace, and big business and at its more repressive labor legislation. Sōhyō's leftward shift and the abandonment of economic goals for an almost exclusive emphasis upon political activity led to dissatisfaction, and in February, 1953, the textile and seamen's unions, along with other right-wing groups, established Minrōren, which hoped to return Sōhyō to its initial principles. This did not work, and in April, 1954, Zen Nihon Rōdō Sōdōmei Kumiai Kaigi (Japanese Confederation of Labor), better known as Dōmei, was formed.

The year 1954 was a crucial one for Japanese unions. Sōhyō was faced with the exodus of the Dōmei unions; internally there was a sharp conflict between Takano and "third force" unions led by Ota Kaoru; and externally there were threats of wage cuts, rationalization programs, and work force retrenchments in connection with the deflation of the post-Korean War period. In July, 1955, the Ota faction replaced Takan with Iwai Akira of the National Railway Workers Union as secretary-general of Sōhyō. The new leadership elevated the importance of economic demands, though these changes by no means meant the abandonment of political policies and goals.

In addition to the government's opposition to certain elements in the labor movement and its general insistence upon tax policies, labor regulation, and a tolerance of monopoly--all designed to give emphasis to increasing the rate of economic growth--the union movement suffered from having reached the easy natural limits of union organization. Most of the major firms had been organized, and only the great sea of medium and small enterprise was left. For example, in the private sector in 1960, 67.7 percent of all employees in establishments with 500 or more employees were organized, but only 1.0 percent were organized in those employing 29 or fewer. And even the 100-499 employee category had only 17.1 percent organized. In 1969 organization in the larger firms had declined to 63 percent, but gains had been made among the smaller firms. The rate for those employing fewer than 29 was 4.9 percent, and it was 33.5 percent for the 100-499 category.

The years since 1955 have not been uneventful: for instance, the historic 1959-61 Miike coal strike and the prolonged attempt to implement ILO convention no. 87, governing rights of public employees, but these events have not given rise to any powerful new directions, and the reestablishment of the prewar pattern of factionalism over ideological issues has continued down to the present, when there are four major trade union groups.

In August, 1970, further changes took place, but their direction was unclear. Makoto Ichikawa, President of Zenchūrō (All-Japan Garrison Forces Labor Union), became the President of Sōhyō and Shogo Ohki, Director of General

Affairs and Planning Bureau of Sōhyō, became the General Secretary. The shift in leadership was prompted by internal discussion which stemmed from organizational stagnation. The expectation is that the change will not cause Sōhyō to become militant and imaginative, but that it will move even more toward the right. This movement toward the right draws some of its impetus from the activities of Zenminkon (National Council of the Chairmen of Private Industry Unions). At its fifth conference in January, 1970, 17 large enterprise unions indicated their desire for a trade union movement free from anti-capitalist activities and class-struggle ideologies. Some representatives hope to have a new unified movement by 1972, a hope which was brightened in November, 1970, when six important unions stated that they would set up a joint organizing committee. This "unification toward the right" will be actively opposed, and consequently the price of unity may be a disjointed Sōhyō. Only time will tell.

The Essence of Japanese Unionism

The point which stands out in Japanese unionism is the key role of the government's attitude toward unions. The limited growth in the 1920's and 1930's followed a relaxation of the government's previous policy of complete opposition, and growth was terminated by a return to a policy of suppression. The postwar boom followed positive government support for unions. And even the postwar decline in membership after 1949-50 may be attributed in part to the more conservative approach of the government.

A second major characteristic has been the important role of "isms" and the factionalism which has been related to them. Japan's unionists, both before and after the war, have been torn between the bread-and-butter unionism of Samuel Gompers, imported by early union leaders who had visited or studied in the United States, and the more colorful and dramatic ideas of socialism and Communism imported from Europe.

The role of the public employee is perhaps more significant in Japan than it is in any other country except Great Britain. This stems partly from the fact that about three out of every four of these public employees are organized, compared with a national average of about one worker in three. The importance of the public employee in unionism is also reflected in their large national unions and their significant role in the policies of Sōhyō. The fourth major characteristic is that decision-making is centered at the enterprise (local) level.

COMPARISON OF UNIONISM IN JAPAN AND THE UNITED STATES

The growth of unionism in both Japan and the United States has been governed chiefly by the attitude of the central government. In the United States until 1937, and in Japan until 1945, the hostile-to-neutral attitude of the government toward the union movement allowed corporations to oppose unions with economic and social weapons, and in the 1920's, in both countries, with paternalistic employment practices designed to bind the workers to the company and to draw them away from the union. In both countries a dramatic reversal of government policy followed the failure of the corporation-dominated order to meet world challenges of the 1930's: depression in the United States and the China incident in Japan. The reversals were followed by a very rapid growth of unionism to its present role. The development of the plans for the American occupation of Japan followed very closely upon the development of New Deal support for labor. It is therefore not unreasonable to argue that the view of the role of the union in a modern state, upon which the reversal of government attitude in the United States rested, was the same view which resulted in the reversal in Japan, admittedly under the pressure of foreign occupation. In the United States the period of peak union-building activity lasted about nine years, from 1936, when about 13 percent of the nonagricultural labor force was organized, until 1945, when 35.5 percent was organized. In Japan it lasted only four years, from a state of no organization in 1945, to 1949, when about 35 percent of the nonagricultural labor force was organized. Since these high points were reached in both countries in the 1940's, the expansion of their labor forces has outpaced the gains in union membership, so that today union membership in both is only about 28 percent of the nonagricultural labor force. (See Tables 3 and 4.)

The countries' labor movements have been divided over the proper program for unions and over issues associated with left-wing political ideologies. The basic issues have been the same--bread-and-butter unionism as opposed to a broader social concern--but the resolution of the issues has been different. During the first 70 years of American union history there was tension between those who thought of gains in the work place and those who thought of gains for all workers or the entire society. This division was exemplified in the conflict between the Knights of Labor and the AFL. Yet the whole

TABLE 3

Trade Union Membership in Japan and the United States, By Major Industry

Area	United States, 1968 Number	United States, 1968 Percent	Japan, 1969 Number	Japan, 1969 Percent
Mining and Quarrying	342,000	1.7	131,694	1.1
Contract Construction	2,541,000	12.6	684,672	6.0
Manufacturing	9,218,000	45.6	4,235,414	37.6
Transportation	2,503,000	12.4	2,058,785	18.3
Telephone and Telegraph	476,000	2.4		
Electric and Gas Utilities	324,000	1.6	216,687	1.9
Trade	1,392,000	6.9	470,675	4.1
Finance and Insurance	50,000	.2	757,260	6.7
Service Industries	1,093,000	4.5	1,280,046	11.3
Agriculture and Fishing	26,000	.1	136,911	1.2
Government	2,155,000	10.7	1,120,730	9.9
Other	90,000	.4	144,508	1.2
Total*	20,210,000	100.0	11,248,601	100.0

*Includes Canadian members.

Sources: Japan Labor Bulletin, IX (March, 1970), 9; U.S. Bureau of Labor Statistics, Handbook of Labor Statistics 1970, p. 335.

TABLE 4

Major Unions in Japan and the United States, by Number of Members

Rank	Union	Members 1969	Union	Members 1968
1	Jichirō (local public service workers)	863,527	Teamsters	1,755,000
2	Nikkyōso (teachers)	548,648	Auto Workers	1,473,000
3	Zensen Dōmei (textile workers)	531,911	Steel Workers	1,120,000
4	Denkirōran (electric machine workers)	481,326	Machinists	903,000
5	Kokurō (national railway men)	276,817	Electrical Workers (IBEW)	897,000
6	Zenkindōmei (metalworkers)	250,302	Carpenters	793,000
7	Shitetsusōren (private railway men)	249,204	Laborers	553,000
8	Zengairen (insurance sellers)	244,950	Retail Clerks	552,000
9	Zendentsu (telecommunication workers)	237,300	Meat Cutters	500,000
10	Zenkensōren (construction workers)	237,006	Hotel and Restaurant Workers	459,000
11	Zentei (postal workers)	233,747	Ladies Garment Workers	455,000
	Total	4,154,738		9,460,000

Sources: Japan Labor Bulletin, IX (March, 1970), 12; U.S. Bureau of Labor Statistics, Directory of National and International Labor Unions in the United States, No. 1665 (1970), p. 69.

union movement in those years was so tenuous that our historical focus tends to be on the existence of unions rather than on their policy divisions. Then, too, for almost 40 years, 1890 to 1930, business unionism was dominant. It was probably this dominance that tended to relegate left-wing ideologies to the footnotes of U.S. unionism. In Japan, however, the union movement of the 1920's, though small, was large enough to allow divisions over policy, here closely allied to the left-wing problem, to loom large upon our historical focus. Japanese unions were caught up in the anti-Communist policies of postwar America, which also had some effect upon U.S. unions. The impact in Japan, however, was probably greater because the leadership role of Communists was larger and more valuable than it was in the United States. There is no simple explanation for the greater role of left-wing political activities in unions in Japan than in the United States. One important factor is the difference in degree of political influence which had previously been granted to the working class. In the United States the drive for an effective political role for the working class had largely been achieved before unions became very large or important and before left-wing political ideas became significant. This was not true of Japan, where universal male suffrage was not granted until 1925 and the potential of effective political representation for the working class was probably not achieved until after the Pacific War.

Within the two union movements the locus of effective decision-making appears to be quite different; in Japan it is in the unit union and the enterprise federation, and in the United States in the national union. But this overstates the difference. In the United States the vast majority of all bargaining contracts are negotiated on an individual company basis. In these situations, especially in industries which are not characterized by a few very large firms, control over contract terms does rest with the local union unit. And it is becoming increasingly common for locals to be given the option to strike over local plant issues after agreement has been reached with a large company on the major contract issues. Thus, in many industries a great deal of control over the contract does remain at the local level, though most of the impetus toward new union policies, goals, and tactics remains with the national officers. In Japan the increasing use of Shuntō (spring wage offensive) means that on a de facto basis, national unions and labor groups are coming to have more and more influence upon the bargaining demands and agreements, though contractual control remains with the enterprise unit or federation.

There are two factors which are relevant to the locus of decision-making. One is the method of initial union organization. The majority of AFL unions were originally organized in a variety of separate locations and afterward federated into a single union. As a consequence, they tended to reserve much of the authority to themselves rather than deeding it to the new national. The most centralized unions, such as the Auto Workers and Steel Workers, were organized largely by the national office, which, in doing so, reserved the power rather than granting it to the newly established locals. In Japan almost all of the unions were self-organized on a unit or establishment basis, and thus it is not surprising that they have kept much of the authority to themselves. A second important factor has been the degree of labor mobility. One of the most serious problems which historically faced the American union movement was the ease with which an employer could substitute other workers for union workers who would not accept his terms. Thus it was essential that the union develop control over enough employers and sources of labor to make the union's dealings with any given employer effective. This implied a decision center which stood above the level of the individual company. In Japan the much more constricted patterns of labor mobility largely precluded inter-company labor mobility (at least within the unionized sectors of the economy), and thus the problem was not one of conditions within an industry so much as it was conditions within the single work place. A third factor has been the attitude of the employers and the extent to which they have resisted efforts toward partial or full multi-employer bargaining. It is probably true that the Japanese firm, with its strong opposition to bargaining with "outsiders" (nonemployees), has helped to maintain the locus of authority within the unit union.

The Strike

Part of the folklore of U.S. industrial relations has been that the strike is the ultimate weapon or tactic of bargaining, a model adopted largely from the idea that war is the ultimate extension of diplomacy. Yet with hundreds of major contracts and thousands of minor ones negotiated in 1968, there were only 5,045 work stoppages, involving less than 15 percent of all union members. (See Table 5.) The average strike lasted 24.5 calendar days, and the average union member who struck lost 18.5 days of work. These data and

TABLE 5

Selected Labor Dispute Characteristics,
Japan and the United States, 1966 and 1968

	Japan		United States	
	1966	1968	1966	1968
Work Stoppages	1,252	1,546	4,405	5,045
Workers Involved (thousands)	1,132	1,163	1,960	2,649
Man-days Lost (thousands)	2.7	2.8	25.4	49.8
Nonagricultural Employment (percent)	3.1	2.9	3.1	3.9
Union Membership (percent)	10.9	10.8	10.9	14.0
Disputes Lasting Four Days or Less (percent)	75.1*	55.5	27.7	24.3
Disputes Concerning General Wages (percent)	52.0	51.7	43.4	50.4
Income-related Disputes (percent)	76.2	81.2	51.2	57.1
Disputes over Principal Management Decisions Concerning Labor (percent)	6.2	6.4	32.2	29.3
Disputes over Job Security (percent)	3.6	1.2	4.1	3.6

*The figure for Japan is five days or less, and the figure for 1966 is actually from 1965.

Sources: Ministry of Labor, Rōdō Sōgi Tōkei Chōsa Nen Hōkoku, 1966 and 1968 [Yearbook of labor dispute statistics]; U.S. Bureau of Labor Statistics, Handbook of Labor Statistics, 1968, pp. 301, 306; Analysis of Work Stoppages, 1968, Bureau of Labor Statistics Bulletin 1646 (January, 1970), pp. 13, 16, 17.

the fact that only 24.5 percent of all work stoppages lasted more than a month clearly suggest that most American strikes are in the nature of tactics rather than ultimate solutions. The role of the strike as a tactic, as a formal part of the collective negotiations, is even more clearly evident in Japan. (See Table 5.)[15] The rate of union member participation in strikes in Japan was the same as in the United States in 1966 but smaller in 1968.[16] Each striker lost an average of only 2.4 days, and between 55 and 75 percent of all strikes in Japan, as compared with only about one-quarter of those in the United States, lasted four days or less. Another principal difference between the two countries relates to the major issue which caused each strike. There is reasonable similarity between the proportion of strikes over general wage increases, about half of them in each country, and over job security, around 3 percent. (See Table 5.) The difference lies in strikes over management decisions concerning labor. The relatively large proportion in the United States, close to one-third, reflects the importance of collective negotiations in the establishment of working conditions and conditions of employment. The tiny figure for Japan, about 6 percent, reflects the relatively small formal role which the union plays in these areas, a phenomenon which is discussed in greater detail in the section on the employment relationship.

The Current State of Unions

In 1955, after a number of fitful efforts, the American Federation of Labor and the Congress of Industrial Organizations merged to form the new AFL-CIO. Initially it included the majority of American unions, though the railroad brotherhoods remained outside and thus maintained their long-standing isolation from the mainstream of American labor. Soon they were joined by the Mineworkers, the expelled Teamsters, and, most recently, by the Auto Workers. The source of these breakdowns is not difficult to find, for the merger solved nothing except to decrease slightly the size of labor's bureaucracy. The issues that had divided a separated labor movement continued to divide a single labor federation.

The causes of the division were complex, somewhat historical, and, unfortunately, intertwined with personalities. Yet in many ways the division continues to be that which split the Knights of Labor from the national craft unions and which divided the AFL from the Industrial Workers of the World. It is whether unions are to be a narrow vested interest, devoted to the well-being of a small group of workers, or whether they are to be vehicles of social concern, passionately devoted to the well-being of all who work.

In Japan even the semblance of unity has eluded the union movement. The largest of the national labor groups is Sōhyō which began in 1950 and to which in 1969 unions representing 37.8 percent of all union members were affiliated. The second largest is Dōmei, which dates from 1954 and which had 17.5 percent of the union members in 1969. The third is the loosely structured Chūritsūroren (Federation of Independent Unions), which shares many goals with Sōhyō and frequently works very closely; it enrolled 12.0 percent of 1969's union members. The fourth has 0.6 percent of the members and consists of a few unions which embrace the pure ideal of industrial unionism and which were among the early ones to withdraw from Sanbetsu. At that time they formed the small center known as Shinsanbetsu. It is not clear whether the International Metal Trades-Japan Council should be considered as a fifth group or not. Its membership of almost 1.2 million members is made up of private-sector industrial unions from all four of the major groups, and in recent years these unions have played an increasingly important role in some aspects of union activity, especially in wage negotiation. In addition to the major groups there are the unaffiliated unions and groupings of all unions whose companies are themselves loosely grouped together. Lastly, in 1969, 32.1 percent of all union members were in unions which were unaffiliated with any trade union group. These allocations of membership represent a decline of about 10 percentage points for Sōhyō and a gain of 4 for Dōmei, when compared to the situation 11 years ago.[17]

There are a number of differences between the major groups, two of which are of central importance.[18] One is the difference in political approach and attitude. Sōhyō is closely tied to the Shakaitō (Japan Socialist party), which is a class-conscious, Marxist, neutralist, and pacifist-oriented party. Dōmei supports Minshu-Shakaitō (Democratic Socialist party), which is opposed to class-consciousness and to Marxist-Leninist socialism and which sees the British Labour party as worthy of emulation. The second major difference is structural. Within Sōhyō there is a heavy concentration of public service employees, many of whose rights to bargain formally and to engage in concerted activity are limited. Only 39 percent of the membership is covered under the Trade Union Law, which governs union activity in the private sector. The remainder are covered under the four laws dealing with trade unions in national and public service and national and public enterprises.[19] In the other federations all but a handful of the members are covered under the Trade Union Law.

As can be seen in Table 3, there are union members in all areas of the Japanese economy, though transportation-communication and manufacturing account for about 56 percent of all unionized workers. The other two major sectors, each with about 10 percent, are service industries and public service. This understates the importance of public employees, who make up about 27 percent of all union members, because it includes government corporation employees in their functional occupational categories. The importance of the government sector becomes clearer upon examination of Table 4, which lists the 11 major unions. There it will be seen that of these unions, which account for about 37 percent of all members, five are composed of workers employed by the government.

The basic strength of the U.S. union movement, as it has been for years, continues to be in manufacturing, with almost 46 percent of all members, and in construction and transportation, each with a little more than 12 percent. (See Table 3.) These strengths are also reflected in the 11 largest unions, which account for about 45 percent of all union members. None of the largest unions represent workers employed in public service. This may change in the future, for recently there has been a seeming upsurge in union orientation among government workers at all levels, especially public school teachers. If this should continue, the next few years could witness dramatic gains in unionism. There are many reasons for this new departure, but certainly chief among them has been the willingness of the respective governmental units to bargain with their employees. Here again, as in the past, it is the attitude of the government which determines whether union membership will prosper or decline.

The size of the Japanese unions in Table 4 is quite respectable, ranging from 200,000 to 800,000, on a relative order of magnitude comparable with those in the United States. Yet the average number of members per union, shown in Table 2, is less than 200. This apparent contradiction stems from the unit union concept used by the government in counting and from the enterprise character of most Japanese unions. The vast majority, about 82 percent of all unit unions, have an enterprise basis of organization.[20] This means that their members are confined to the employees of a single shop, establishment, or enterprise. When a firm has a number of branches, the unit unions will typically join together. The joint organization will be either a central organization which has local branches or a federation of local unions. The former is the more common form. These enterprise federations often are the dominant voices in the national unions.[21] The unit union is difficult to describe because it combines within itself functions which in the United States are those of both the local union and the national union. It might be said to resemble an intermediate organization like the Ford or General Motors departments of the United Auto Workers of America,[22] but there is an essential difference. The U.S. local or the intermediate department is an administrative component, but the Japanese unit union is autonomous. In other words, the locus of decision-making lies at the local level.

Public Labor Policy

Japan's basic labor legislation was dictated by the Occupation authorities, and not surprisingly its provisions are very similar to those in the United States at that time.[23] This meant that the principal emphasis was placed upon legislation which guaranteed labor the freedom to organize without interference from either the government or the employers; in fact, the right was written into the Constitution. Procedures similar to those under the Wagner Act in the United States were established to handle unfair labor practices. In one important respect the original Japanese legislation went far beyond that in the United States, for it placed few restrictions upon the freedom of government employees to organize, bargain, and engage in work stoppages. In the United States, it was to be another 15 years before there would be a serious encouragement of the collective activities of governmental employees, and even now the legality of strikes by these employees is seriously limited or, as in the case of federal employees, prohibited.

Under the threat of a general strike on February 1, 1947, General MacArthur denied the strike weapon to public employees. In 1948 this was given legislative sanction in the National Public Service Law, which denied collective bargaining and the right to strike to government employees. Similar legislation came to be applied to local government employees and to employees of government enterprises. Legally this means that now Japanese and U.S. legislation and practice are essentially similar. The biggest difference is that unions of

Japanese government employees play an active and important part in their country's union movement, whereas American public employees are largely outside the main current of American unionism.

In the absence of bargaining, wages for civil servants are determined in both countries by reference to wage levels which are paid in private enterprise. In theory both systems of determination are the same, but in practice the evolution in Japan of Shuntō in the private sector, which provides an easily identified estimate of the average wage increase in the unionized sector of the private economy and the important position of government employees in the union movement, has meant that wages in the public sector are much more closely tied to the results of collective bargaining than is true in the United States. This is discussed in more detail in Chapter 3.

The activities of the U.S. Conciliation Service and the conciliation function of the labor relations commissioners under Japan's Labor Relations Adjustment Law are quite similar. The services of a trained conciliator to assist the parties in finding a solution to an industrial dispute are provided. It is possible that these conciliators play an important role in setting wage patterns within the boundaries of the final and serious demands of the respective sides, but because privacy and informality attend these activities, it is not possible to gauge their importance. It is clear, however, that the conciliator does not represent the government's views and that he must work within the context provided by the private parties. This means that the only important government role dealing with wages in either country is to be found under minimum wage legislation.

In the United States minimum wages are set under one of three pieces of legislation. These are the Fair Labor Standards Act (Wage and Hour Law), which determines a national minimum wage for workers employed in interstate commerce; the Walsh-Healy Act, which provides for special industry rates for workers engaged in producing items purchased by the federal government in amounts over $10,000; and individual state minimum wage laws, which cover employees in intrastate commerce. Several circumstances have combined to make the Wage and Hour Law minimum the only important and effective one. This results largely from the expansion in its coverage and partly from court interpretation. In addition, most determinations under the Walsh-Healy Act either use the federal minimum wage or, by the time they are promulgated, tested, and approved through court action, are out of date and inconsistent with actual labor market conditions. Construction wages under the Davis-Bacon Act, where the required minimum rate is usually the union scale, are an exception. The level of the minimum wage represents a political decision by Congress and is taken without regard for any formal criteria, though until the recent increase to $1.60 new levels merely brought the current minimum in line with the original 1938 level updated for average changes in productivity and prices.

In Japan the Labor Standards Law, besides allowing for minimum wages, also covers the regulation of a wide variety of working conditions, more than the U.S. Wage and Hour Law. In this law Occupation authorities did not follow the American model, but used the British pattern of allowing the Labor Standards Bureau to set wages regionally and nationally upon the basis of the recommendations of wage councils. The law's coverage excluded workers in household and family undertakings, which initially greatly reduced its potential for meaningful application. This is essentially the same as in the United States, where the lowest-wage industries are very often in intrastate commerce. There they are immune from federal law and are left only to the weak or nonexistent state minimum wage laws. In addition to the weakness of coverage, the Wage and Hour Law was not vigorously applied, and even by 1954 no minimum wage had been put into effect. In 1959 a minimum wage law for low-wage and nonorganized workers was passed, and in October, 1969, it covered 7.8 million workers. However, the most common determination of a minimum until legislation in 1968 was by the voluntary action of employers. In 1969 about 63 percent of covered workers were under minimums established by tripartite wage councils, but this should increase because the 1968 amendments allowed the inter-enterprise agreements to continue only until June, 1970. Thus the establishment of a truly national minimum wage remains an unfulfilled goal of the union movement.

Additional legislation affecting the labor market would be unemployment insurance, public employment offices, and manpower adjustment programs. Typically these laws directly affect only a small portion of the labor force and probably have only limited impacts upon the functioning of the labor markets. Obviously there are a number of administrative differences between Japanese and U.S. legislation in these three areas, but only one difference would seem to be significant. Unemployment insurance in Japan is national in scope, whereas in the United States it is a combination of federal and state activities, which leads to some rather disparate regional situations.

THE EMPLOYMENT RELATIONSHIP

In any economy there is a diversity of relationships between an employer and his employees, ranging from the highly personal relationship of an employer to a lifelong family servant to the institutionally casual relationship of the traveler and the porter in a railroad station. Yet for the majority of the regular jobs in an economy there are some shared characteristics of what is appropriate behavior for both employee and employer. It is to these that we now turn.

The U.S. Employment Relationship

The basic element in the employment relationship in the United States is the concept of a contract. This means that each party to the relationship, employer and employee, has a set of duties to the other, and nothing more and nothing less than the fulfillment of these duties is required. There have been a number of changes in the parties' respective duties and in the contractual conditions during the past 100 years, but no change in the basic concept. There has also been a shift away from a unilateral determination of working conditions by the employer to more of a joint determination, often in conjunction with a union. Today Workman's Compensation covers most employees (though not railroad workers).

Despite such changes in the conditions of employment and the sources of their determination, the essence of the nature of the employment relationship has remained unchanged. It is a contractual one, in which the employee agrees to offer a given amount of labor for a given price. As a contractual arrangement, it has usually been considered inappropriate to use any but job-related criteria as a basis of payment. Consequently family allowances and other paternalistic payments have been uncommon. Additionally, the off-job behavior or activity of workmen has been outside the legitimate concern of the employer. It is true that the early textile mill operators built dormitories for their unmarried female employees and appointed house mothers to worry about the girls' morals (as if the long hours in the mill did not provide sufficient protection), and company housing was not uncommon in many industries. But such items were generally short-lived, and both unions and workers have constantly sought to preserve the division between their lives inside and outside of their place of employment.

Unlike most business contracts, which run for a fixed term, the employment contract with rare exceptions, such as those for indentured servants, was on a day-to-day basis. Both employer and employee were free to terminate the contract at will and for any reason. Nor, in most cases was a prior termination any barrier to the employer's being able to engage new employees or to the employee's securing a new job at wages comparable with or better than what he would have received if he had not left his previous employer. Until shortly after World War I the high rates of turnover which seemed to be one by-product of the employment-at-will aspect of the employment contract did not present any difficulties to employers. There were few, if any, organized efforts to reduce high rates of turnover.

Then in the 1920's two kinds of changes in the duration of the employment relationship began to take place. On the one hand, employers recognized that the turnover of more skilled employees represented a cost, especially in plant operations unique to a single industry. This led to the introduction of certain employee benefits which had as one object the tying of the employee to a specific employer. On the other hand, the unions began to press more and more for the right of the employee to hold his job subject to only two conditions, his satisfactory performance and the existence of work. These conditions were quickly written into the labor contract when, in the 1930's and 1940's, labor unions grew very rapidly. As a response to corrupt political practices and concerns over academic freedom, similar but more extensive protections of job rights became standard at all levels of government and educational systems.

An increased length of tenure within the firm meant that upward mobility would have to take place by intra-firm rather than inter-firm movement. This meant that along with increased tenure of employment, there was an increasing demand by employees and unions for policies of promotion from within. The adoption of policies of internal mobility tended to reduce drastically the number of ports of entry into a firm's job structure, especially among blue-collar workers but increasingly also for white-collar and professional employees.

Despite the increased responsibility of the employer to provide a given employee with continued work, no similar movement took place upon the employee's side. He was and is free to leave at will. The positive benefits in terms of supplementary payments and opportunities for promotion and the negative difficulty of limited ports of entry in other firms, however, may reduce mobility, especially at older ages. Thus, in 1961 about one person in 10 changed his employer during the year, but for those aged 55 to 64, only one in 25 changed employer. Median job tenure for males in 1968 was 4.8 years, but 15 years for those aged 55 to 64. The annual quit rate seems to have declined from 1948 to 1965, after which it has risen slightly.

The source of the contractual basis of the employment relationship is not clear, probably because it has been with us for so very long. Perhaps it lies in the great famines and pestilence of the 14th century, ending in the Black Death of 1348, which, because it resulted in a serious shortage of labor, caused the old seignoral obligations to be commuted quickly into money payments. Perhaps it lies in the contractual nature of the American colonization: early political and economic rights were determined by a contractual relationship between the colonists and the companies which underwrote the expense. Even their theology involved a contract between God and the faithful. And at the practical level the early economy involved a large number of workmen who arrived in America as indentured (contractual) servants.

The Japanese Employment Relationship

The essence of the employment relationship in Japan is the responsibility of the worker to the company and of the company to the workers. These reciprocal relationships have been termed "management familyism" by Hazama Hiroshi,[24] and the elements of the relationship--lifetime tenure, scheduled wage increases, and fringe benefits to encourage loyal commitment--are perhaps better known as Nenkō Joretsu Seido (age and length of service-based wage system). While this nenkō system is said to characterize Japanese industrial relations, it must be recognized that not all, perhaps not even a majority, of Japanese workers are included. The wages of regular workers in large corporations, governmental employees, including those in government corporations, and university employees are determined in this manner. The excluded workers would be the temporary employees of large corporations (many of whom may have long tenure with a single firm), day workers, and most employees of medium and small enterprises. In a 1965 survey of 312 firms, all of which employed at least 100 workers, it was found that 95 percent had a wage system which involved the periodic increase in the wages of all employees.[25]

Since in the private sector about 37 percent of all employees work for establishments of 100 or more, this would provide a minimum estimate of the number covered by nenkō.

Differences in the wage system is not the only aspects which separate the industrial relations of the smaller and large-scale firms. Recently Okamoto Hideaki has identified four categories of establishments: household firms, limited workshops, specialized factories, and oligopoly concerns.[26] While not having a clearly identified correspondence, these four would tend to be equivalent to the size groups less than 30, 30-99, 100-499, and 500 and up used by the Ministry of Labor. Okamoto suggests that only in the household and oligopoly concerns would length of time served be the key determinant in prestige and, presumably, in income. The limited workshop and specialized factory would rely more upon open recruitment from the outside labor market, as opposed to internal promotion and training, in staffing, and more upon skills and ability, as opposed to age or years of employment, in the setting of wages.

This view, at least for the specialized factory, (100-499 employees), tends to be at variance with what was reported in the Ballon, Sakurabayashi, and Tsunekawa survey, which found few differences in personnel policies among firms employing between 100 and 999 persons. A possible reconciliation of these two views has been provided by Tsuda Masumi, who noted that personnel policies among medium-sized firms varied, depending upon whether they were related to larger firms, especially between the shita-uke gaisha (firms which act as subcontractors) and firms which are independent of these or similar ties to particular large corporations. The independent firms tend to develop nenkō-type personnel policies, whereas the shita-uke gaisha do not.[27]

The system of nenkō, whether practiced by Mitsubishi or one of Okamoto's household firms, tends to begin in a similar manner. The initial employment decision will be dependent upon family ties, in the case of the household firm, and upon educational ones, for the larger firms.[28] Illustrative of this, rather than being an accident, is the fact that almost all of the current Japanese Cabinet members are graduates of Tokyo University. Yet the role of educational, personal, and years-of-service ties in the determination of initial employment and subsequent promotion should not be overemphasized. And an appreciation for the importance of ability and success in determining employment and promotion should not be neglected. Among the firms in the survey cited earlier, only 4 percent did not use some differentiated system in the awarding of periodic increases. Among the 312 firms, 63 percent varied wage increases depending upon minute differences in employee performance appraisal. The individual also finds that to some extent his opportunities for promotion will be affected more by the passing of years and his initial position than by almost any other aspect. Yet 67 percent of the firms in the survey felt that the periodic wage increase system prevented desirable promotion and placement, suggesting that some changes may be in the offing.

There are other aspects of the system in addition to wages. The company will probably provide an inexpensive dormitory for single employees, company-owned apartments for married couples, and assistance in the ownership of a home.[29] For plants in new areas there may even be a company-developed subdivision, including land set aside for cultural and educational facilities. Company hospitals and other fringe benefits, including gifts on special occasions and other evidence of the concern of the employer for the workers, will also be provided. In general this maximum involvement of the company in workers' personal lives, especially in the economic aspects, is looked upon favorably by both labor and management.[30]

The Source of Nenkō Seido

There is no clear and widely accepted understanding of the origin of Nenkō Seido. In his widely read book James C. Abegglen argued that it was a direct outgrowth of Tokugawa feudalism: "The distance between the manorial lord in a nonmonetary economy exchanging services with his followers and the Japanese firm using wages as only part of the exchange of obligations with its workers is not great."[31] Yet such a view is, in the minds of many Japanese scholars "... too broad and too general to explain the individual features of labor relations in Japan."[32] And Koji Taira has stressed that high turnover rates among factory workers were common before the Pacific War, which suggests that the nenkō system was not part of the cultural heritage.[33] Clearly, then, the answer must be in the evolution of labor market institutions, and it is to these that we turn.

Ōkōchi Kazuo, formerly President of Tokyo University and the dean of Japanese labor scholars, has emphasized the dekasegi (working away from home) nature of ordinary factory employment, as opposed to skilled craftsmen, which followed the Meiji Restoration.[34] A dekasegi worker was usually a second or third son or an unmarried daughter whose labor was not needed on the family farm. These men and women would be recruited for factory labor by agents who traveled through the countryside. When business turned down in the city and these workers became unemployed, they returned to their family home, to be maintained and to contribute whatever work they could. Since these workers tended to be both unmarried and surplus agricultural labor, their initial wages could be very low and clearly were incapable of supporting a wife and family. The wages in industry were low because the supply of these workers was large relative to the demand for their labor. Having been recruited from a rural background, they respected family obligations and the system of having principal decisions made by their seniors after joint consultation. Thus it was natural for contractor-agents to treat them in a similar manner. Only a few of these workers would remain with their new employer to become skilled and valued workers. In the years during which a few workers achieved this key status, they would also assume family responsibilities. Consequently, it became necessary for the employer to establish a separate wage system for them, one which would both bind them to the employer and allow them to carry out their family obligations. Hence the development of an age and service-based wage system. This description as it applies to the textile industry is quite accurate. When one considers that until 1929 textiles accounted for more than half of all manufacturing employment and that it wasn't until 1932 that male employees became a majority of those employed in factories, it is not surprising that labor relations in textiles should have played a major role in the shaping of concepts in Japan's early industrial relations.

A slightly different position is taken by Fujita Wakao and Hazuma Hiroshi, who found the source of nenkō in the organization of government-owned enterprises during the early Meiji era, which was associated with the appointment of feudal vassals as white-collar workers after they had received some training.[35] A linkage of nenkō patterns with an earlier era is also given by Kawada Hisashi, who noted that mines during the Tokugawa period were operated by yamashi who directly hired a few key workers and then let the common labor jobs to labor contractors.[36] This was essentially the approach adopted by the early factory owners following the Restoration.

Opposition to the view that nenkō had its genesis during the Tokugawa is based mainly upon the argument that it represents a managerial decision based upon economics and that its application during the postwar years is much more extensive than it was in an earlier era.[37] It is argued that between the wars, nenkō was applied only to managerial and clerical employees and certain key members of the production work force, and then only in the larger factory operations. This view of the development is as follows.[38]

During the 19th century an apprentice machinist would work a few years in Tokyo, move to Osaka for a few more years, and then to Kure and the naval shipyards before returning to Tokyo. Only in this way would he receive proper and complete training. Similar patterns were followed by other skilled groups, while the unskilled were largely governed by the dekasegi pattern described earlier. So long as the principal need of the emerging factories was for a large number of unskilled workers and a few persons trained in traditional skills, there was little reason for the firm to alter its response to traditional labor market institutions which made the firm dependent upon the oyakata (middlemen), who controlled channels of apprenticeship and who had their own ties with specific rural areas and their dekasegi workers.

With the advent of the new century and the boom of the World War I years, the needs of the firms began to change. The new capital equipment meant new skill requirements, some of which workers could satisfy only with training obtained on the machinery specific to a single plant. Thus the managers recognized that a greater degree of employment stability and tenure among at least a portion of the work force was desirable, especially for skilled jobs unique to the firm. In 1910 Hitachi set up an extensive in-plant training program, and after World War I a number of other companies established their own programs. The initial results were not very satisfactory. The foremen in the companies were generally oyakata and, not wishing to give up their own system, they had nothing to do with the teaching. The apprentices became unhappy because they did not learn, and many left the company. Only about one-fifth actually completed the courses, and of those who did not complete the course, five-eighths left to join an oyakata. Management then sought to co-opt the oyakata by offering them long-tenure employment, regular salary increases, titles, etc. Many oyakata accepted these offers. This resulted in their shifting their operation into the firm. Thus relations which until then had involved external labor market factors were internalized within the firm.

Since the former oyakata now had the highest status within the firm and since their control and reward systems had utilized length of service, it was to be expected that this system too would be internalized.

The internalizing of a nenkō system was probably a small price for the firms to pay to overcome the resistance of the oyakata to the demands of the new age.[39] It also had a number of other advantages. It provided stability and made use of the social cohesion of the oyabunkobun relationships. It allowed the firm to safeguard its technical and trade secrets. Additionally, it provided management with a new weapon against the rise of unionism.[40] The defense against unionism was two-fold: a lifetime employment system indirectly provided an effective employment blacklist against union agitators, and it allowed the firm to increase the compensation of those workers, skilled craftsmen, who had the most to gain from unionism without at the same time raising the wages of all employees. Lastly, it allowed the firms, in an era of rapid social change, to strengthen historical ties and to give expression to feelings, like the one quoted below, which they obviously shared.

> ... Working conditions and other improvements for workers have not often depended upon the power of a well organized labor union, but have depended upon the ethical considerations of managers. Thus laborers have always been connected with managers through ethical ties.[41]

While it is clear that a key worker and nenkō reward system was well institutionalized by the late 1920's, it touched only a minority of the blue-collar labor force. In the steel industry it appears that only after the age of about 40 could a worker be said to have achieved really permanent status. Until then, on the basis of his lack of loyalty or his failure to obtain the requisite skill level, he could be forced to leave the firm.

Potentially this wage and human relationship system could have been swept away in the confusion and depression of 1945. These vast changes, coupled with the rapid rise to power of the labor unions, might have produced a new system, for certainly Japanese management was not unaware of the advantages of an occupational wage system. And with American occupation they could have had ample assistance in setting up a new system. The fact that they did not alter their system, but extended the concept of the regular employee and the employee whose wages rose with age or service to almost all of their blue-collar labor force, suggests that there were powerful forces acting in favor of the old system. Clearly the widespread acceptance of the system would have been a strong factor in its retention in a time of stress. With its emphasis upon skills associated with a single plant, the system would have encouraged the retention of men familiar with a capital stock--which, because of the war damage, must have been quite particularized to a given plant. Once new capital began to be introduced, adherence to nenkō protected the older workers, who might otherwise have been replaced. Such protection was as desirable to the Japanese union leaders as protection against technological unemployment was to become to American union leaders in the late 1950's.[42] Needless to say, it also benefited management, for, to the extent that the system tied the worker more closely to the company, it made it easier to introduce technological changes.[43] It also lessened the chance that the enterprise union would become overly concerned with conditions in the subcontracting plants and in other medium and small enterprises which produced parts or subassemblies.

The Japanese Wage System After 1950

The nenkō system was reestablished on a more extensive scale after World War II, but it was not many years before its usefulness was questioned. Two sets of factors have been seen as undermining the nenkō system: those associated with technological change and those associated with a shortage of labor, especially new school graduates. One of the first discussions of the impact of technical change came in 1957, and by the early 1960's they were commonplace.[44]

In 1961 Nikkeiren's quarterly newsletter suggested that during the next 10 years there would be a shortage of unskilled labor. As a consequence of this, the dual structure of the labor market would be eliminated and there would be an accelerated tendency toward the adoption of a job-ability type of wage system.[45] At the time that was written, an estimated 5 percent of the larger employers in the Tokyo area utilized a job evaluation system in the determination of their standard or basic wages. It was also about that time (October, 1962) that the Manpower Study Section of the Economic Research Committee, in an interim report to the government, suggested that the nenkō wage system be replaced by a job-related wage system. The Liberal Democratic party adopted the suggestion, and in 1965 the Division of Wages of the Ministry of Labor was recommending to all enterprises that they adopt a formula similar to the one used by the Yawata Steel Company.

Such a formulation essentially would give job-related factors a weight of about 15 percent in the determination of the basic wage.[46]

In January, 1966, the plenary session of the Wage Study Commission headed by Nakayama Ichiro of the Japan Institute of Labor issued a report on productivity and the wage system. The report suggested that additional progress in the improvement of the work force could not be achieved under the traditional wage system, and it recommended that more efforts should be devoted to moving toward job-based pay systems.[47] The apparent slow movement toward more extensive use of job-based wage systems was again underscored in 1967, when, with abundant evidence that an era of a shortage of unskilled labor had long since arrived, Higuchi Koki could suggest that it might take another 10 years for the principle of "same wage-same job" to come into full existence.[48] This estimate may have assumed a too rapid rate of change. The president of Kitachi Shipbuilding and Engineering Company wrote in 1969, "... The time has come for a change..." [in wage system practices], a statement which is consistent with the idea that nenkō-centered systems still dominate Japanese personnel practices.[49] Indeed, in 1970 Esso Standard (Japan), which had used a pure merit system, introduced seniority-related factors into its wage system.[50]

The move away from pure nenkō systems began in the 1950's, when some firms introduced Shokumukyu formulas (job-classified wage rate systems). Though few in number--perhaps only 1 percent of the firms in the Kantō area were using them--these systems appeared to clash excessively with the more traditional approaches, and since then the changes have tended to emphasize shokunokyu (ability-classified wage structure) systems.

The exact extent of the use of non-nenkō factors by various companies is difficult to determine. The Jūjō Paper Company, which some consider to have had the most advanced wage system in Japan, in 1962 used job-related factors to determine 70 percent of base wages. At the same time in the Tokyo area, 37 firms, out of a sample of 74 which used job analysis, appeared to accord a median weight of about 40 percent to those factors.[51] It was in 1958 that the Japan Steel and Tube Company first used job evaluation, but it was not until 1962 that the three largest companies in iron and steel substantially reformed their traditional wage structures. The reform was modest; only about 15 percent of average monthly wages were redistributed on the basis of job evaluation. Even this modest amount was opposed by the union, controlled by the older workers, and in 1966 probably less than 20 percent of a worker's wage was affected by job evaluation measures in the Yawata and Fuji Steel Companies.[52]

In 1968 basic wages made up 85 percent of average monthly contract earnings. This was little changed from recent years, but was significantly higher than the 67.7 percent in 1956.[53] A basic nenkō wage system was utilized in determining about 10 percent of the base wages, and a basic job-ability system accounted for about 13 percent. The remaining 77.5 percent was based upon integration formulas which included elements that were both personal and job-related. These percentages were little changed from those recorded in 1963, except for a rise of about 2.5 percent in the importance of basic job factors, and a similar decline in the integrated formula area. Preliminary results from the 1968 survey suggest few changes from 1967, except among firms employing more than 5,000 workers, where there was a trend toward greater use of job-based rates. It seems clear that there will continue to be some erosion in the use of nenkō factors in the years ahead, but the pace and degree of this erosion would seem to depend upon the extent to which the forces underlying both the drive for a new system and the basic structure of nenkō change.

One view has been that nenkō and other seemingly special features of Japanese industrial relations were attributable largely to a lack of modernization. Consequently, with modernization extending into more and more sectors of the Japanese economy, it could be anticipated that factors associated with job evaluation would become more prevalent. The influence of one factor associated with modernization, advanced technology, has already been mentioned. A 1967 survey of a number of industries, however, suggests the great complexity of any tie between technology and the wage system. Most industries reported some reduction in the time necessary for a worker to obtain a given skill level, but there did not appear to be a clear tie between these changes and reported alterations in the method of paying wages. For example, in finance and insurance there were no reported changes in the wage system; in petrochemicals there was a slow movement toward a job-based wage system, but the nenkō one still predominated; and in heavy electrical appliances serious problems associated with worker expectations and subjectiveness in the introduction of a job-based system were reported.[54] Moderating these influences is the fact that nenkō is intimately tied to shūshin koyō (lifetime employment) and the Japanese social system.[55] In the absence of major alterations in these patterns, the most appropriate expectation would seem to be the growth in importance of job-related factors, but for the dominant pattern to be some complex blending of personal, nenkō, and job factors.

Comparative Employment Relationships

It would be difficult to argue that the differences between a Japanese blue-collar employee under nenkō and an American, with his seniority promotion system and fringe benefits tied to years of service and with protection against subcontracting and technological change, are very large. Yet the highly mobile professor who moves easily among universities, consulting, and government with his vested pension plans represents a significant contrast with his Japanese counterpart, who probably received all of his college and graduate education in the major university where he teaches and will undoubtedly retire never having taught at any other university. Clearly, then, there are both vast and insignificant differences between Japanese and American practice, depending upon the labor market. The dissatisfaction over aspects of nenkō, as shown in the survey which was cited, and the changes toward an occupational wage system which have already taken place in some Japanese firms suggest that Japan is moving closer to U.S. practice, largely as a result of management recognition of the advantages inherent in great flexibility of promotion and wage payment. At the same time, American management has recognized the importance and value inherent in protecting the worker against major unforeseen changes associated with technological development, thus bringing American practice closer to nenkō. Yet when all this has been said, there remain two differences in lifetime employment in the countries. The Japanese employee accepts an obligation to provide lifetime service in a way that his American counterpart does not.[56] And the nature of the company's honor in maintaining lifetime employment opportunities is much more at stake in Japan than in the United States.

NOTES

1. Clark Kerr, John T. Dunlop, Frederick H. Harbison, and Charles A. Myers, Industrialism and Industrial Man (Cambridge, Mass.: Harvard University Press, 1960).

2. Abraham J. Siegel, "Method and Substance in Theorizing About Worker Protest" in Universities National Bureau for Economic Research, Aspects of Labor Economics (Princeton: Princeton University Press, 1962) pp. 21-52; and Arthur M. Ross and Paul T. Hartman, Changing Patterns of Industrial Conflict (Cambridge, Mass.: Harvard University Press, 1960).

3. An application of a convergence hypothesis to some aspects of the Japanese labor market will be found in Bernard Karsh and Robert E. Cole, "Industrialization and the Convergence Hypothesis: Some Aspects of Contemporary Japan," Journal of Social Issues, XXIV, 4 (1968), 45-63.

4. The formulation of the hypotheses is that of Solomon B. Levine; see his "Postwar Trade Unionism, Collective Bargaining, and Japanese Social Structure," in R. P. Dore, ed., Aspects of Social Change in Modern Japan (Princeton: Princeton University Press, 1967), pp. 246-50.

5. Arthur M. Whitehill, Jr., and Shin-ichi Takezawa, in their recent comparison of industrial relations in Japan and the United States, concluded with a general assessment of their empirical findings. In doing this, they did not attempt to use any of various models, models which they referred to as "arbitrary." See their The Other Worker (Honolulu: East-West Center Press, 1968), p. 343.

6. Ministry of Labor, "Special Survey of Retirement Age Workers," reported in the Japan Labor Bulletin, VII (August, 1968), 2. The normal retirement age in Japan is 55, in the United States 65.

7. Bernard Karsh, "The Exportability of Trade Union Movements: The Japan-U.S. Trade Union 'Cultural Exchange Program,'" in The Changing Patterns of Industrial Relations (Tokyo: Japan Institute of Labor, 1965), pp. 55-68.

8. Adolf Sturmthal, "Industrialization and the Labor Movement," in Labor Relations in the Asian Countries (Tokyo: Japan Institute of Labor, 1967), p. 52.

9. Americans often seem to think of their own country as the proper model, but America has one of the least typical union movements in the world.

10. An elaboration of most of the events mentioned here may be found in Henry Pelling, American Labor (Chicago: University of Chicago Press, 1960); Gerald N. Grob, "Knights of Labor and the Trade Unions, 1878-1886," Journal of Economic History, XVIII (June, 1958), 176-92; Irving Bernstein, The Lean Years (Baltimore: Penguin Books, 1966); David Brody, Steelworkers in America (Cambridge, Mass.: Harvard University Press, 1960); Jonathan Grossman, William Sylvia, Pioneer of American Labor (New York: Columbia University Press, 1945).

11. Official records record a rise of 617,618 members between July 1, 1885, and July 1, 1886. Norman J. Ware, The Labor Movement in the United States, 1860-1890 (New York: Vintage Books, 1964), p. 66.

12. Factual material on the growth of Japanese unions is largely based upon Kazuo Ōkōchi, Labor in Modern Japan, Economic Series, 18, (Tokyo: Science Council of Japan, 1958); Iwao F. Ayusawa, A History of Labor in Modern Japan (Honolulu: East-West Center Press, 1966); Solomon B. Levine, Industrial Relations in Postwar Japan (Urbana: University of Illinois Press, 1958); George O. Totten, III, "Collective Bargaining and Works Councils as Innovations in Industrial Relations in Japan During the 1920's," in Ronald P. Dore, ed., Aspects of Social Change in Modern Japan (Princeton: Princeton University Press, 1967), pp. 203-43; Robert Evans, Jr., "Evolution of the Japanese System of Employer-Employee Relations, 1868-1945," Business History Review, XLIV (Spring, 1970), 110-25.

13. George O. Totten, III, The Social Democratic Movement in Prewar Japan (New Haven: Yale University Press, 1966), p. 213.

14. The company-dominated image of the American term "company union" should not be transferred to the linguistically similar Japanese term Kigyō Kumiai (enterprise union).

15. For a brief discussion of the strike as a tactic, see Robert Evans, Jr., "Shuntō, Japanese Labor's Spring Wage Offensive," Monthly Labor Review, XC (October, 1967), 23-28.

16. Since all American union members cannot strike in a given year because of the use of no-strike grievance clauses and multi-year contracts, whereas most Japanese workers participate in three negotiations a year (general wages and two bonuses), the effective participation rate is much smaller in Japan.

17. "The 1969 Basic Survey of Trade Unions," Japan Labor Bulletin, IX (March, 1970), 9-12.

18. A more complete discussion of these differences may be found in Alice H. Cook, Japanese Trade Unionism (Ithaca: Cornell University Press, 1966).

19. A brief summary of the union status of governmental employees may be found in Yasuhiko Matsuda, "Government Employees in Japan," Japan Labor Bulletin, III (October, 1966), 4-8, and III (November, 1966), 4-8.

20. Masumi Tsuda, The Basic Structure of Japanese Labor Relations (Tokyo: Musashi University, 1965), p. 89.

21. Ibid., pp. 93-95.

22. Levine, Industrial Relations in Postwar Japan, p. 90.

23. A more complete discussion will be found in ibid., pp. 137-73 and in Changing Patterns of Industrial Relations, (Tokyo: Japan Institute of Labor, 1965), pp. 216-47.

24. Hazama Hiroshi, Nihonteki Keiei no Keifu [A genealogy of the Japanese system of management] (Tokyo: Nihon Noritsu Kyōkai, 1963), pp. 103-07.

25. Robert J. Ballon, Makoto Sakurabayashi, and Ichiro Tsunekawa, "Wage Survey of Male Blue Collar Workers," Sophia University Socio-Economic Institute, Industrial Relations Section, Bulletin 14 (April, 1967), p. 3.

26. Hideaki Okamoto, "Enterprises in Japan: A Sociological Perspective," Japan Labor Bulletin 6 (July, 1967), pp. 4-8.

27. Tsuda, op. cit., p. 84.

28. The employment process in large firms and other aspects of nenkō are described in James C. Abegglen, The Japanese Factory (Glencoe, Ill.: The Free Press, 1958). The descriptive material is accurate, but parts of the analysis may be unduly affected by the period of the interviews, 1956, just as high postwar growth rates were beginning. Also the emphasis upon the cultural source of nenkō has been called into question by a number of Japanese scholars.

29. In 1958 a survey of 1,053 companies revealed that 69.6 percent maintained bachelor dormitories, 82.7 percent family housing, and 42.5 percent a housing loan system.

30. Whitehill and Takezawa, op. cit., p. 359.

31. Abegglen, op. cit., p. 116.

32. Tsuda, op. cit., p. 20. Similar views have been expressed by Noda Kazuo in his "Traditionalism in Japanese Management," Rikkyō Daigaku Shakaigakubu Ken Kyū Kiyō, ōyō shakai Kenkyū Dai Rokushū Bessatsu [Rikkyō University Faculty of Social Science Research Bulletin, Applied Social Science Research], 6 (March, 1963), 154-56.

33. Koji Taira, Economic Development and the Labor Market in Japan (New York: Columbia University Press, 1970), pp. 159-63.

34. His ideas are presented in summary form in Tsuda, op. cit., pp. 6-9. See also Tsuda Masumi, "Nenkō Joretsu Chingin to Nenkō Seido" [Age- and service-based wages and the wage system], in Shinohara Miyohei and Funehasihi Naomichi, eds., Nihon-gata Chingin Kōzō no Kenkyū [Research on the structure of Japanese wages] (Tokyo: Rōdō Hōgaku Ken Kyū Sho, 1962), pp. 235-87; Shōwa Dojinkai, ed., Wagakuni Chingin Kōzō no Shiteki Kōsatsu [Japanese wage structure] (Tokyo: Shiseido, 1960).

35. This is discussed in Tsuda, op. cit., pp. 75-76.

36. Hisashi Kawada, "Continuity and Discontinuity: An Approach to Industrial Relations Systems," in The Changing Patterns of Industrial Relations (Tokyo: Japan Institute of Labor, 1965), p. 71.

37. Akira Katakami, "Types of Joint Consultation and Their Relations to Collective Bargaining in the Industrial Relations of Japan," Bulletin of University of Osaka Prefecture, series D, X (1966), 61.

38. In addition to the works cited in notes 31-37, the following have been useful in preparing this section: Makoto Sakurabayashi and Robert J. Ballon, "Labor Management Relations in Modern Japan: A Historical Survey of Personnel Administration," in Joseph Roggendorf, Studies in Japanese Culture (Tokyo: Sophia University, 1963), pp. 245-60; Totten, "Collective Bargaining...," pp. 203-43; Eitaro Kishimoto, "The Characteristics of Labour-Management Relations in Japan and Their Historical Formation," Kyoto University Economic Review, XXXV (October, 1965), 33-55, and XXXVI (April, 1966), 17-38. Solomon B. Levine, "Labor Markets and Collective Bargaining in Japan," in William W. Lockwood, ed., The State and Economic Enterprise in Japan (Princeton: Princeton University Press, 1964), pp. 633-67.

39. This is the essence of Levine's argument.

40. This point is strongly emphasized in Kishimoto, op. cit., p. 27.

41. Nakumura Mototada, ed., Nihon Kōgyō Kurabu Nijūgo Nenshi [Japan industrial club 25-year history], (Tokyo: Nihum Kōgyō Karabu, 1943), I, pp. 182-83.

42. The rationalization of employment (the transfer or layoff of surplus labor) was a major union concern in the decade 1945-55, a principal cause of strikes, including the longest in the postwar period, and the central economic policy focus of the initial Sōhyō leadership.

43. The worker with strong allegiance to the company is more favorable to automation than are other workers. Kunio Odaka, "Implications of Dual Allegiance in the Modernization of Industrial Relations in Japan," in The Changing Patterns of Industrial Relations (Tokyo: Japan Institute of Labor, 1965), p. 108.

44. Tsuda Masumi, Rōdō Mondai to Rōmu Kanri [Labor problems and labor management] (Kyoto: Japan Academic Association for Social Policy, 1959).

45. Japan Federation of Employees Association News, 9 (August, 1961), 4.

46. Tsuda, The Basic Structure..., pp. 101-02.

47. Japan Labor Bulletin, VI (March, 1967), 2.

48. Koki Higuchi, "Industrial Relations in Transition," The Oriental Economist, XXXV (August, 1967), 489.

49. Takao Nagata, "Japan's Labor-Management Relations," Management Japan, III (1969), 28.

50. Japan Labor Bulletin, IX (May, 1970), 2.

51. Japan Federation of Employers Association News, 12 (December, 1962), 5-6.

52. Kazutoshi Koshiro, "Industrial Relations in the Japanese Iron and Steel Industry, II," Japan Labor Bulletin, V (July, 1966), 7-8. For a discussion of changes in the promotion policies among leading companies which also stressed ability and down graded a nenkō approach, see Kamata Isao et al., "Kaihyō Kigyō no Shoshin sei Kaku" [Promotion policies in representative companies], Chūō Kōron [Public opinion review] (September, 1966), pp. 306-25.

53. Based upon the results of various "Chingin Rōdō Jikan Seido Sōgō Chō Sa" [Wage and Hour Survey], as reported in Rōdō Tōkei Nenpō [Yearbook of labor statistics].

54. "Sangyō betsu in mita gijutsu kakushin to Chingin Seido no Dā Kō" [Trends in technical changes and the wage system] (1967). (Unpublished.)

55. The tie between the shūshin and nenkō systems is discussed in Hazama Hiroshi, "Fukuri Kokka ni okeru Keiei" [Prosperity and management], Chūō Kōron (March, 1962), pp. 274-83.

56. Several years ago (August 30, 1963) Life ran a story on a Hitachi engineer. He was quoted as saying that he would not change jobs even for a large raise because of what the company had done for him. It would be almost impossible to find an American engineer who would make a similar statement.

CHAPTER

2

EMPLOYMENT AND MANPOWER

Over a few years employment changes within a nation are so many and so varied and the characteristics of manpower problems so complex that it is difficult to select the most appropriate topics. This is especially true for the United States and Japan because the specific issues which have been the concerns of professional economists, the policy perlexities of government officials, and the events deemed newsworthy by the newsmen in the two countries seem so utterly different. A single example will illustrate the point. In Japan there is a great concern over the shortage of young workers, especially middle-school graduates, while in the United States the concern has been over the inability of young workers to find jobs.

This chapter therefore concentrates upon the relevant concerns in the two economies and at the same time establishes the basis for some fruitful comparisons. Such a principle may be found in the mechanism and organization of the labor market. This is because situations which result from dramatic interactions between labor demand and labor supply and, on rare occasions, changes in major institutional arrangements in the labor market give concern to the economist, problems to political leaders, and stories to newsmen. A concentration upon labor market mechanisms, the interaction of demand and supply schedules for labor, and the organization of the labor market should allow proper coverage and provide a basis for comparison.

THE LABOR MARKET MECHANISM

Within the demand for labor the principal elements of a dynamic atmosphere are associated with the changing nature of the industrial, occupational, and geographical location of jobs, especially newly created jobs. On the supply side there is seemingly less potential for dramatic change, though different subgroups within the labor force may offer a greater or lesser degree of their labor in the market, depending upon other opportunities, cultural restrictions, and variations in schooling and retirement practices.

In the classic economic world the importance of labor market mechanisms was very minor, for the assumption was always made that wages were sufficiently flexible and mobility sufficiently rapid and extensive that markets were quickly cleared. The attributes of alternative employment were thought to interact with employee attributes and taste in such a way that the net advantages of jobs were usually inversely related to wages. Such a view of market response is no longer tenable, for it can be seen that many types of employment and wages remain superior upon all accounts. Consequently, the market mechanism must be seen as more than the classic channels through which employees flow in the process of establishment of equilibrium. It is in addition a rationing system which allocates jobs among the potential supply of applicants. A natural result of such a rationing process is for society to view those individuals who are excluded from the more favorable types of employment as a disadvantaged sector or "a problem." It would be possible for two countries to have very similar employment mechanisms which applied roughly similar criteria in the labor allocation process but produced disadvantaged groups whose superficial characteristics were quite distinct. This, as will be argued later, is largely true of the United States and Japan. First, and as a basis for analyzing the market mechanisms, a special emphasis will be placed upon changes in employment opportunities, variations in labor supply, and special market situations.

CHANGES IN EMPLOYMENT OPPORTUNITIES

Agricultural Employment

The broad sweep of the shifts in industrial employment in the United States is shown in Table 6. The most outstanding long-run movement is the movement out of agriculture. Only 100 years ago more than half of the laboring population was engaged in extracting the natural resources of the land, sea, and forests. From 1870 until 1930 there was a steady decline of roughly 5 percent per decade in the proportion of agricultural employment. The sharpest drop, 6.8 percent, came between 1880 and 1890. Between 1930 and 1940 there was only a very modest change, 2.9 percent. Indeed, during the worst years of nongrowth and extensive unemployment there was a net return to agriculture. The years after 1940 again show a rapid decline, which became even more pronounced in the 1950's, when the proportion employed on the farm was halved. Measured in terms of persons, the decline was about 24 percent.

Data on changes in the industrial distribution of employment in Japan for essentially the same period are provided in Table 7, though here the beginning year is 1872 rather than 1870. Only limited reliance can be placed upon the data prior to 1920 because really accurate Japanese population data were not available until the census of 1920.[1] Consequently, data for earlier years must depend upon estimates. Those used in Table 7 have been widely quoted, but they are based largely upon linear projections backward from the census of 1920 and hence must be interpreted with caution.

Two things stand out in the tables. The first is the dramatic decline in the proportion of the labor force employed in agriculture. The second is the seeming influence of the Pacific War in arresting and reversing the movement out of agriculture in Japan. Thus, in Japan there were almost as many people relative to the size of the labor force employed in agriculture in 1950 as in 1930, despite the fact that agricultural employment declined in the 1930's.

In both countries the most dramatic relative shift in employment has been in agriculture, where precipitous declines have occurred. The relative American farm population declined 48. 9 percent, from 53. 5 percent in 1870 to 4. 6 percent in 1969. In Japan the decline was 57. 1 percent, from 75. 0 in 1875 to 17. 9 in 1969.[2] Proportionately there was a tenfold

TABLE 6

Industrial Distribution of Employment, United States, 1870-1969
(percent)

Industry	1870	1890	1910	1920	1930	1940	1950	1960	1969
Agriculture	53.5	43.4	31.6	27.6	21.9	19.0	12.5	6.7	4.6
Mining	1.4	1.9	2.6	2.6	2.0	2.0	1.6	1.0	.9
Construction	--	--	--	--	--	4.6	6.1	5.9	4.7
Manufacturing	20.5	23.7	28.5	30.3	28.9	23.7	26.0	27.1	26.4
Transportation, Communication	4.2	6.0	7.1	7.3	7.9	7.0	7.9	6.9	6.0
Trade	6.8	8.8	9.7	10.0	12.5	16.6	18.6	18.2	19.9
Finance	--	--	--	--	--	3.3	3.4	4.2	4.8
Public Administration	.7	.9	1.2	1.7	1.8	3.1	4.5	5.0	16.6
Professional and Related	2.6	3.8	4.6	5.1	6.7	7.5	8.5	11.7	--
Other Services	9.7	9.6	10.1	8.0	10.1	11.6	9.3	9.3	14.9
Not Reported	--	--	--	--	--	1.6	1.5	4.0	--
Clerical	.6	2.0	4.6	7.3	8.2	--	--	--	--

Note: The nonagricultural data do not reflect the distribution of the self-employed, 6.7 million, and unpaid family workers, .7 million.

Sources: Data for 1870-1930 are from the 16th Census, 1940, "Comparative Occupational Statistics for the United States, 1870-1940," p. 101. (Between 1870 and 1930 the industrial classifications used were reasonably comparable.) Data for 1940-60 are from the 18th Census, 1960, General School and Economic Characteristics, U. S. Summary Final Report PC (1)-1C, pp. 1-223. Data for 1969 are from Manpower Report of the President 1970, pp. 228, 265.

TABLE 7

Industrial Distribution of Employment, Japan, 1872-1969
(percent)

Industry	1872	1890	1910	1920	1930	1940	1950	1960	1965	1969
Agriculture	75.0	69.2	55.0	51.6	47.4	42.4	46.5	30.0	23.4	17.9
Fishing	3.2	2.4	2.3	2.0	1.9	1.7	1.9	1.6	1.3	.9
Mining	--	.4	1.5	1.6	1.1	1.8	1.7	1.2	.7	.5
Construction	1.0	1.7	2.7	2.7	3.3	3.0	4.3	6.1	7.1	7.4
Manufacturing	5.9	10.2	16.3	16.5	16.0	21.2	15.9	21.8	24.5	26.8
Trade	8.1	8.7	11.8	9.8	14.0	12.7	12.1	17.6	20.2	22.6
Transportation and Communication	1.0	1.1	.9	4.2	4.4	4.7	5.1	5.6	6.6	6.7
Public and other services	4.3	3.3	5.6	9.8	11.6	11.8	12.4	14.9	16.1	17.4
Others	1.6	1.7	2.1	1.9	.2	.7	--	--	--	--

Sources: Data for 1872-1910 are estimates based upon the 1920 census and projected backward: Hijikata Seibi, "Shokugyō Betsu Jinko no Hensen o tsūjite mitaru Shitsugyō Mondai" [The unemployment problem as observed by changes in the gainfully occupied population], Shakei Seisaku Jihō [Review of social policy] (September, 1929), pp. 78-79. 1920-40 are from Irene B. Taeuber, The Population of Japan (Princeton: Princeton University Press, 1958), p. 87. 1950-65 are from an every-five-year population census, quoted in Japan Institute of Labor, Japan's Labor Statistics (Tokyo, Ministry of Labor, 1970), pp. 30-31. The 1969 data are from Rōdōryoku Chōsa Hōkoku [Annual report on the labor force survey], (1969), p. 10. The agricultural estimates for 1872, 1890, and 1910 are from revised agricultural-nonagricultural estimates of James I. Nakamura, Agricultural Production and the Economic Development of Japan, 1873-1922 (New York: Columbia University Press, 1966), pp. 142-50.

shrinkage in the United States and but a fourfold one for Japan. In part these different absolute and percentage rates reflect the great divergence in the two countries' situations in 1870. The proportion of agricultural employment in Japan was 1.4 times that in the United States. Indeed, agricultural employment in Japan in 1920 accounted for almost the same proportion of total employment as it did in America half a century earlier. Once Japan reached the position where only half of her people were engaged in agriculture, the rate at which people moved off the farm was much more rapid than it was for the United States. In the United States it took from 1870 to 1940 to reduce the proportion of the labor force engaged in agriculture from 53.5 percent to 19 percent. Yet in Japan it took a mere 17 years: from 46.5 percent in 1950 to 19.3 percent in 1967. Thus both countries have experienced dramatic declines in the proportion of agricultural employment. The pattern of movement in the United States has been one of fairly steady decline from 1870 to 1960. In Japan there was a similar steady decline from 1870 until the end of World War I, when for practical purposes relative declines in agriculture ceased; in 1950 decline began anew.

A second difference between the two countries has been in the change in persons employed in agriculture and the number of farms. In Japan the number of farm families was fairly stable at 5.5 million from 1870, except for the immediate postwar years, when it rose to 6.2 million. The farm household population remained at about 29 million from 1880 to 1923. It rose gently to 31 million in 1940, peaked at 37.9 in 1949, and then began to fall rather rapidly.[3] In the United States the number of farms rose from 4 million in 1880 to 6.5 million in 1920. It stabilized there for about 20 years and then began a rapid decline to its 1970 figure of 2.9 million.[4] The farm population since 1920 has followed a generally consistent pattern: around 30 million from 1920 to 1940, then dropping to 23 million in 1950 and 11 million in 1967. In the United States the rapid and continuous decline in the relative employment in agriculture has been accompanied since 1940 by a rapid movement out of agriculture by farm families and the consequent enlargement of average farm size. The similar decline in Japan has had only a very moderate impact upon the number of farm households and the resulting size of individual farms. This has meant that the basic burden of Japanese farming has fallen upon the very young, the very old, and particularly the women of the family. This can be seen in the fact that the principal male or the householder in 79 percent of all farm households engages in some off-farm employment.

Nonagricultural Employment

The growth in U.S. manufacturing between 1870 and 1920 and again between 1940 and 1960 was relatively rapid. Yet these changes amounted only to changes in industrial distribution of about 10 percent in the first period and about 4 percent in the second period. The other principal shifts came in trade, which has about doubled its proportion of employment since 1920. Professional and related employment also doubled in the same period, while public administration increased slightly more, about 2.5 times. Some of these latter increases resulted from the reallocation of clerical employment, which was carried as a special category until 1930, to the other industry groupings. The era from 1870 to 1960 can be broken down into two subperiods, with the end of World War I acting as the watershed. In both of these periods, except for 1930-40, there was a very steady outpouring of employment from agriculture. In the first period, 1870-1920, much of the downward movement in agriculture was taken up by gains in transport and communication and in manufacturing. Since 1920 the biggest gains have come in trade and in professional and related services.

Between 1872 and 1910 the proportion of Japanese employed in manufacturing increased rapidly, but the next 20 years saw little change. The Pacific War had an impact upon manufacturing analogous but inverse to that in agriculture. The proportion employed in manufacturing in 1950 was only just equal to what it had been in 1930, despite the rapid shift in favor of manufacturing employment during the 1930's. By 1960 manufacturing had regained its 1940 position, though because of population growth there were 3 million more workers in manufacturing in 1960 than there had been in 1940. The other major areas of change have been trade and public service. The former has more than doubled its proportion of employment since 1920, and there has been perhaps a 60 percent increase in the role of public and other services.

Looking only at the most recent distributions of industrial employment, it can be seen (see Tables 6 and 7) that the trade and transport and communication sectors of the two economies are approximately equal in relative employment. The patterns of employment growth in wholesale and retail trade in both countries since 1920 have also been equal. The transport, communication, and public utilities sectors have had opposite growth experiences. In the United States the trend has been downward since 1920, while in Japan there has been a modestly rising trend.

The manufacturing sectors are also about equal in size: 26.8 percent for Japan in 1969 and 26.4 percent for the United States in 1969. This represents for Japan the upper point of a fivefold expansion since 1872, but for the United States it is only 5.9 percent above the 1870 figure. The relatively service-oriented position of the U.S. economy can be clearly seen in the relative sizes of the total public, private, and professional service categories, which in the United States make up about one-third of total employment, a proportion about twice that in Japan.

Occupational Employment

The changes in occupational employment in the United States largely mirror the industrial shifts. (See Table 8.) Between 1900 and 1969 the percentage of farm managers and farm laborers declined from 19.8 and 17.6, respectively, to only 2.3 and 1.9, respectively. The combined proportion of laborers and operatives in total employment has remained fairly stable, though the relative proportions have undergone pronounced shifts. In 1900 approximately half of the total were operatives and half were laborers. By 1960 there were three operatives for each laborer. The proportion of craftsmen has grown, but only a little, and most of that growth occurred prior to 1920. Service workers and managers have both increased, with perhaps the gain after 1940 deserving to be called a marked rise. Other than in agricultural occupations, the only dramatic changes have come among professional and clerical workers. The former tripled its 1900 proportion of 4.2 percent to 13.6 percent in 1969, while the rise in clerical employment was even more pronounced, from 3 percent in 1900 to 17.2 percent in 1969.

On balance, the occupation pattern over time is the same as the industrial one. The era to about 1920-30 shows an increase in machinery-based occupations (operatives, craftsmen, transport), while the more recent years have been characterized chiefly by expansions in the proportions of clerical, professional, and service jobs.

The occupational distribution in Japan, as in the United States, mirrors the changes in the industrial distribution. (See Table 9.) The proportion of craftsmen, operatives, and laborers rose rapidly in the 1930's as agricultural employment declined, only to be reversed in the subsequent decade. Over the years from 1930 to 1969 the biggest relative gains came in professional employment, which more than doubled; in clerical, which

TABLE 8

Occupational Distribution of Employment, United States, 1900-69
(percent)

Occupation	1900	1910	1920	1930	1940	1950	1960	1967	1969
Professional	4.2	4.7	5.4	6.8	7.5	8.6	10.8	13.0	13.6
Farm Manager	19.8	16.5	15.3	12.4	10.4	7.6	4.0	2.6	2.3
Manager	5.9	6.6	6.7	7.2	7.3	8.8	10.2	9.8	10.0
Clerical	3.0	5.3	8.1	8.9	9.6	12.3	14.5	16.6	17.2
Sales Worker	4.8	4.7	4.9	6.3	6.6	7.0	6.5	6.1	6.0
Craftsman or Foreman	10.5	11.6	13.0	12.8	12.0	14.2	12.9	13.1	13.0
Operative	12.8	14.6	15.7	15.7	18.4	20.4	18.6	19.0	18.7
Private Household Worker	5.4	5.0	3.4	4.1	4.7	2.6	3.3	2.4	2.1
Service Worker	3.6	4.6	4.5	5.7	7.1	7.9	9.3	10.3	10.3
Laborer	12.5	12.0	11.7	10.9	9.4	6.6	6.0	5.0	4.9
Farm Laborer	17.6	14.4	11.7	8.8	7.0	4.4	3.9	2.2	1.9

Notes: Unemployed persons are entered in their last occupation. Up until 1967 the labor force was defined in terms of those 14 years old and older. Beginning in 1967 it included only those 16 years old and older.

Sources: Data for 1900-50 are from the Historical Statistics of the United States, 1957, Table D 72-122. Data for 1960, 1967, and 1969 are from Handbook of Labor Statistics, 1970, p. 36.

TABLE 9

Occupational Distribution of Employment, Japan, 1930-69
(percent)

Occupation	1930	1940	1950	1955	1955	1960	1966	1969
Professional	2.5	4.0	4.3	4.9	4.6	5.0	5.1	5.6
Administrative, Management	.2	.6	1.7	2.1	1.8	1.7	2.5	2.6
Clerical	4.7	7.3	8.6	8.7	9.0	11.2	13.7	14.3
Sales	13.3	9.1	8.2	10.8	11.1	12.1	12.8	13.2
Farmer, Logger, Fisherman	49.4	44.0	47.7	40.4	40.0	32.7	24.1	18.8
Miner	.8	1.1	1.2	.9	.7	.7	.4	.3
Transport, Communication	1.5	1.5	1.4	1.8	1.7	2.4	4.3	4.5
Craftsman, Production Worker, Laborer	19.8	25.3	22.0	24.0	25.4	28.1	30.7	32.2
Service Worker	7.6	5.8	4.5	6.3	4.8	6.1	7.2	7.5
Other	.2	1.2	.1	--	--	--	--	--

Sources: Data for 1930-55 are adapted from Kokusei Chōsa ni yoru Shokugyō Jinko no Saikōsei [A reconstruction of Japanese census data on occupational employment], Census Research Series 70 (Tokyo: Japan Institute of Labor, 1965), pp. 67-68. Data for 1955-1960 are from Nihon Tōkei Nenken, 1966 [Japan statistical yearbook], p. 55. Data for 1966 are from Rōdō Ryoku Chōsa Hōkaku, 1966 [Annual report on the labor force survey], pp. 50-51. The 1969 figures are from Japan Institute of Labor, Japan Labor Statistics (Tokyo, 1970), p. 41.

almost tripled; and in transport and communication, which tripled. In the case of transport and communication, almost all of the gain has been in the last 9 years. Thus in terms of dramatic shifts this sector can take its place with agriculture.

Comparative Distributions

The shifting employment proportions can be placed into the simple development model of progress from a primary base through secondary and finally into tertiary employment. It would appear that from the 1870's to 1920 Japan followed the initial stages of this model by undergoing some shift from primary toward secondary employment. From 1920 to 1950, with the exception of the forced draft experience of the China incident and Pacific War years, the period was largely one of running very fast merely to stay in one place. Since 1955 Japan appears to be moving simultaneously into both the second and the third stages.

The general pattern in the United States for both industrial and occupational distributions of employment has been to follow the conventional movement away from primary areas of the economy--agriculture, forestry, fishing, and mining--and into secondary types of employment, with an emphasis upon manufacturing and the provision of transportation and communication. In turn this stage is followed by movement into tertiary areas, with their emphasis upon personal service. In terms of capital investment it has meant largely a shift from land to machines to people. Viewed in this way, the United States economy was by the turn of the century already well into the second, or machine, stage of development. By 1920-30 the economy was beginning to become more and more of a service economy.

The distribution of occupational employment in the two countries runs largely true to what would have been expected on the basis of the industrial distribution. The clerical proportions are approximately equal, and both represent major increases. The most outstanding differences are in the professional and managerial classes. Part of the difference is definitional, with the U.S. definition being wider than the one used in Japan. A second major difference is in the treatment of agriculture. In Japan 98.7 percent of those in agriculture are classed as craftsmen, while 58.1 percent of farmers in the United States are listed as managers. Other industries show less extreme differences, and in manufacturing the difference is almost nonexistent: 4 percent of the Japanese and 5.1 percent of the Americans are managers. A similar situation exists for professional workers, with the closest correspondence coming in the service industry, where 33.4 percent of the Japanese and 34.1 percent of Americans in services are professionals.[5] Whether this smaller proportion of managerial and professional employees represents a shortage in Japan or a surplus in the United States is not clear, though a case could be made for the latter. We are left with the observation that the two principal differences between the employment structure in Japan and the United States are (1) Japan has only partly entered the service phase of economic growth, while the United States appears to be well into that phase; and (2) in Japan the ratio of professional and managerial personnel to total employment is much smaller in most industrial sectors than is true of the United States.

WOMEN IN THE LABOR FORCE

Among U.S. labor economists there is general agreement that one of the largest labor force and employment changes has been the major increase in the proportion of women employed. It is to this that we now turn.

The United States

Between 1947 and 1969 the number of women in the U.S. labor force has grown from 16.6 million to 30.6 million, an increase of 85 percent. Compared with the increase in the male labor force, the female increase has been over four times as large, 85 percent to 21 percent. In addition to the growing national population, this expansion of the female labor force has been accomplished by a gain in labor force participation of 10.9 percent. The rise has been almost uninterrupted from 31.8 percent in 1947 to 42.7 percent in 1969. The percentage shift in the male labor force has been half that of the female labor force and its direction has been opposite, the labor force participation of males declining from 86.8 percent in 1947 to a low of 80.9 percent in 1969. On a combined basis this has meant that the total labor force has expanded by about 23 million persons, from 60.9 million in 1947 to 84.2 million in 1969, while aggregate labor force participation has inched upward from 58.9 percent to 61.1 percent.

Except for the very youngest age group, the labor force participation of all classes of women has risen. This is shown in Table 10, which presents the participation rates for women by age groups. There it can be seen that the major shift has occurred in the age group 55-64. Among women of those ages the increase in the participation rate has been 16.1 percent, an expansion of almost 60 percent. The second largest increase was to be found among the age group 45-54. The 15.8 percent increase also brought that group the distinction of having the second highest level of participation in 1969, 53.8 percent. Until 1957 the highest participation group had been the 20-24 year age group, a position it regained in 1967. The exceptions to these rapidly rising trends in participation are to be found among the very young and the very old. The participation rate for ages 16-19 has remained largely unchanged, while that for those over 65 rose briefly from 8.1 percent in 1947 to a post-war high of 10.9 percent in 1956 and since then has declined. In 1969 it was 9.9 percent.

Japan

Unlike the United States, where the trend among all female age groups has been toward a rising labor force participation, in Japan the general movement among the youngest and oldest age groups has been toward a decline in labor force participation.[6] This has been partly counter-balanced by increased participation among women 40-60 years of age. (See Table 10.) The most dramatic change has undoubtedly been among those aged 15 to 19. In 1950 this group's participation rate was 56.0 percent. In the next 15 years it declined to 37.7 percent. This would largely seem to reflect the fact that a larger number of women are going on to attend high school. In 1952 the ratio of female middle school graduates to female high school graduates who were entering the labor force was 3.4 to 1. By 1969 there were about 290,000 more female high school graduates than female middle school graduates who were entering the labor force. Approached from another point of view, in the early 1950's about half of each year's female middle school graduates went on to high school and half sought employment. In 1969, for every female middle school graduate who went into the labor force, 4.1 girls went on to higher education.[7]

This monumental shift in continuance of education does not appear to be largely in response to labor market conditions, at least not as it affects new school graduates. This is because

TABLE 10

Female Labor Force Participation Rates, Japan and the United States, 1950-69 (percent)

	Japan					
Age	1950	1955	1960	1965	1965	1969
15-19	56.0	50.1	49.7	37.5	35.8	35.0
20-24	64.0	68.2	69.4	69.5	70.2	70.0
25-29	48.3	51.8	50.1	46.6	49.0	47.0
30-39	50.0	51.3	53.1	52.6	--	--
30-34	--	--	--	--	51.1	48.9
35-39	--	--	--	--	59.6	57.6
40-49	53.2	55.0	56.7	62.4	--	--
40-54	--	--	--	--	60.2	61.9
50-59	48.2	48.8	49.3	54.8	--	--
55-64	--	--	--	--	45.3	44.8
60 and over	27.2	27.0	26.9	25.1	--	--
65 and over	--	--	--	--	21.6	18.5
	United States					
	1950	1955	1960	1965		1969
16-19	39.2	40.7	39.8	38.0		43.5
20-24	46.1	46.0	46.2	50.0		56.8
25-34	34.0	34.9	36.0	38.6		43.8
35-44	39.1	41.6	43.5	46.1		49.9
45-54	38.0	43.8	49.8	50.9		53.8
55-64	27.0	32.5	37.2	41.1		43.1
65 and over	9.7	10.6	10.8	10.0		9.9

Note: The survey sample unit in Japan was changed from the 1960 to the 1965 census and enumeration was altered from self-plus-interview to interview only.

Sources: Japan--Japan's Labor Statistics (Tokyo: Japan Institute of Labor, 1967), p. 27; and for 1965 and 1969, Annual Report of the Labor Force Survey (1969), p. 3. United States--Handbook of Labor Statistics (1970), p. 29.

the relative wages of middle school graduates rose much more rapidly than did those of high school graduates. Between 1954 and 1969 the starting wages of female middle school graduates rose 5.6 times, but for high school graduates the increase was 4.3 times. Measured absolutely, the increase in monthly wages between 1954 and 1969 for female high school graduates was 1,721 yen, greater than that for middle school graduates.

The employment of women, the proportion of which has remained essentially constant, has shifted in approximately the same manner as the combined male and female employment. This means that the greatest change has been the movement out of agriculture. In 1950, 60 out of every 100 employed women were engaged in agriculture and forestry. In 1969 the figure was down to only 24 in 100. The biggest increase came in manufacturing, which now employs 25 out of every 100 women, more than twice the 12 out of 100 of 1950. A similarly large increase took place in trade and finance, and more modest ones in services and public service, where the increase was from 11 per 100 in 1950 to 18 per 100 in 1969. These were also three areas where women as a proportion of total employment increased. Women now make up over one-third of all manufacturing employees. For trade and finance the increase was from 38.8 percent to 46.0 percent of all employees, and there was a similar shift in services and public services, 36.7 percent to 50 percent of all employees. The relative income position of the employed woman has also improved slightly. Between 1952 and 1968 the ratio of male to female earnings declined from 2.23 to only 2.15. Similar modest declines were to be found in the specific industrial areas where there were marked increases in female employment. There are, of course, variations in income between age groups and firm size which must also be considered. In 1968 the economy-wide male-female wage ratio for 18-19-year-olds was 1.28, but this rose to 2.83 for those aged 40-49. In general the ratio of male to female wages is somewhat smaller in the larger firms. In 1968 there was only a 40 percent differential at age 20-24 in firms employing more than 1,000, but it was 51 percent in firms of 30-99 employees.

The general picture which emerges from this is that there has been very little change in the female labor force activity in Japan which has been unique to women. In company with men, women have increasingly gone to higher schools. There have been modest declines, especially since 1960, in labor force participation among women in the prime childbearing years 25-39 which are probably attributable to the declines in the amount of small-scale enterprises which would utilize family labor, since it has typically been common for most women working for large firms to cease employment upon marriage. Indeed, a recent well-publicized legal case concerned the right of the Sumitomo Cement Company to discharge a woman who had promised to resign upon getting married but who, upon marriage, refused to resign. While the decision was a victory for women's rights, for the District Court of Tokyo held in December, 1966, that the company could not discharge the woman, it is not apt to change the situation in the near future. Women in professional employment are, however, more apt to continue working while they are married, since they are usually employed in firms which operate under a nenkō system and thus cannot drop out of the labor force and then return in quite the way that American female professionals can. There are, of course, some modest stirrings toward a return to the labor force among women who left employment upon marriage or the birth of children. Some large electrical concerns will employ older women on either a full-time or a part-time basis. And with increasing shortages of low-wage (that is, primarily young) workers, it can be anticipated that part-time employment will increase; yet even in 1968 only 6.5 percent of regular women employees were scheduled to work less than 35 hours a week, a modest increase from the 5.0 percent level of 1964.[8]

Comparative Female Participation

The most obvious difference in the labor force behavior of women in the two countries is the fact that there was a slight decline in overall female participation in Japan until 1965 and then again between 1968 and 1969. In the United States there has been a marked increase in participation in the postwar decades. There is a degree of similarity in that it is in the ages above 40 in the United States where the largest overall increases have taken place, and it is in the same portion of the age distribution that there has been growth in Japanese female participation. On an absolute difference basis, the greatest difference is to be found in the age group 15-19 (16-19 in the United States). Among that age group in the United States there was an increase of 4.3 percent in labor force participation between 1950 and 1969. But in Japan the decline was 21.0 percent. There would appear to be a simple explanation for this difference. We noted earlier that there had been a dramatic shift in the number of Japanese girls who entered the labor market as high school graduates rather than middle school graduates, a reflection of the fact that the proportion of girls who graduated from middle school and went on to high school had increased dramatically. In the United States there has been no comparable shift in education for women. The median years of education of the female labor force aged 18-24 rose only from 12.4 years in 1952 to 12.6 years in 1969.

Despite the very rapid rise in labor force participation among U.S. women, the absolute levels of labor force participation among women in Japan exceed those in the United States. (See Table 10.) It would be tempting to explain this fact in terms of differences in income levels between the two countries, since the income level of the household is an important factor in labor force participation. Yet the differences in income levels between the United States and Japan, with the U.S. level two to three times that of Japan, would tend to swamp the modest differences in participation. We would also be confounded by the fact that as the absolute levels of income have risen in the United States, so has labor force participation, while in Japan remarkable increases in per capita income have had but a modest impact on the participation of women.

The factors which underlie these trend movements in America are relatively easy to identify and discuss, yet they have been difficult to assess properly. In the absence of longitudinal studies of the labor force participation of cohort groups over a period of years, most of the many recent studies of female or married women's labor force participation have tended to utilize cross-sectional data, and then a reconciliation of the cross-sectional results with the secular trends has been attempted.[9]

In general the results have been that the two primary determinants have been the level of husbands' income and the wage levels or employment opportunities for women, with the latter having the much stronger influence. Additionally, the presence of young children has been important and there is some evidence that women may move into and out of the labor market in response to short-run family consumption needs. In 1963 women entering or reentering the labor force were asked about the principal reasons for their decision. Sixty-two percent of them gave answers associated with needing or wanting the income. For married women the figure was marginally larger, with 65 percent of them giving financial needs or desires as the reason for their seeking employment.[10] The areas of fastest growth in employment--clerical, professional and service occupations--have all been categories which contain a large number of jobs available to women, and it is thus not surprising that the employment of women in these areas grew faster than did overall female employment.

Thus we can conclude that a combination of increased education for women, the expansion of occupations wherein women find extensive employment, and supply elasticities which favor a response to female wages over increases in husbands' income have resulted in substantial increases in female labor force participation in the postwar years. If one compares labor force participation for married women, one finds that these rates are markedly higher in Japan than in the United States. The pattern is similar to those for all females. The sole exception is the age group 20-24, where in 1969 for all women the Japanese rate is 13.2 percent higher than the one in the United States but for married women of the same ages it is 5 percent lower in Japan. This probably results from a later marriage age for Japanese women.

THE OPERATION OF THE LABOR MARKET

The function of a labor market is to allocate workers of various qualities and characteristics among a variety of occupations and employers, both at one point in time and over time. The actual mechanisms which are utilized and the institutional intermediaries which develop may appear to be quite dissimilar in different cultures or with the passage of time. Yet, despite the dissimilarities, the basic functions of a labor market remain the same. Consequently, by maintaining the focus on these functional areas, it is possible fruitfully to compare labor markets which upon casual reflection may appear to have few similarities. The important functions which must be examined are (1) the methods of seeking employment, (2) job tenure and the related aspects of occupational and industrial mobility, (3) the observable impact upon the labor market of cyclical movement in the economy, and (4) the employment relationship. This last factor was discussed in Chapter 1 and will not be repeated here. Therefore, the remainder of this chapter will be concerned with job-seeking, mobility, and measures of unemployment.

Job-Seeking in Japan

Perhaps in no other aspect of these two countries' labor markets are the differences as marked as they are in the reception accorded to new entrants into the labor market. In Japan in 1969 there were almost eight job openings available for every male and 3.9 openings for every female high school graduate. In the United States in March, 1968, the unemployment rate for 18- to 19-year-olds who had completed eighth grade (middle school) was 17.4 percent, and it was 7.5 percent for 18- to 19-year-old high school graduates. This latter rate was almost 3.3 times higher than the unemployment rate for high school graduates of all ages. The reasons for these completely divergent patterns are probably several, but chief among them would seem to be variations in the significance of initial job-seeking and in lifetime labor mobility, two facets to which we now turn.

For a variety of reasons as discussed in Chapter 1, the larger and potentially the more stable Japanese employers have sought to choose the majority of their new employees from each year's groups of new graduates.[11] In practice this has never been possible, and since 1953 only 30-37 percent per year of all newly hired employees among firms employing 30 or more have been new graduates. Until 1965, of the remaining new employees 10-15 percent were occupationally inexperienced, but in recent years it has been closer to 20 percent.[12] Among the 50-55 percent who have had previous employment experience, usually about half of them have worked in the same or in closely allied occupations. Yet because of the importance which major firms, universities, and governmental units have placed upon hiring new graduates and the fact that such a large proportion of the newly hired are new graduates, the market for graduates has tended to become specialized and self-contained. In 1969, when there were 4.8 jobs for each new middle school graduate and 5.7 jobs for each new high school graduate, there were only 1.25 jobs for each non-new graduate who was registered with the Public Employment Offices.

The self-contained nature of this market may also be seen in the wage-setting mechanism, which is separated from that applied to the regular employees. Most companies separately determine the amount of wage increase which they will offer to next year's new school graduates and that which they will offer to the union during negotiations. This separation stems partly from the times of graduation and bargaining.

With graduation in March, the employment process for graduates takes place during the fall, while the major union-management negotiations are concentrated in the spring. The separation also stems from management's belief that wages for new school graduates are none of the union's business. To a degree the unions agree, though in recent years a number of unions have been formulating demands for minimum starting wages. In general, however, these demands for minimum wages have not been given great emphasis by the unions, and their character is more apt to be a tactic in the overall union goal of raising average wages than a serious desire to affect the graduates' labor market.

In addition to the marked improvement in the number of jobs which the new graduate finds being offered to him, there have been rapid increases in the starting wage. Between 1954 and 1969 the wage for male high school graduates entering manufacturing increased over fourfold, going from 6,317 yen to 26,357 yen. For male middle school graduates, the increase was from 3,808 yen to 21,053 yen. The two rates approximately maintained a 3,000-4,000 yen differential between them, but this meant marked declines in percentage wage differentials. In 1954 the beginning wage for a high school graduate was about 68 percent higher than the wage of a middle school graduate. By 1969 the difference was only 25 percent.[13]

Another shift in this labor market has been in the proportion of new graduates who have found employment in the larger firms. In 1957 only 16 percent of the middle school graduates were going into firms of 500 or more employees, but in 1969 36.7 percent were hired by this class of firm. For firms of 100 or more, the shift was from 36.3 percent in 1957 to 62.3 percent in 1969. During the same period there was no real change in the proportion of all employees who worked for firms of over 500 employees. Among industries the biggest change has been the movement away from agriculture, forestry, and fishing, which in 1953 employed a little more than one-third of all new middle school graduates and about 15 percent of all new high school graduates. By 1969 only 6.1 percent of new middle school graduates and 4.5 percent of new high school graduates were entering these industries. The principal gainer was manufacturing, especially among the middle school graduates. In 1953 38.1 percent of middle school graduates were employed in manufacturing, but in 1969 58.1 percent were employed in manufacturing. For high school graduates the respective figures were 26.1 percent and 36.2 percent. Trade was a relatively large gainer among high school graduates, but its employment of new middle school graduates declined. The service sector, including public service, had an opposite experience, increasing its employment of middle school graduates but decreasing that of high school graduates.

Job-Seeking in the United States

We have seen that in Japan there are extensive data on the labor market for new school graduates. This reflects employer recognition that this labor market is largely functionally separate from other employment markets. In the United States, where the new graduate market is not nearly so separate, we know much less about it. Indeed, reflecting the United States' own history, the primary research interest in job-seeking has focused upon the response of workers who were discharged after long years of service because their firms were in declining industries.

Upon closer examination of U.S. practice, it would appear that in some sectors of the market, job-seeking and placement tend to be organized in a manner very similar to that in Japan. Two of these sectors are beginning clerical jobs and the market for college graduates. Representatives of large firms visit high schools and colleges in order to seek out new employees. Since over the years there will tend to be a continuing relationship between the teachers, professors, and placement bureau personnel, both sides have an incentive to develop a rational and well-informed labor market which will provide potential employees with more information and will be more efficient in sending the better students to the better jobs. The similarity to the Japanese pattern is also found in the setting of salaries for the new employees. This can be seen very clearly among large employers of clerical employees, where the firms are very much aware of their competitors' wage offers in the new graduates' labor market. There is also rapid adjustment by the follower firms to the lead of the key wage setters.[14]

There also seems to be a tendency for firms to separate the setting of initial wages from the determination of wage increases for those already employed. A good example has been in the engineers' labor market in the United States, where, during periods of apparent engineer shortage, a marked narrowing has occurred between the wages paid to newly graduated engineers and to engineers currently employed.

As previously mentioned, one aspect of job-seeking which

has been of interest to Americans has been the way in which workers find jobs. Nine major studies may be cited.[15] In general these studies show that informal methods of search using friends and relatives, and going from company employment office to company employment office, are the most important. These patterns are especially pronounced in situations where unemployment in the general geographical area is high. With high unemployment levels, probably three out of four workers found their jobs by using informal methods. In a tighter labor market the overall use of informal systems probably declines to about 60 percent of all job placements. The decline apparently comes about because employers make more of an effort to find workers by using advertisements and employment services. Also, in a tight labor market there are many entrants who are new or returning to the labor market, and with their lesser job market experience, they are more apt to turn to formal methods of job-seeking. In one recent study of job-seeking differences by race, it turned out that differences between the use of informal systems were not very important, but that there were variations in the kinds of formal institutions which were used. A significantly greater proportion of the blacks used the state employment service rather than private employment services.

Comparative Job-Seeking

In both countries there are formal systems for initial job placement for the graduates of public schools and of universities. In the United States these specialized market procedures are most fully developed for college graduates. To the extent that formal hiring procedures operate among lower school graduates, they do so for clerical employees, especially women, who often receive specialized clerical training in high school. The use of these formal channels is also most common among firms which employ a large number of clerical workers. Among other employers, the predominant American tendency seems to be to wait until a combination of the advice of friends and relatives and the individual's own job-seeking have brought the prospective worker to the employer's door. In Japan the specialized procedures are operative for graduates at all levels of education and for the complete range of firms, from the largest Tokyo-based firms, which fly workers in from Kyūshū, to the neighborhood kimono shop, which will be in the employment market only once every few years. On the one hand, this represents major difference in the operation of the labor market in the two economies, one which means that this aspect of the labor market is more rational and well-organized in Japan than in the United States. Viewed in an alternative manner, the friends and relatives who in the United States would unite to send a potential employee to a particular employer would in Japan be the ones to whom the employer would turn to for assistance in selecting new employees. In Japan this has meant that employers have tended to draw their new employees from particular geographical areas or schools. In the United States, too, the information channels of friends and relatives have created specialized paths along which geographical mobility takes place,[16] though the paths are not as clear and well-defined as they are in Japan.

Inter-Firm Mobility in Japan

In Chapter 1's discussion of the employment relationship, it was pointed out that the idealized employment relationship was one that involved lifetime employment, loyalty between employee and employer, and a nenkō wage pattern. While this ideal is far from realized in practice--and, indeed, even whether it should be an ideal is coming to be questioned--it is still the predominant relationship among the largest and highest-paying employers. As a consequence, it is to be expected that employee turnover would be less among the larger firms and higher among the smaller ones. The expectation turns out to be correct. The number of separations among those employed by 500-employee and larger firms was only 1.8 per 100 in 1965, but it was 2.8 per 100 among establishments with 30-99 employees. Thus the separation rate among the larger firms was only 65 percent of what it was among the smaller ones. This ratio has increased extensively since 1953, when the larger firm separation was only 42 percent of the smaller (1.3 per 100 versus 3.1 per 100). If only regular or indefinite-term employees are considered, then the separation rate for the 500-and-over class of employer was .9 percent per month in 1965, while the rate for the 30-99 size class was 1.8 percent per month. Here too the differential has become smaller over time, largely as the result of a higher turnover rate among employees of the larger establishments. In 1956 the monthly separation rate of regular employees was but .5 percent per month in the large firms, which was about one-third the rate in the smaller firms.

The foregoing is what would be anticipated from our discussions of the employment relationship, but it also stems from the unwillingness of the larger employers to pay the same wages to an experienced worker that he would have received if he had obtained all of his experience with the new employer. To some extent this policy is being modified in those firms which are experiencing labor shortages, but even there it typically takes the newly hired experienced worker several years to catch up with his age and skill class. These general policies were recently illuminated in a survey of wage practices.[17] Approximately 80 percent of the surveyed firms hired some experienced workers, and among this group nine out of 10 paid them lower wages than their counterparts who had always been employed by the firm. About 16 percent of the companies said that the newly hired experienced worker's wages would catch up with his counterparts in two or three years, 47 percent said it would take more than three years, and 33 percent said the wages would never catch up. Among the larger employers the "never catch up" answer was given by 41 percent of the firms.

Additional evidence on the limited mobility between firms comes from a survey of the Tokyo-Yokohama industrial district in 1954. There it was determined that in factories employing 100 or more, 78 percent of the workers had worked only in large factories, 16.4 percent had worked in small factories prior to going to work in the large ones, and 5.6 percent had moved from a large firm to a small one and back to a large one again. Among small firms, 47.7 percent of the workers had worked only in small factories, 21.4 percent had moved from a small one to a large one and back again, and 30.9 percent had moved from a large factory to a small one.[18] A 1960 survey in Tokyo also recorded greater movement from large firms to small ones than vice versa.[19] Thus we get a picture of the small factory acting as a sponge to absorb labor not taken into the more desirable, larger, and higher-paying factories.

The limited amount of inter-firm mobility among experienced workers tends to be concentrated among the younger members of the labor force. Less than half of all new job mobility in 1965 involved the movement of experienced workers, while 58 percent represented the employment of persons who a year previously had been outside the labor force. Among males between the ages of 40 and 54 only 2.8 percent changed employers within a year, but for those aged 20-24 the mobility was three times as great, with 7.5 percent changing employers.[20] (See Table 11.) Among women, the mobile workers were

TABLE 11

One-Year Job Mobility, Japan and United States, 1965
(percent)

Age	Japan		United States	
	Male	Female	Male	Female
18-19	10.2	8.1	31.7	29.0
20-24	7.5	8.2	28.5	14.9
25-34	4.4	6.0	13.8	8.5
35-39	3.3	4.7	--	--
35-44	--	--	7.4	5.3
40-54	2.8	4.2	--	--
45-54	--	--	5.2	4.7
55-64	.5	3.2	3.8	2.4
65+	.3	.3	2.7	1.8
Total	4.7	6.5	9.9	6.9

Note: For Japan these are percentages of those whose jobs were different in July, 1965, than in July, 1964, divided by those employed on both dates. For the United States they are percentages of those who were employed in January, 1965 and 1966 and who changed occupation.

Sources: Economic Planning Agency, Economic Survey of Japan, 1967-68 (Tokyo: Japan Times Ltd., 1968), p. 152; Samuel Saben, Occupational Mobility of Employed Workers, Special Labor Force Report 84 (June, 1967), p. 34.

also concentrated among those less than 30 years of age. A similar finding with regard to lower mobility among older workers is contained in a recent article by Odaka Konosuke, in which he analyzes the job histories of two samples of Japanese workers.[21] One sample of approximately 2,000 was drawn on a national basis in 1955 and the second of 1,300 was drawn in Tokyo in 1960. From these, Professor Odaka has provided some rich insights into the mobility process. The following discussion, which is drawn from his article, is limited to the 1960 sample, since much of the comparative material from the United States refers to the 1960's.

The long-term occupational and industrial mobility of a labor force can be presented either in terms of the average number of changes per worker or in terms of a transition matrix which shows the percentage of each occupational industrial work group which has moved to the various other occupations or industries. Odaka calculated ten-year matrices for the age ranges 20-30, 30-40, and 40-50. Matrices for the entire period 20-50 were obtained by multiplying the component parts. A summary of these tables is given in Table 12. There it can be seen that the greatest movement out of an industry has occurred in agriculture, not a surprising fact, considering the drastic decline in the proportion of agricultural employment. Leaving agriculture aside, it can be seen that, on the average, the probability of an employee's remaining within the same industry during the ages 20-30 is about .7. Over the longer period, ages 20-50, it appears that in general the probability of no inter-industry movement is greater than .5.

These survey data also support the conclusion obtained in the Tokyo-Yokohama survey of mobility between small and large firms: that it is easier to move from a large-scale manufacturing firm to a small one than it is to go from a small one to a large one. Thus only 1 percent of those who were employed in manufacturing firms of less than 10 employees at age 20 were working in firms of more than 1,000 employees at age 30. Yet 12 percent of the 30-year-olds employed in the less-than-10-employee manufacturing firms had been employed in larger (1,000 or more) firms at the beginning of the decade.

In addition to questions of inter-industrial movement there are also questions of the probabilities of long service in any given employment. This is shown in columns 4-6 of Table 12. There it can be seen that the probability of not changing jobs in a 10-year period ranges from a low of .24 for 20-30-year-olds in agriculture to a high of .73 for 30-40-year-olds employed in construction. With rare exceptions, most notably

TABLE 12

Male Job Mobility, Japan

Industry	Percent in the Same Industry as at Age 20			Percent Employed Who Did not Change Jobs for 10 Years		
				Age		
	At 30	At 40	At 50	20-30	30-40	40-50
Agriculture	26.4	11.2	7.6	24.5	35.3	54.6
Construction	85.4	72.6	66.1	43.8	72.7	70.0
Manufacturing*	72.8-89.6	60.2-74.4	51.6-65.2	38.2	51.7	59.2
Trade and Service	74.5	66.1	63.0	39.7	50.7	66.3
Professional Service	78.7	67.5	65.8	52.5	56.0	60.0
Transportation and Public Utilities	63.0	49.9	32.1	53.4	61.2	41.9
Public Administration	56.6	34.9	23.2	52.6	44.7	36.8

*The table from which these figures were taken presents data on manufacturing by size of firm.

Sources: The basic data are the job histories of a sample of Tokyo residents in 1960, covering 1912-60. These data are adapted from tables in Konosuka Odaka, "The Structure of Japanese Labor Markets," Riron Keizai Gaku [Economic studies quarterly], XVIII (June, 1967), 29-32.

in public administration, the probability of not changing jobs is greater for the older age groups. For example, in trade and service the probability of not changing jobs is .40 for 20- to 30-year-olds, .51 for 30- to 40-year-olds, and .66 for 40- to 50-year-olds. In general the relative size of the probability of job change is consistent with the probability of inter-industrial mobility. It does not seem possible to characterize any particular industrial sector, save agriculture, as having an outstandingly high or low rate of job shifting.

It is difficult to characterize these findings as indicating a high or low level of mobility because we lack any acceptable standard by which to judge. Yet with some 4.6 percent of the nonagricultural labor force changing jobs in 1965, with about half the labor force changing jobs at least once in 10 years, and with about half of these decade moves involving inter-industry mobility, it would appear that the elasticity of labor supply has been quite extensive. Certainly it is much greater, especially among employees of smaller firms, than is implied by the catchy phrase "in for life," which some people have used to describe Japanese employment practices.[22]

Job Mobility in the United States

The character of job mobility has several dimensions, including the amount of employee mobility, the probability of changing jobs over a 10-year period, and changes in occupation or industry. It is these which will be discussed here. As can be seen in Table 13, there is a very high level of annual job changing in the United States, with approximately one-quarter of the work force having started their current employment within the past year. The magnitude of job shifting is in large part a function of the age of the work force, since young people have much shorter job tenure than the average. Among those 20-24 years of age who were working in January, 1966, 23.8 percent had not been employed a year previously and 26.9 percent had worked for a different employer. Among persons 55-64 years of age the comparable percentages were 4.2 percent and 6.8 percent.

A similar emphasis upon youth and shortness of job tenure may be observed in Table 14, which shows the proportion of workers by industry in 1968 who began their current jobs at least 10 years earlier. While it is clear that a much larger proportion of those over the age of 45 have held the same job for 10 years than is true of those between 25 and 44 years of

TABLE 13

Male Occupational Mobility, United States
(percent)

Initial Occupation	Same Occupation in 1962 as First Job	Same Occupation in 1966 as in 1965	Occupation Changes Involving a Change in Industry *
Professional	62.5	89.3	49.7
Manager	35.7	91.0	58.1
Clerical	17.6	78.6	61.2
Sales	15.5	86.5	91.0
Craftsman	38.6	87.6	67.6
Operative	25.8	80.4	77.1
Service	19.8	80.4	78.7
Laborer	14.2	72.3	87.0
Farmer, Farm Laborer	28.8	93.0	--

*Industry and occupation changes are based on three-digit groupings.

Sources: Column 1 is from Peter M. Blau and Otis D. Duncan, The American Occupational Structure (New York: John Wiley and Sons, 1967), p. 498. Columns 2 and 3 are from Samuel Saben, Occupational Mobility of Employed Workers, United States Bureau of Labor Statistics, Special Labor Force Report 84 (1967), pp. A7, A-16.

TABLE 14

Male Job Tenure, United States, 1968

Industry	Percent Who Began to Work for Current Employer at Least 10 Years Ago	
	Age 25-44	Age 45 and over
Agriculture	37.6	70.7
Mining	34.6	57.5
Construction	21.0	37.1
Manufacturing	37.2	62.5
Transportation and Public Utilities	36.4	70.4
Trade	19.2	47.2
Services and Finance	14.0	42.0
Public Administration	29.5	55.6

Source: Edward J. O'Boyle, Job Tenure: How it Relates to Race and Age, January, 1968, United States Bureau of Labor Statistics, Special Labor Force Report 112 (1969), p. A-12.

age, there are also marked differences among industries. Among younger men, the variation is from a low of 14 percent in services and finance to a high of 37.6 percent in agriculture. For men over the age of 45, the range is from 37.1 percent in construction to 70.7 percent in agriculture. In general the rank order of job tenure by industry is the same for both age groups, and the order of magnitude is such that the percentage of non-job changers is twice as high among the older workers as among the younger ones.

A high degree of job mobility and a shortness of job tenure are conducive to high rates of change of industry or occupation, but they may also merely represent, as does a whirlpool, rapid movement in a small space. Some insight into occupational mobility is provided by the data in Table 13. There it can be seen that from 72.3 percent of laborers to 93 percent of farmers and farm laborers had the same occupation in 1966 that they had had in 1965. Over a somewhat longer period, from the time of a first full-time job to the job held in 1962, the proportions in the same occupation are rather smaller, from a low of 14.2 percent of laborers to a high of 62.5 percent of professionals. There is some degree of correspondence in the rank orders of the two columns, but the differences in magnitudes between short-run and long-run occupational mobility are quite large. Thus there is a high degree of retention in the professional category in both periods, with the figure for the longer time period being 70 percent of the level for the one-year period, yet for sales workers the long-period retention is only 18 percent of the one-year figure. It is also instructive to note that the two occupations, professionals and craftsmen, which have the most developed formal educational requirements are the ones for which there seems to be the smallest amount of long-period occupational mobility. Since the median occupational retention rate from the first job to the job held in 1962 is only 25.8 percent, it seems reasonable to conclude that U.S. labor markets are characterized by a high degree of occupational mobility.

Comparative Job Mobility

Once the worker has become employed, there is significantly less job separation in Japan than in the United States. This can be seen in the simple turnover rates, which apply primarily to manufacturing. In 1969 the U.S. rates of job accessions and separations were 4.7 and 4.9 per 100, respectively. These were about double the Japanese rates of 2.6 and 2.4 per 100 employees. A similar conclusion is obtained by an examination of the data in Table 11. There it can be seen that the degree of job change by the employed members of the labor force within a year is about twice as high as in Japan for males but about the same for women. Much of this represents job turnover among younger members of the labor force. In the United States less than 5 percent of nonagricultural employees over the age of 45 changed jobs in 1965, compared with about half that percentage for Japanese over 40. The greater job stability in Japan was also evident from a comparison of the proportion of workers who had not changed jobs over a 10-year period. The 10-year job stability rates for males aged 30 to 40 in Japan are significantly higher than those for American males ages 25-44. Taking manufacturing as an example, in Japan 51.7 percent of the men did not change jobs in a 10-year period, but in the United States only 30.3 percent had made no job change.

Interestingly enough, however, when the comparison is between Japanese males aged 40-50 and American men over the age of 45, a different picture emerges. The Americans appear to change jobs less often. This may stem from the fact that the data in the United States refer to a recent 10-year period (1956-66), while the Japanese data refer to 10-year periods over the working life of the individuals. Among the older workers the results are affected by the dislocation associated with the China incident and the American occupation. This last point should not obscure the process which is at work in the United States. In the United States there tends to be a great deal of job movement in the early years of the individual's labor market experience. After about the age of 35 the movement settles down to relative stability at around 7 percent of the labor force and long tenure becomes the rule. In Japan a similar initial employer sampling among those employed by the larger firms does not exist. Yet there are some tendencies in this direction, as indicated by a three-year survey (1969) by the Ministry of Labor of middle school and high school graduates, which showed that over 50 percent of them had left their original employer by the end of three years. As could have been anticipated, the rates for smaller enterprises were much higher than those for larger ones. Between 1966 and 1969 the rate for those employing 0-4 was 70 percent, but only 38 percent for those employing more than 1,000. Thus, while Japanese turnover rates are lower because of the youthful job-seeker's mobility in the United States, at older ages the differences are less pronounced. This can also be seen in the following example. The median years on the job for American foremen in 1966 was 12.8 years. In 1964 among Japanese foremen in manufacturing the length of service was 13.3 years. Odaka Konosuke, whose data on long-term mobility were cited earlier, also compared Japanese results with some American studies[23] and, on the basis of those comparisons, he concluded that there was less job mobility among Japanese workers than among Americans.

It is difficult to compare mobility between industries and occupations because in the United States the mobility data relate to occupations and in Japan they relate to industries. Yet there is sufficient overlap among certain occupations and industries to allow some calculations and comparisons to be made. Within the professional classes of employment there appear to be few differences between Japan and the United States.

In both countries close to two-thirds of those who held

professional jobs at youthful ages were still employed in those areas in late middle age. In Japan the comparison was between jobs at age 20 and at age 40 or 50, while in the United States it was between first job and the job held in 1962. Among the other groupings, however, there appears to be significantly more mobility in the United States. The occupational retention figures for the United States among sales workers was 19.8 percent, and among service workers it was 15.5 percent. The Japanese figure for trade and service combined, between the ages of 20 and 50, was 63 percent. A similar result is noted for construction work. In the United States only 26.2 percent of 1962's construction craftsmen had held their first job there, while 72 percent of the 40-year-old Japanese construction industry workers had worked in construction at age 20. Indeed, the most interesting comparison may be the order of magnitude of the numbers in column 1 of Table 12 and column 2 of Table 13. The first figures indicate the degree of industrial retention in Japan between the ages of 20 and 30, while the second concern the occupational retention in the United States over the course of one year. Excluding agriculture, the Japanese range is from 56.6 percent to 85.4 percent, and the U.S. one is 72.3 percent to 91 percent. We thus conclude that, in addition to greater job mobility, there has also been a much greater occupational and industrial mobility in the United States.

Two other modest elements of mobility deserve at least mention in passing: geographical mobility and the shift from blue-collar status to white-collar status. In Japan in 1960 the proportion of the population (persons one year or older) who were inter-prefectural migrants was 2.81 percent. In 1963 in the United States 6.8 percent of a similar population moved across county lines, and 3.6 percent moved across state lines.[24] Since the appropriate American unit with which to compare the Japanese prefecture lies somewhere between a state and a county, it would appear that geographical mobility is about twice as great in the United States as it is in Japan.

Odaka argues that the blue-collar and white-collar labor markets in Japan are quite closed one from another and cites the fact that Yule's coefficient of association for white-collar workers in manufacturing was .898.[25] The only exception noted was some tendency for blue-collar workers to move into management jobs. A similar situation exists in the United States. Surveys of inter-generational occupational mobility yield comparable results.[26] Among persons whose first jobs were white-collar ones, three-fourths of them held white-collar jobs in 1962. Among initial blue-collar workers, only one-fourth of them had moved into white-collar jobs by 1962, and the Yule coefficient for the general class of white-collar workers was .81. As in Japan, the movement from blue-collar jobs to management was somewhat easier. Among 1962's managers, 43 percent of them had initially held a blue-collar job.

On balance, then, we must conclude that all kinds of employment-related mobility are much greater in the United States than in Japan, with the exception of the boundary between blue-collar and white-collar unemployment and occupational mobility among professionals. The principal determinant of these differences lies in the much greater mobility among the younger elements of the labor force, for after the age of 35-40 the differences between the two countries are much smaller. The difference among the young is in turn explained by the different importance which is placed upon being trained by the firm from an early age. In Japan this has been highly esteemed in a way which has not been true in the United States. To the extent that Japanese firms come to place less importance upon early recruitment and alter their methods of wage payment to reflect this change, it is to be anticipated that Japanese and U.S. patterns of mobility will draw closer together.

Unemployment in Japan

It is sometimes helpful to think of the labor market mechanism as ranking all potential employees in terms of their suitability for employment and then allocating jobs to the most highly qualified and from there downward toward the least qualified, until the number of jobs has been exhausted. Those who remain without jobs will become the unemployed and/or will retire from the labor force. In an actual economy such a buffer group is clearly not static, but involves a great deal of turnover as individual workers become employed and others enter the ranks of the unemployed. Yet most studies of the unemployed show that a disproportionately high percentage of those who are unemployed during the course of a year or who are unemployed several times during the year are those whose personal characteristics, such as education and physical handicaps, make them among the less desirable employees. Thus, when the economy enters a recession, it is anticipated that the ranks of the unemployed will swell and, conversely, that they will contract during a boom. The boom may also be expected to draw other marginal workers into the labor force.

In Japan, especially among the larger employers who offer lifetime employment to a large proportion of their employees, there have evolved several systems other than unemployment (via a layoff) to handle the problem of fluctuations in the demand for their output. These systems have also allowed the firms to pay high wages to their permanent employees and, at the same time, to obtain the benefits of low labor costs which are derived from operating in a society which seemingly has had a chronic labor surplus since the middle of the Tokugawa period, some 300 years ago. The first system has been the extensive use of subcontracting firms. These firms, small in scale, have recruited their labor in the small-firm labor market and have paid the much lower wages typical of that market. In addition, the level of fringe benefits has typically been less for workers in these firms. In addition to the subcontractor's employees, some of whom, as in the shipyards, may work alongside the parent company's workers in the parent plant, the large firm has also employed temporary workers. Technically, a temporary worker is one hired for short-term periods, but in many cases the first short-term period has been followed by more short-term periods, giving rise to permanent temporary workers. Lastly, there have been temporary workers employed by the day. In these three situations the workers' employment conditions and tenure of employment have been much poorer than those of the firm's regular employees.

Unemployment during the postwar years has generally decreased. It has gone from a high of 1.8 percent to below 1 percent in 1961 and stabilized in 1969 at 1.1 percent. The same general pattern characterizes unemployment compensation recipients as a proportion of those eligible to receive unemployment compensation. In 1955 the unemployment compensation ratio was 5.6 percent, and it had declined to 2.4 percent in 1969. Concurrently the number of day-work employees was becoming smaller. In 1955 there were 569,000 new applicants for day work at the Public Employment Security Offices. Each year for the next decade the number of new applications for day work declined, until in 1968 there were only 134,691 applications. The yearly total of monthly placements of day workers, which had been 4.8 million in 1955, reached a peak of 5.8 million in 1960 and then drifted downward to 3.4 million in 1968.

The same kind of trend may be seen in the proportion of indefinite-term new hires to definite-term new hires. This is consistent with other observations of the use of temporary workers. In the late 1950's there had been a tendency to utilize them extensively in certain industries, especially those undergoing rapid increases in employment. In 1957, 26.3 percent of the employees in electrical machinery firms were temporary employees, while in autos it was 19 percent.[27] A prime example was Toyota, which employed 230 temporary workers in 1956, but 5,100 or 52 percent of their total employment, in 1961. More recently the use of temporary workers has been in decline, and on June 1, 1966, for the economy as a whole, temporary and daily employees made up only 5 percent of all employees in private establishments.

In a country in which only 63 percent of the employed labor force are classed as employees and where some 17 percent of the employed are unpaid family workers, including some 8 percent of those employed outside agriculture and forestry, it is highly likely that persons who would have been listed as unemployed or possibly outside the labor force in a more developed economy, such as that of the United States, would in Japan find work and be classified as self-employed or as unpaid family workers. Some indication of the possible magnitude of this may be seen in some data from before the Pacific War. During the 1920's, when employment opportunities grew slowly and manufacturing employment increased only about 7 percent, the number of individuals employed as green grocers grew by 52 percent, fish dealers increased 47 percent, confectioners and bakers rose 202 percent, the number of tea dealers expanded by 54 percent, and leather and leather product dealers almost doubled, growing 92 percent.[28]

Turning to more recent years, during the boom years 1956-59, the number of unpaid family workers in wholesale and retail trade and in the service industry declined. In trade there was a decline of 21,000 persons, and in the service industry there was a decline of 9,000. Between 1959 and 1965, when the growth rate was not as spectacular as in 1956-59, the number of unpaid workers in these two areas increased by 113,000 in trade and by 41,000 in services.

As might be anticipated in an economy which concentrates its initial employment offers on new graduates, the older workers form one of the primary groups for whom unemployment is a problem. In October, 1968, the ratio of job applicants to job openings at the public employment offices was .7, yet for those between 50 and 55 years of age it was 2.1 and for those over 55 it was 6.9. Additionally, the jobs which older workers obtain often involve lower wages than they had previously received. In 1968, 23 percent of men over 50 who were newly hired experienced a decline of more than 30 percent in their wages, whereas only 5.8 percent of males between the ages of 20 and 34 experienced such a large reduction in their earnings. The other major group which may be identified as experiencing employment problems are those who live in the relatively less developed regions in Japan. In 1968 the overall ratio of active job applications to active openings, exclusive of new graduates, was .9. The median rate for the 46 prefectures was 1.0. The lowest ratio was 0.2 in Aichi-ken prefecture, whose capital and major city is Nagoya. Two of the worst levels, 4.9 and 5.8, were in Aomori-ken and Kagoshima-ken, located at the extreme north of the main island of Honshū and the southern end of Kyūshū, respectively.

On balance, then, it would appear that the Japanese economy, through the imaginative use of unpaid, temporary, and day-work employees and subcontractors has provided a very flexible labor force. Yet it is also an economy whose excess demand and supply position may only partly be understood by an examination of the unemployment rate.

Unemployment in the United States

The normal pattern of labor displacement during economic downturns has been to lay off blue-collar workers and to adopt a policy of attrition for white-collar employees. This has usually meant that blue-collar workers and new or returning entrants to the labor force have borne the brunt of cyclical unemployment. It has been their unemployment rates which have risen relative to overall unemployment rates during recessions. This can be clearly seen by looking at the rate of unemployment among operatives. Experienced workers in this occupation in postwar years have constituted between 18 and 21 percent of total employment, but between 20 and 32 percent of the total unemployment. Professionals, who constituted 7 percent of total employment in 1948 and over 13 percent in 1969, have contributed only 2 to 5.5 percent to the ranks of the unemployed. During years of relative boom, especially those involving a strong growth in manufacturing employment, the unemployment rate for operatives has been only slightly higher than the average unemployment rate. In 1966, for example, it was 25 percent higher than that of the experienced labor force. Then during recessions, the operative unemployment rate dramatically outpaces the average. During the recession year 1958 the operative unemployment rate exceeded the rate for all experienced workers by 60 percent. Similar patterns may be observed for young male workers and for blacks, especially younger blacks.

Depending upon the underlying strengths and weaknesses in the economy, there have been minor movements in the relationships among the unemployment rates of various groups. The extent to which there had been major shifts in the incidence of unemployment was the basis of the long debate over structural unemployment which raged between 1960 and 1966.[29] The general conclusions of that debate were that there had not been any sudden changes in the character of unemployment in the late 1950's, but that over the course of the postwar period, a greater incidence of unemployment had come to rest upon very young workers and nonwhite workers.

Partially associated with the structural unemployment debate was another one, this one on the impact of economic downturns upon entrance into the labor force, especially by secondary workers. This was the so-called "discouraged worker-added worker" controversy. It centered about the question of whether a downturn drew workers into the labor force in order to supplement family incomes reduced by the unemployment of the principal earner (the added worker), or whether a downturn discouraged potential workers from trying to seek employment. The data are still not adequate for the definitive answer to the question, but the weight of the evidence supports the view that the number of discouraged workers exceeds the number of added workers.[30] Thus it appears that, to a modest degree, the unemployment rate understates the extent of the excess supply of workers during a recession and at the height of a boom it understates the degree of excess demand for labor.

Comparative Unemployment

A comparison of unemployment in the two countries is not especially meaningful. The U.S. experience in the postwar period has been a series of expansions and the recessions of 1948-49, 1953-54, 1957-58, and a long period of excess labor supply from 1959 to 1965. Consequently, unemployment levels in the 1966-69 boom were roughly the same as those in the best years of the immediate postwar period, 1952-53. In Japan after 1955 there was a steady downward trend in umemployment until 1961, since which it has been essentially unchanged, though unemployment compensation rates do give evidence of some recessions, or, more properly, years of slowdown in the rapid rate of growth which has been Japan's recent experience. The chief difficulty in a comparison does not lie so much in the divergent experience of labor shortage or surplus, though this is important. It lies in the fact that, whereas in the United States most of the excess supply of labor shows up in higher unemployment rates, especially among blue-collar workers, the use of temporary employees, unpaid family workers, and subcontractors within a company's own plant, and the large area of self-employment provide large segments in the Japanese economy which can absorb excess labor supply which in the United States would appear as higher unemployment rates. In the absence of some technique which would allow one to estimate the extent to which movements into and out of self-employment and such represent opportunities for useful employment instead of a substitute for unemployment, it will be impossible to gauge accurately changes in the excess supply of or demand for labor. An alternative to numbers are the writings of the economic and business press. On the basis of these data the conclusion would have to be that the recent experience of the two countries has been completely dissimilar, for in Japan they speak of a labor shortage and suggest the importation of Koreans, while in the United States (until 1966) they speak of high rates of unemployment and defend the exclusion of Mexicans and other low-wage groups.

SUMMARY

This chapter has considered the shifting occupational and industrial categories of employment, female labor force participation, and mobility. In general the conclusions in each section have been that there are some significant differences amid similarities. Among areas of employment the differences may be said largely to reflect the lower level of economic development in Japan. The lower levels of GNP are also a factor in the differences in labor force participation among women. Divergent mobility patterns would appear largely to reflect alternative approaches to structuring the labor market. Thus, one would anticipate that as Japan's economy grows, it will move increasingly into a service orientation, and as a consequence the employment and occupational distributions will increasingly approach those of the United States. Female labor force participation is more difficult to characterize. It seems likely that the pressure on the graduates' labor market will increasingly open up opportunities for women to return to hired employment after some years in retirement associated with family duties. This, combined with the increasing size of refrigerators and the spread of other consumer durables lessening the hours required to maintain a home, should result in some modest rise in the rate of Japanese female labor force participation. This will make the time trends of Japan and the United States more similar, and the increasing level of participation in the United States will bring the two countries' absolute levels of female labor force participation closer. A similar approach also seems likely to characterize U.S. and Japanese mobility patterns. At younger ages a rising level of turnover in Japan and an increasing emphasis upon seniority and career patterns for older Americans will cause the mobility patterns to approach one another.

NOTES

1. The reader interested in a discussion of Japanese population data should consult Irene B. Trauber, The Population of Japan (Princeton: Princeton University Press, 1958).

2. The recent decline is discussed in Tsuchira Rokurō, "Agricultural Changes," Japan Quarterly, XVI (January-March, 1969), pp. 53-60.

3. Ryoshin Minami, "Population Migration away from Agriculture in Japan," Economic Development and Cultural Change, XV (January, 1967), pp. 183-201.

4. Statistical Abstract of the United States, 1970, p. 582.

5. Nihon Keizai Chōsa Kyōgikai [Committee on Japanese economic surveys], Shōwa 40 Nendai no Koyō Mondai [Current employment problems], (Tokyo: Daikyō Purinta, 1967), I, 324-27.

6. This and a number of other labor force and employment aspects for the early postwar years are discussed in Umemura Mataji, Sengo Nihon no Rōdō Ryoku [Postwar Japanese labor force] (Tokyo: Iwanami Shoten, 1964).

7. Japan Institute of Labor, *Japan's Labor Statistics* (Tokyo, 1970), p. 48. The figures for those going on to high school include any who are both students and workers.

8. Tadashi Henami Akamatsu, "Women Workers and Retirement After Marriage," *Japan Labor Bulletin,* VIII (May, 1969), 7.

9. An excellent discussion of the problems associated with female labor force participation and the results of a number of econometric estimations are contained in Glen G. Cain, *Married Women in the Labor Force* (Chicago: University of Chicago Press, 1966).

10. Carl Rosenfeld and Vera C. Pernella, "Why Women Start and Stop Working: A Study in Mobility," U.S. Bureau of Labor Statistics, Special Labor Force Report 59 (September, 1965), A-5.

11. In 1966, 25 large firms hired 77 percent of their new male employees directly from schools. James C. Abegglen, ed., *Business Strategies for Japan* (Tokyo: Sophia University, 1970), p. 42.

12. Japan Institute of Labor, *op. cit.*, pp. 54-55.

13. Data are from various *Shoninkyū Chōsa* [Census of initial salaries], published by the Ministry of Labor.

14. George P. Shultz, "A Nonunion Market for White Collar Labor," in Universities National Bureau of Economics, *Aspects of Labor Economics* (Princeton: Princeton University Press, 1962), pp. 127-29.

15. A summary of these results may be found in Melvin Lurie and Elton Rayack, "Racial Differences in Migration and Job Search: A Case Study," *The Southern Economic Journal,* XXXIII (July, 1966), 94.

16. *Ibid.*, pp. 84-85.

17. Robert J. Ballon, Makoto Sakurabayashi, and Ichiro Tsunekawa, "Wage Survey of the Male Blue Collar Workers," Sophia University Socio-Economic Institute, Industrial Relations Section, Bulletin 14 (April, 1967), pp. 22-23.

18. Miyokei Shinohara, "Formation and Transition of the Dual Economy in Japan," Hitotzubashi Journal of Economics, VIII (February, 1968), 8.

19. Tominaga Kenichi, "Shokugyō Idō no Yukue" [The state of occupational mobility], Chūō Kōron [Public opinion review] (March, 1962), p. 326.

20. A recent survey of over 2,000,000 middle and high school graduates showed that over 25 percent had changed jobs within a year and over 50 percent had changed at least once within the first three years. Japan Labor Bulletin, VIII (May, 1969), 2; IX (March, 1970), 2-3.

21. Konosuke Odaka, "The Structure of Japanese Labor Markets," Riron Keizai Gaku [Economic studies quarterly], XVIII (June, 1967), 25-42.

22. In 1958, 36 percent of the regular employees of shipyards had more than 10 years of service, but only 2 percent of the employees of subcontractors working in the yards had that much service. The respective figures for five years of service were 80 percent and 11 percent. Kobayashi Kenichi, Gendai Nihon no Koyō Kōzō [The structure of employment in contemporary Japan] (Tokyo: Iwanami Shoten, 1966), p. 72.

23. Odaka, op. cit., pp. 38-40. The American studies with which comparisons were made dealt with the late 1940's, when it appears that there may have been more job mobility in the United States than at the present. The unemployment rates for 1948 and 1966 were equal, yet the quit data in 1948 was 3.4 and it was only 2.6 in 1966.

24. Shigemi Kono and Mitsuru Shio, Inter-Prefectural Migration in Japan, 1956 and 1961: Migration Stream Analysis (New York: Asia Publishing House, 1965) p. 11; John B. Lansing and Eva Mueller, The Geographical Mobility of Labor (Ann Arbor, Mich.: Institute for Social Research, 1967), pp. 14-15

25. Odaka, op. cit., p. 37.

26. Peter M. Blau and Otis D. Duncan, The American Occupational Structure (New York: John Wiley and Sons, Inc., 1967), p. 498.

27. Rinjikō ni Kansuru Jitchi Chōsa no Kekka Gaiyō [Summary of the results of a survey of temporary employment] (Tokyo: Ministry of Labor, 1957).

28. Shinohara, op. cit., p. 30.

29. See Robert A. Gordon, "Unemployment Patterns with Full Employment," Industrial Relations, VIII (October, 1968), 46-72, and the material cited therein.

30. The literature on this point is surveyed in Jacob Mincer, "Labor Force Participation and Unemployment: A Review of Recent Evidence," in Robert A. Gordon and Margaret S. Gordon, eds., Prosperity and Unemployment (New York: John Wiley and Sons, Inc., 1966), pp. 73-112.

CHAPTER 3

AGGREGATE WAGE PATTERNS AND RELATIONSHIPS

The dominant questions of macroeconomic policy in the years before 1940 centered on expansions and contractions, booms and busts. Inflation was associated with war, gold, and loose banking practices, while the wage question usually referred to a generally low level of wages or to their decline during periods of financial crisis or extensive unemployment. After 1940, with the exception of the period at the immediate end of the war, the spectre of mass unemployment and dizzily falling wages seems to have been banished. As a replacement there emerged the problem of wages and prices which rise too rapidly and too often. This problem forms the basis of this chapter, which contains a discussion and analysis of the aggregate wage patterns for Japan and the United States in the postwar period.

It begins with a discussion of the analytical basis of the aggregate wage problem. This is followed by a brief comparison of the movement of wages and related variables in the two countries over the postwar years, in order to provide the reader with some frame of reference in which to place the specific analyses. Two principal methods of aggregate wage analysis which may be identified in the historical context of postwar labor economics--pattern bargaining and the Phillips curve--are discussed. In addition there is a section on a less often used labor supply analysis, a method of analysis which is particularly appropriate for a comparison of these two countries. The chapter closes with a consideration of one policy issue particularly related to aggregate wage determination, the question of wage-price guidelines. Much of the material on wage changes pertains only to the manufacturing sectors of the economies. This concentration of effort follows largely from the availability of data and published studies and in part from the feeling in both countries that manufacturing is the key economic sector and that, as a consequence, the wage-setting patterns and mechanisms which are applied in the remainder of each economy are derived from events in manufacturing.[1]

THE BASIS OF THE AGGREGATE WAGE PROBLEM

Periods of true equilibrium in an economy are probably never observed. Yet, initially it is conceptually helpful to consider an industry as being in short-run equilibrium. In such a circumstance its workers will be receiving the value of their marginal product and there will be neither an excess supply of nor an excess demand for labor. Any observed unemployment will measure the level of frictional unemployment in the economy. An industry's equilibrium position in the next period will reflect the influence of altered tastes for goods, new investments, variations in the labor force, technological change, and the interactions generated by these forces. In such a context it is difficult to predict the new equilibrium wage and employment position for the economy or for any specific sector.

For the economy as a whole, the experiences of Japan and America suggest that, cyclical difficulties aside, the normal situation is one where the new equilibrium involves increased employment and higher real wages. In the United States, the number of nonagricultural wage and salary workers has grown from 43. 8 million in 1947 to 74. 3 million in 1969, and weekly wages for these employees went from $58. 59 in 1957-59 dollars to $89. 75 in 1957-59 dollars. In Japan, employment in nonagricultural activities rose from 23. 2 million in 1954 to 41. 4 million in 1969, and the index of real wages (on a 1960 base of 100) has gone from 77. 7 to 160. 9. It is possible that the growth in real wages resulted primarily from a falling price level and relatively constant money wages. This possibility mainly has only theoretical interest, for in the postwar experience of the two economies, the general trend has been a rising consumer price level. Historically, there may have been periods, namely the post civil war period for the United States and the 1870's and late 1920's in Japan, when it was relevant.

If all of these forces--technology, changing tastes, shifts in the labor force, new investment, etc. --were to affect all industries equally, the estimation of new equilibrium points would be greatly simplified, but this is seldom, if ever, the case. There will be different impacts depending upon the circumstances of the industries. For example, between 1953 and 1969 average hourly earnings in American manufacturing rose by 84 percent, but ranged between 70.0 percent in furniture and 111 percent in tobacco manufacturing. Alternatively, the average increase was 145 cents and ranged between 96 cents in apparel and 185 cents in transportation equipment. The interesting questions then become (1) What are the sources of rapid wage growth in some sectors? (2) What impact or interactions do these imbalances generate in the rest of the economy?

Normal theoretical considerations immediately suggest those factors which have already been mentioned, especially technological change and investment, and profits, the latter often being closely related to technology and investment. Reflecting a more traditional view, expectations in the immediate postwar years would have been that the initial impetus to higher wages in a favored sector would be tempered by an increased labor supply as workers moved from the more laggard sectors to the more dynamic ones. Observed reality did not seem to conform to this expectation. The laggard industries seemed to be increasing their wages almost as rapidly as the leading sectors, and a similarity of wage changes by industry was observed which exceeded expectations formed on the basis of the wide differences in the profit, productivity, and growth experiences of the industries.

A variety of interactions were suggested in an attempt to explain these unexpected similarities in wage changes. Most of these involved institutional factors. While unions were the institutional factor which was most widely discussed, the same wage patterns would have been observed if equity considerations, worker morale, or potential employee mobility had been important elements in the firm's wage-determination decision. Even granting the importance of institutional agents in transmitting new wage levels throughout a system, the questions of how the initial wage increase was stimulated remained to be more satisfactorily answered, and the exact mechanics of the transfer of wage pressure between industries remained to be illuminated.

Thus much of modern U. S. work upon aggregate wage determination can be seen as attempts to estimate the importance and relative size of productivity, profits, unemployment, and wage-setting mechanisms in producing the postwar wage patterns. Most of these studies of the process of aggregate wage determination stressed a combination of institutional and market forces. Usually, though, any single author has given greater emphasis to either markets or institutions. Yet all have acknowledged that bargaining and wage determination have taken place within the context of the forces of the labor market, the profit-productivity matrix of the firms, and various institutional frameworks.[2]

POSTWAR AGGREGATE WAGE PATTERNS

The Base Year in Japan

The immediate post-surrender years in Japan were ones of great dislocation and a failure of the economy to produce at the level of its limited potential. The dislocation resulted from a combination of the militarily inflicted physical destruction and the uncertainties associated with defeat, a depleted stock of capital goods, the exhaustion of human resources, and the policies of the United States.[3] The latter, primarily the Occupation policies, were framed in terms of vindictiveness toward an aggressive power. The policies had the aim of fundamentally reforming Japan's basic industrial structure in order to inhibit her future capacity for aggression, to compensate in some measure for the suffering of the countries she had defeated, to punish Japan, and lastly to make the economy more democratic. Therefore, these policies were not conducive to rapid recovery. The failure of the economy even to be able to feed itself in these years became evident in the extent of U. S. aid required, at its peak $535 million in 1949. A combination of events, the high cost of aid as seen by the United States, the growing estrangement between the United States and the Soviet Union, and the extreme nature of some of the proposed Occupation policies gradually led to modifications in certain of the most economically inhibiting Occupation policies. In time these modifications of economic policy, coupled with the natural resilience of the people, generated economic recovery. An additional important stimulation toward recovery came in June, 1950, with the invasion of South Korea by the North Koreans.

Apart from the political ramifications which resulted in

further modifications of U. S. policies toward Japan, the economic impact upon Japan's economy from U. S. spending associated with the Korean War was fantastic. Employment, and especially exports, boomed. Industrial production, which had fallen from a prewar peak of 148 in 1937 (1934-36 = 100) to a low of 31 in 1946 and had recovered only to 84 in 1950, bounced up to 153 in 1953. On a 1960 base, the 1937 peak figure was 37. 7 and 1953's was 40. 7. The index of real national income (1934-36 = 100) had recovered by the early 1950's, reaching 107 in 1951. Due, however, to population growth, the per capita index did not reach the level of the early 1930's until 1954.[4] The exact year in which the Japanese economy completed its recovery from military defeat is still a subject for debate. It probably depends in large part upon which aspect of the economy is of specific interest, though 1952-54 is generally accepted as marking the end of recovery and the beginning of postwar growth.[5] In view of these unsettled conditions within Japan, it would seem most meaningful to begin our comparative analysis with the year 1952, when it can be argued that at least the bulk of the return to normalcy had been accomplished.

The Base Year in America

Despite the fact that during World War II many economists made pessimistic predictions concerning unemployment and depression in the immediate postwar period, the U. S. economy did not experience either major dislocations or a depression after the war ended. The most visible measure of economic change in the immediate postwar period was the decontrol of prices and wages and the consequent release of the war's pent-up inflation. This led to quite rapid rises in the cost of living, the index of which for urban workers (1957-59 = 100) went from 62. 7 in 1945 to 83. 8 in 1948, a 33. 6 percent increase in three years. By 1948 the immediate postwar inflation seems to have run its course. In that year unemployment stood at a historically satisfactory 3. 8 percent, and real gross national product was up from its 1946-47 plateau. Thus, this year would seem to mark the end of recovery from wartime and reconversion and the beginning point for postwar growth. It was also a year when the dispersion of industrial wages was close to its maximum point of compression. This complicates any discussion of changes in wages, since part of the movement in wages in subsequent years may reflect a natural return to equilibrium and not the response to changes in other variables.[6]

Whether it is wiser to compare the United States and Japan over the same number of years, 1952 forward, or over the same economic period, the era of postwar growth, is a difficult question. In this case it is compounded by the wage compression problem, but more importantly by the impact of the Korean War, which was probably an excess stimulus to the U. S. economy but a necessary ingredient to the recovery of the Japanese economy. In general, I feel that economic consistency has more to recommend it than does chronological consistency. Consequently, the U. S. experience is analyzed over the years since 1948.

Wage Changes in Japan

Between 1952 and 1969, average monthly wages in Japanese establishments employing 30 or more have risen from 14, 103 yen to 64, 333 yen, an increase of almost 450 percent.[7] (See Table 15.) Hourly wages rose from 73. 4 yen per hour in 1952 to 338 yen in 1969, a rate of increase slightly above the rate for monthly wages, reflecting a modest decrease in the number of hours worked. In part these rapid increases reflect nominal increases, for especially in recent years the cost of living has also been rapidly rising. The index of real monthly wages (1960 = 100) has grown only 126 percent, rising from 71. 3 in 1952 to 160. 9 in 1969.

Looking at increases in money wage levels, there appear to be two different periods, 1952-60 and 1961 to the present. With the exceptional 15. 3 percent rise in monthly wages in 1952-53 and the abnormally low 3 percent gain in 1957-58 excluded, the money wages in the first subperiod generally rose 5 to 7 percent per annum. In the post-1960 period, however, the annual increase is on the order of 10 percent in each year through 1966. Since then it has averaged closer to 14 percent. The growth rate of real wages presents a very different picture, a fact which would seem to minimize any simple and direct relationship between wage and price increases. For real wages (see Table 15) the very rapid jump of 8. 3 percent in 1952-53 was followed by no increase in the subsequent year, since rising consumer prices wiped out that year's wage gain. In 1955-56 there were substantial gains associated with the Jimmu boom, the economic expansion named after the legendary first Emperor of Japan. (The name implies that the growth in those years could be compared with the growth associated with the formation of Japan.) Wages in real terms during 1958-67

TABLE 15

Wages in Japan and the United States, 1948-69

Year	Japan Average Monthly Nonagricultural Wages (yen)	Japan Index of Real Monthly Wages (1960=100)	Japan Index of Real Hourly Wages (1960=100)	United States Private Non-agricultural Hourly Wages	United States Index of Real Wages (1960=100)
1948	--	--	--	$1.22	72.2
1949	--	--	--	1.28	76.2
1950	--	--	--	1.34	78.7
1951	--	--	--	1.45	79.2
1952	14,103	71.3	73.9	1.52	81.1
1953	16,336	77.2	79.4	1.61	85.1
1954	17,497	77.2	80.1	1.65	87.1
1955	18,343	82.1	84.5	1.71	90.5
1956	19,987	88.0	89.6	1.80	94.0
1957	21,324	89.3	93.2	1.89	95.0
1958	21,161	92.4	93.1	1.95	95.5
1959	22,608	96.9	94.0	2.02	98.5
1960	24,375	100.0	100.0	2.09	100.0
1961	26,626	105.7	104.6	2.14	101.4
1962	29,458	109.1	110.4	2.22	103.9
1963	32,727	112.2	114.4	2.28	105.4
1964	35,812	119.3	121.1	2.36	107.9
1965	39,360	121.9	125.4	2.45	109.9
1966	43,925	128.5	133.0	2.56	112.0
1967	48,714	138.0	142.0	2.68	114.0
1968	55,405	150.0	154.0	2.85	114.0
1969	64,333	160.9	170.9	3.04	118.0

Notes: The Japanese data apply to firms employing 30 or more workers. The samples which underlie columns 1 and 2 differ slightly. Column 3 is obtained by dividing Column 1 by average monthly hours and by the price index for urban workers. The sample establishments were changed in May, 1955, and in January of 1958, 1961, 1964, and 1967.

The wages are total cash earnings, which include contractual payments and special cash payments, which consist of summer and year-end bonuses and any other non-contractual payments. Retroactive payments are included.

U.S. wages are gross hourly earnings. They do not include bonuses or retroactive payments. Real wages were obtained by dividing money wages by the consumer price index (1957-59 = 100).

Sources: Japan Institute of Labor, Japan's Labor Statistics (Tokyo, 1970), pp. 70, 110, 128; U.S. Department of Labor, Handbook of Labor Statistics, 1970, pp. 203, 285.

may be characterized as involving an every-other-year cycle in which a modest 3 percent wage gain would be followed by a 5 percent or higher gain in the next year. The only breaks in this pattern came in 1961-63, when both years witnessed only modest increases in monthly real wages, and 1967-69, when the increases were on the order of 8 percent.

There was divergent experience within the various sectors of the economy. Manufacturing, despite what might have been anticipated from assumptions concerning its key role, grew somewhat less rapidly than did the economy as a whole until 1965. The leading sector until 1965, when it was replaced by manufacturing, was construction, which essentially held its position of leadership over the entire period. Construction was followed by transportation and communication, and then by utilities, in both of which wages rose more rapidly than in manufacturing until 1965. The sectors with the slower rates of wage advance to 1969 were mining and finance and insurance, though their patterns have not been as consistent as those of the leading sectors. Mining wages grew as rapidly as manufacturing until about 1959-60, but have fallen behind since that time, primarily in 1961-62. Wages in wholesale and retail trade grew less rapidly than manufacturing until 1961, especially in the years 1953-56. Between 1961 and 1965, however, wholesale and retail trade wages outpaced those in manufacturing and have followed them in 1965-69. The experience of finance and insurance was that wages grew somewhat more rapidly than in manufacturing from 1952 to about 1955. Since then wages in this sector have gradually slipped behind the pace in manufacturing, most notably since 1963.

Within the manufacturing sector there has also been a wide divergence in the growth rates of wages. Between 1953 and 1960 the industry in which wages grew most rapidly was the chemical industry. There the overall gain in wages was 68 percent, as compared with a manufacturing average of 65 percent. The slowest rate of increase was in rubber, where it was a niggardly 19 percent. Since 1960, however, the laggard rubber industry has been transformed into the pace setter, doubling its wages between 1960 and 1965, though its rate after that has been somewhat more modest. Meanwhile, the iron and steel industry became the most sluggish, with increases after 1960 amounting to only 45.6 percent by 1965, a pattern which it too has changed since 1965, when its experience has been slightly above the average. The 1965-68 wage leader was the machinery industry, with 56 percent.

Wage Changes in the United States

Gross hourly earnings for workers in private nonmanufacturing employment went from $1.23 in 1948 to $3.04 in 1969. (See Table 15.) In real terms (deflating by consumer prices) this was an increase from $1.46 to $2.39. This represents a growth in the real wages of the working man of 64 percent in the 21 years from 1948 to 1969, 45 percent since 1952. Money wages rose by over 4 percent per annum in seven of the 10 years from the recession of 1948-49 to the recession of 1957-58. Since then, only after 1965 has the rate of money wage increases been above 4 percent. The use of wage increases deflated for price changes presents a different picture. In the early period there was quite a bit of fluctuation, from the 0.5 percent gain in 1950-51 and 1957-58 to the high of 5.5 percent in 1948-49. The median annual real wage increase for 1948-58 was 2.8 percent. After 1958, with the sole exception of the 3.6 percent real rise in 1968-69, there was only a dreary succession of low real wage increases. The median year-to-year increase was 1.9 percent.

The wage increase pattern for major sectors within the private nonagricultural sector was, for the most part, very similar to the overall pattern. An exception was construction, where the rate of increase has outpaced the others. Construction wages went from $1.71 in 1948 to $2.82 in 1958 and to $4.78 in 1969. After accounting for price changes, these represent a 37 percent increase between 1948 and 1958 and 40 percent between 1958 and 1969. A second modest exception was retail trade, where the pace of wage advance has been somewhat faster than the average since 1960. Class I railroads and telephone communication had a reverse experience. In the case of telephone communication, the period of rapid growth was 1948-55, and for Class I railroads it was 1948-1958.

Comparative Wage Changes

Between 1952 and 1960 the experience of both economies with price inflation was relatively nominal, though in Japan consumer prices rose roughly twice as much as in the United States. (See Table 16.) In Japan the increase was 21 percent, and in the United States it was 12 percent. Since then, however, the differences have been much greater in Japan: between 1960 and 1969 consumer prices rose 64.9 percent, or

TABLE 16

Consumer Prices, Japan and the United States, 1948-69

Year	U. S. Consumer Price Index (1957-59=100)	Japan Consumer Price Index (1960=100)
1948	83. 8	--
1949	83. 0	73. 0
1950	83. 8	68. 0
1951	90. 5	79. 0
1952	92. 5	82. 6
1953	93. 2	88. 0
1954	93. 6	93. 7
1955	93. 3	92. 7
1956	94. 7	93. 0
1957	98. 0	95. 9
1958	100. 7	95. 5
1959	101. 5	96. 5
1960	103. 1	100. 0
1961	104. 2	105. 3
1962	105. 4	112. 3
1963	106. 7	121. 0
1964	108. 1	125. 6
1965	109. 9	135. 2
1966	113. 1	142. 0
1967	116. 3	147. 8
1968	121. 2	155. 5
1969	127. 7	164. 9

Note: In 1965 Japan expanded its index from 28 cities to all cities with a population of 50,000. Consequently, figures for 1966-68 are based upon the percentage growth of the new series.

Sources: U. S. Department of Labor, Handbook of Labor Statistics, 1970, p. 285; Japan Institute of Labor, Japan's Labor Statistics (Tokyo, 1970), p. 128.

slightly in excess of 7 percent per annum. In the United States, prices increased by only 27.7 percent, about 40 percent as much. Consequently, the fact that during the years between 1952 and 1960 money wages in Japan grew by 70 percent, or almost twice as rapidly as the 38 percent in the United States, comes as no surprise. In the second period, the difference was about 4 to 1 in favor of Japan, 164 percent to 46 percent. Even so, a little arithmetic will suggest that even after accounting for the impact of price increases, the real wage experiences in the United States and Japan were rather dissimilar between 1952 and 1960. In Japan real wages rose by approximately 40 percent, or 5.0 percent per year. For the United States, the gain was only 23 percent, or 2.9 percent per year. Comparing the "normal" pre-1960 periods, 1952-60 for Japan and 1948-60 for the United States, one observes a closer correspondence between the experience of the two countries, an annual growth of 5.0 percent to 3.3 percent. In the years after 1960 the more favorable relative position of the Japanese laborer is improved even more. Real wages in Japan rose 60.9 percent (6.7 percent per year) between 1960 and 1969, but rose only 18 percent (2.0 percent per year) in the United States. For Japan these calculations were based upon monthly wages uncorrected for hours of work. In the United States the data are average hourly wages. Correcting for hours only tends to emphasize the magnitude of the change before and after 1960, for during the 1950's hours worked in Japan rose by 5 percent, but after 1960 they fell by almost the same amount (6 percent). Thus, in real hourly terms Japanese wages grew at 4.5 percent per year, compared with a U.S. rate of 3.3 percent during the years of postwar growth before 1960. After 1960 the differences became much wider, 7.8 percent for Japan and only 2.0 percent for the United States.

Productivity in Japan

The immense growth of the economy and of real wages in Japan has gone forward largely upon the basis of dramatic increases in average physical labor productivity, which has grown slightly less than four times since 1955. The gain in the index of productivity for all industries (1960 = 100) was from 64.5 in 1955 to 249.6 in 1969. For manufacturing, the index rose from 64.5 in 1955 to 259.3 in 1969.

Accustomed as we are in America to thinking of a relationship between movements in labor productivity and wage gains, it is instructive to examine this pattern for Japan. Considering the period as a whole, there is a correlation between changes in money wage rates and productivity, but largely because of the influence of the last few years. During 1955-66 there was no correlation. This was due largely to the inflationary influence of the post-1960 years, which may also have generated, on a feedback basis, large money-wage increases to counter the depressing impact of the rising prices upon standards of living. There is, however, a strongly significant rank-order correlation between yearly wage gains in real terms and annual productivity advances during these years.

While there is a rank-order correlation between annual increases in real wages and productivity, the truly outstanding factor, in the American context, is the magnitude of the degree to which the productivity increases have consistently outrun the real wage increases. The index of real wages between 1955 and 1969 rose from 82. 1 to 160. 9 (1960 = 100), but productivity went from 64. 5 to 259. 3 (1960 = 100). In other words, real wages essentially doubled and labor productivity increased by about twice as much. On a year-to-year basis, the cumulative real wage gain (1956/55-1969/68) was 71. 8 percentage points, and the productivity gain was 157. 9 percentage points. This 2 to 1 ratio of each year's gain in productivity to the gain in real wages is quite stable over the 10-year period. The years 1957, 1959, 1963, and 1967 stand out as ones in which the gains in productivity were larger than normal compared with the increase in real wages, while 1958 is the only year when wages grew more than productivity. In 1968 and 1969 real wage gains relative to productivity gains were also impressive.

Productivity in the United States

The productivity index in U. S. nonagricultural sectors has risen from 76. 5 in 1948 to 134. 7 in 1969 (1957-59 = 100), a 76 percent increase over the period. (See Table 17.) Between 1948 and 1958 the gain was from 76. 5 to 99. 7. In the second period, 1958-69, the increase was from 99. 7 to 134. 7.

Looking at the relationship between productivity and wage gains per year, it is evident that the degree of price inflation has been such as to destroy any strong money wage-productivity pattern. There is a modest rank-order correlation between year-to-year gains in productivity and gains in wages. The rank-order coefficient, though statistically significant, is a

TABLE 17

Labor Productivity, Japan and the United States, 1948-69

Year	Japan		United States	
	Index of Labor Productivity, All Industries (1960=100)	Index of Labor Productivity, Manufacturing (1960=100)	Index of Private Nonagricultural Output per Man-Hour (1957-59=100)	Index of Output Per Man-Hour, Manufacturing (1957-59=100)
1948	--	--	76.5	76.4
1949	--	--	79.5	79.3
1950	--	--	84.4	85.0
1951	--	--	86.3	86.9
1952	--	--	87.0	87.3
1953	--	--	89.6	90.2
1954	--	--	91.6	91.8
1955	64.5	64.5	95.7	97.2
1956	73.1	73.4	95.2	96.2
1957	78.7	78.9	97.2	98.2
1958	78.6	78.6	99.7	98.1
1959	88.3	88.5	103.1	103.7
1960	100.0	100.0	104.4	105.5
1961	110.6	110.2	107.4	107.9
1962	114.4	113.3	112.3	114.3
1963	125.7	124.0	115.7	118.9
1964	143.5	141.4	120.0	124.7
1965	151.1	148.9	123.6	129.8
1966	170.2	163.0	127.9	131.8
1967	198.0	190.0	129.9	132.1
1968	225.9	217.1	134.2	139.2
1969	259.3	249.6	134.7	142.6

Note: The index for Japan was obtained by dividing the output estimated by the Ministry of International Trade and Industry by total man-days from the same source. In the United States the figures are based upon establishment data.

Sources: Japan Productivity Center, as presented in Japan Institute of Labor, *Japan's Labor Statistics* (Tokyo, 1970), pp. 122-123; U.S. Department of Labor, *Handbook of Labor Statistics, 1970*, p. 158.

not overly large. Looking at the pre-1958 data and the post-1958 data separately does not result in an improvement in the relationship between money wages and productivity, though for the years 1948-58 there is an almost significant negative relationship. An analysis of the two periods, using real wages and productivity, yields the results that in the early period there was not a significant relationship, while for the latter the rank-order correlation improves to .77, which is significant at the 1 percent level. If the changes in productivity and wages are compared, it can be seen that for the postwar years, 1947-1969, the productivity increase of 2.7 percent per year has been outpaced by the real compensation increase of 2.8 percent per year. This is almost all a product of events in the first period, for from 1957 to 1969 real compensation grew at 2.6 percent per year and productivity at 3.0 percent per year. The years 1960 to 1965 were those when the increase in productivity markedly outraced real wage gains.

Comparative Productivity

Looking at productivity increases, one observes that Japanese productivity grew at 11 percent per year in the earlier period and almost 1.5 times faster after 1960, especially after 1965. In the United States, however, there is some difference in the productivity increases in the two periods. The first period was one of somewhat variable growth which averaged about 2.8 percent per year, while after 1958-59 output per man-hour in the private economy increased in a somewhat more stable manner but at a slightly faster rate. The relationship of increases in productivity to wage gains in the output per man-hour is also quite different in the two countries. In Japan over all the post-reconstruction years, productivity grew much more rapidly than did wages. When wages are measured monthly, there appears to be no difference between the two periods in the degree to which gains in productivity outpace wage increases, though the use of hourly real wages suggests that the margin in favor of productivity is somewhat smaller after 1960 than it was before. In the United States the pattern is reversed, for the late 1940's and early 1950's were years in which wages outran productivity; after the recession of 1958 the gain in productivity clearly surpassed the rate of real wage change until 1966. The gain was roughly 3.1 percent per year to 2.7 percent per year.

The Labor Force in Japan

The Japanese labor force in this period was also undergoing considerable change, some of which was discussed in Chapter 2. Here there is need to outline only briefly the trends in total labor supply and the tightness of the labor market. (See Table 18.) The labor force in 1960 was about 4.6 million larger than it had been in 1954, while labor force participation had declined only marginally, from 69.8 percent to 69.2 percent. In the succeeding eight-year period, 1961-69, the size of the labor force expanded somewhat more slowly, about 250,000 fewer persons per year. A principal factor in the slower growth was the decline in the labor force participation, which fell by 3.7 percent. The impact of the continuing high rate of economic growth and the decline in the relative size of the labor force can be seen in the unemployment rate determined by the labor force survey, which declined from an approximate annual level of 1.5 percent in the five years before 1960 to .8 or .9 percent in the years after 1960. The unemployment compensation recipient estimate of unemployment shows less improvement. It averaged 3.9 percent for 1955-60 and 3.0 percent for 1961-69, while the separation rate in manufacturing rose from 1.9 percent in 1955-60 to 2.4 percent in 1961-69.

The Labor Force in the United States

The supply aspects of the U.S. labor market are varied. (See Tables 18 and 19.) Looking only at the unemployment rate, the postwar years apparently can be divided into several subperiods. One begins in 1947 and runs to 1953. These years were characterized by full employment periods, in which the measured rate of unemployment fell to below 4 percent. The subperiod from 1954 to 1957 or 1958 was apparently one with full employment, but the unemployment rate was slightly above 4 percent. The third period, beginning in 1958 and continuing until early 1965, was one in which the measured unemployment rate was continually above 5 percent. The last period is the Vietnam boom of 1966-69. Use of the quit rate in manufacturing as a measure of labor market tightness suggests three periods, one running from 1948 to 1956, a second from 1957 to 1965, and the Vietnam years. Yet supply in terms of gross labor force participation was quite stable at about 60 percent, with a low of 59.4 percent in 1948 and a high of 62.1 percent

TABLE 18

Labor Force and Labor Force Participation Rates, Japan and the United States, 1948-69

Year	Japan: Labor Force, 15 and Older (thousands)	Japan: Labor Force Participation Rate (percent)	United States: Total Labor Force 16 and Older (thousands)	United States: Civilian Labor Force 16 and Older (thousands)	United States: Labor Force Participation Rate (percent)
1948	--	--	62,080	60,621	59.4
1949	--	--	62,903	61,286	59.6
1950	--	--	63,858	62,208	59.9
1951	--	--	65,117	62,017	60.4
1952	--	--	65,730	62,138	60.4
1953	37,890	70.0	66,560	63,015	60.2
1954	40,550	69.8	66,993	63,643	60.0
1955	41,940	70.8	68,072	65,023	60.4
1956	42,680	70.5	69,409	66,552	61.0
1957	43,630	70.7	69,729	66,929	60.6
1958	43,870	69.7	70,275	67,639	60.4
1959	44,330	69.0	70,921	68,369	60.2
1960	45,110	69.2	72,142	69,628	60.2
1961	45,620	69.1	73,031	70,459	60.2
1962	46,140	68.3	73,442	70,614	59.7
1963	46,520	67.1	74,571	71,833	59.6
1964	47,100	66.1	75,830	73,091	59.6
1965	47,870	65.7	77,178	74,455	59.7
1966	48,910	65.8	78,893	75,770	60.1
1967	49,830	65.9	80,793	77,347	60.6
1968	50,610	66.0	82,272	78,737	60.7
1969	50,980	65.5	84,239	80,733	61.1

Notes: In Japan the labor force participation rate is based upon the labor force as a percentage of those 15 and older. A person is considered employed if he worked at least one hour during the survey week.

The participation rates in the United States are for the total labor force, including the military forces. The figures for the labor force are not strictly comparable because of changes in 1953 and 1962 in order to incorporate decennial census benchmarks. In 1960 the inclusion of Alaska and Hawaii added about 300,000 to the civilian labor force.

Sources: Labor Force Survey of the Bureau of Statistics, Office of the Prime Minister, as reported in Japan Institute of Labor, Japan's Labor Statistics (Tokyo, 1970), pp. 26-27; U.S. Department of Labor, Handbook of Labor Statistics, 1970, p. 25.

TABLE 19

Unemployment and Quit Rates,
Japan and the United States, 1948-69

Year	Japan: Unemployment by Compensation Data (percent)	Japan: Unemployment by Survey Data (percent)	Japan: Rate of Separation, Manufacturing (percent)	United States: Quit Rate, Manufacturing (percent)	United States: Unemployment Rate (percent)
1948	--	--	--	3.4	3.8
1949	--	--	--	1.9	5.9
1950	--	--	--	2.3	5.3
1951	--	--	--	2.9	3.3
1952	--	--	2.3	2.8	3.0
1953	4.6	1.3	2.0	2.8	2.9
1954	5.6	1.7	2.1	1.4	5.5
1955	5.6	1.8	1.8	1.9	4.4
1956	3.9	1.7	1.8	1.9	4.1
1957	3.3	1.4	1.9	1.6	4.3
1958	4.3	1.4	2.0	1.1	6.8
1959	3.6	1.5	2.0	1.5	5.5
1960	2.9	1.1	2.1	1.3	5.5
1961	2.7	1.0	2.5	1.2	6.7
1962	3.0	.9	2.4	1.4	5.5
1963	3.5	.9	1.3[a] 2.3	1.4	5.7
1964	3.5	.8	1.1 2.6	1.5	5.2
1965	3.2	.8	1.2 2.3	1.9	4.5
1966	3.0	.9	1.3 2.2	2.6	3.8
1967	2.8	.9	1.3 2.4	2.3	3.8
1968	2.6	--	1.2 2.3	2.5	3.6
1969	2.4	--	1.1 2.7	2.7	3.5

[a]Revised in 1967, at which time the basis for the survey was changed and no more data were released. Thus on the old base .9 was the correct figure and on the new one 1.3. Recalculations on the new base were made back to 1963.

Note: Japanese unemployment survey data are derived from a survey very similar to that used in the United States. Unemployment compensation data are based on the proportion of those eligible for unemployment compensation who were receiving such compensation.

Sources: Labor Force Survey of the Bureau of Statistics, Office of the Prime Minister, as reported in Japan Institute of Labor, Japan's Labor Statistics (Tokyo, 1967), pp. 15-16, and Japan Labor Bulletin (May, 1970), p. 5; U.S. data are from U.S. Department of Labor, Handbook of Labor Statistics, 1970, pp. 25, 116.

in 1969. Masked within this stability were significantly divergent movements in male and female participation rates. The male participation rate in the initial year of approximately 87 percent was maintained until 1956, when it began to decline. By 1967, this rate had dropped about 6 percent to 80. 9 percent. The female participation rate, on the other hand, has more or less steadily risen over the entire 21-year period, going from 31. 8 percent in 1947 to 34. 8 in 1952, 36. 9 in 1956, and reaching 42. 7 percent in 1969, thus becoming equal to more than half the male rate. With gross participation stable, the total civilian labor force has grown approximately 33 percent, from 60. 6 million in 1948 to 80. 7 million in 1969. The growth appears to have been fairly steady, though the impact of the cyclical patterns in the economy is visible. The years since 1962 stand out as ones in which growth has been relatively large, 1. 7-2. 5 percent per year, compared with a median in the postwar period of 1. 5 percent.

Comparative Labor Force

Other than the modest declines in Japanese labor force participation since 1962, there are no striking differences in overall labor force growth. The figures for Japan do cloak the very rapid growth in the number of persons who are employed by others, as contrasted with being self-employed or unpaid family workers. In 1950, out of 35. 6 million employed and experienced unemployed Japanese, only 14 million, or about 39. 4 percent, were employees. The remainder consisted of 9. 3 million self-employed and 12. 3 million unpaid family workers. In 1969 the total work force had grown to 50. 4 million, but the number of employees had more than doubled to 32. 0 million, or about 63 percent of the total. The number of self-employed declined to 9. 9 million, and unpaid family workers declined to 8. 4 million.

The principal difference in labor force behavior lies in the tightness of the market. In Japan the 1950's were a period of a growing relative labor shortage, a shortage which continued almost unabated during the 1960's. In the United States the firm labor markets of the late 1940's and early 1950's were followed by almost a decade of relative oversupply in the labor market.

Summary

In summary, it appears that the labor economies of the United States and Japan have had somewhat different experiences during the postwar years. In Japan real wages have grown rapidly over the entire period, but have consistently and significantly lagged behind productivity growth. Until about 1960 this pattern occurred in connection with moderate increases in consumer prices, a relative abundance of labor, and large increases in the proportion of the working force who were classed as employees. In the United States the wage increases have been much more modest and largely in the context of stable prices, except in the last few years. Until around 1960 the gains in real wages were greater than those in productivity, and the employment side of the labor market was in balance. After 1958, with a looser labor market, in part the seeming result of increased labor supply, productivity increased more rapidly than did real wages until the Vietnam boom began.

It is possible that the differences in the magnitudes of the growth in real wages largely reflect differences in the degree of economic maturity (income per capita) of the countries and that in terms of wage relationships the two nations are quite similar in their response to relative labor surplus. The relevance of such a view should become more apparent in the examination of the aggregate wage-setting systems in Japan and the United States.

AGGREGATE WAGE ANALYSIS

Interest in the United States in the problems of aggregate wage determination may be said to have begun in the immediate postwar period, in the context of certain unique events which occurred then. One of these events was the series of widespread industry-union contract negotiations, which in many industries were conducted with all firms at the same time. The first of these initially annual contract sessions was in 1946 and centered on the demands of the automobile and steel unions. Initial settlement came, however, in the oil industry (22 cents an hour) and in meat packing (16 cents an hour). These were followed in February by a Wage Stabilization Board recommendation for an 18.5 cents an hour increase in the steel negotiations. Technically speaking, the Board should then have considered, on an individual basis, the increases being asked in all subsequent contract negotiations, but in fact the Board offered blanket approval for any contract up to a wage increase of 18.5 cents. Consequently 18.5 cents an hour quickly became the dominant settlement figure in 1946. The second set of negotiations came in 1947, and this yielded a dominant settlement of 15 cents an hour.

The degree of uniformity in the annual wage settlements among the various industries began to dwindle in 1948. The concept of an annual negotiation of wages and conditions of work was also reassessed. Its continuance received a death blow in 1950, when the United Auto Workers and General Motors pioneered their "living" agreement, a contract of five years' duration with productivity and cost-of-living wage increase formulas built into the basic agreement. The five-year contract subsequently proved to be of excessive length for the realities of the American economy and the political nature of the union movement. It is probable, however, that it propelled the turn toward longer contracts, which generally were two or three years in duration. Consequently, while in 1951, 70 percent of all union contracts were for one year, by 1956, 65 percent were for two years or longer, and the average in 1970 was two years and nine months. The timing of negotiations within the year also changed, as both company and union tried to obtain the most appropriate termination dates in terms of their assessment of their own strength and the particular conditions of their industry. One prominent example was the shift of the United Auto Workers' negotiations with the major automobile companies from around midyear into the heart of the new auto season in the fall. Thus, in 1969 there were 3,700 major contract expirations, but the most in any single month was 851 in September, or 23 percent of the total.

The immediate postwar experience with annual negotiations, in many cases on an industry-wide basis, led to an interest in the question of union influence on aggregate wage determination and directly to a system of analysis which may be classed as "pattern bargaining."

PATTERN BARGAINING

United States

The concept of pattern bargaining, which perhaps draws its most profound theoretical statement from Arthur Ross's

Trade Union Wage Policy, is essentially expressed as follows: within certain industries there are firms whose terms of negotiation are emulated or followed in setting the terms for the remaining firms within the industry. An alternative view is that there are only a few key negotiations in the entire U. S. economy and that these settlements spread to the leading firms in other industries and thence down the industry chain to the smallest firms. In its most general form, few would quarrel with the proposition that most wages are determined by pattern setters in the same way that the truth of "As Maine goes, so goes the nation" is accepted, for clearly there is a general business climate which affects all industries and there are product and labor market forces which tie industries and firms together. Indeed, one of the early pattern bargaining studies went to some effort to demonstrate the degree to which wage leadership in the steel industry was exercised by the United States Steel Co. in the nonunion era of the 1920's.[8]

In the same way the rise of a limited paternalism in the industrial relations practice of major corporations in the 1920's, the rise of "company unions" in the post-NRA period of the 1930's, and the efforts to reduce turnover in American manufacturing in the 1920's are eloquent proof, if any is needed, that labor policy and wage leadership among major firms is not a recent phenomenon. What was needed and was new in the postwar years was a vehicle by which the wages in the labor leadership sector could easily and clearly be transmitted to situations whose circumstances were very different. This was usually but not always thought to be the role of trade unionism, especially the large national industrial unions, most of which were in the CIO.

Early students of pattern bargaining asked two questions: What is the mechanism by or through which the pattern settlements were made? and What explains the degree to which any given key settlement is followed by an outside firm? A third question was added later: What are the determinants of the original "key" settlement?

With regard to the question of the role of the wage leader's bargain in affecting the decisions of other negotiations within a broadly defined industry or the orbit of a particular union, there are two principal studies which define the situation. One concerns the steel industry and the other the automobile industry in Detroit.[9] In general, both reported that the key bargain played a major but complex role in the union's overall approach to its subsidiary negotiations. In pattern deviation, factors like the degree of closeness of the secondary firm to the narrowly defined industry of the pattern setter and the size of the secondary firm appeared to be the most important explanations. In other words, the key bargain was seen by the union as a framework for its negotiations, and not as an ultimatum to be delivered to subsequent firms. In the auto union negotiations, it was noted that the smaller firms, and those organized by the auto workers union but not actually in the auto industry, were the most apt to depart from the pattern. In the case of steel in 1960, 10 years after pensions were first obtained in basic steel, one-fourth of the nonsteel firms in Indiana Harbor, Indiana, organized by District 31 of the United Steel Workers of America did not have pensions in their contracts. It was noted earlier that the annual negotiation round tended to become nonoperative in the early 1950's. This breakdown was accompanied by an increase in pattern deviation, at least in steel and autos. In the case of Detroit and the United Auto Workers, there was almost a doubling in the number of firms which settled for less than the pattern settlement between the periods 1946-49 and 1955-57. The change was from 35 percent of the settlements under pattern to 62 percent under pattern. The shift was even more pronounced when measured in terms of employment, for in 1946-49 only 9 percent of the employees were covered by negotiated settlements below the pattern, but in 1955-57 some 62 percent of the employees were in that category.

The finding that in part the pattern settlements of the postwar and highly unionized years were but a continuation of an earlier situation in a nonunion era and the importance of detailed product market similarities and labor market proximity have been echoed in subsequent publications. This suggests that the extent to which occupations tend to be highly specific to a few industries, as opposed to being very general in their characteristics and required aptitudes, may also be very important. In other words, a firm with a high proportion of employees such as still operators, found in oils and chemicals, will react differently from one employing mostly assemblers, a rather ubiquitous occupation. A more recent study in the Chicago area has again confirmed this, finding that the greater the uniqueness of the occupational category, the more important the influence of the pattern or the key settlement in the firm and, conversely, the less important were possible divergent trends in the local labor market.[10]

Turning to the problem of pattern development across industry lines, there are again two principal studies, one by John E. Maher and the second by Otto Eckstein and Thomas A.

Wilson, which was expanded by Frank C. Ripley.[11] Maher argues that among major firms in several industries a pattern of wage settlements exists for the period 1946-57 which is consistent only with influences which transcend the simple ones of demand and supply. The ties are seen to be similar to those which would be operative within an industry or those firms represented by the same union: an input-output nexus, similarities in internal technology, the importance of the state of the general economy for these firms' business, and the institutional channels of communication. The proof of the existence of the pattern, as seen by Maher, lies in the great similarity of negotiated settlements in firms as divergent in industry and physical location as Phelps Dodge, General Electric, Ford, and North American Aviation, which also have great differences in profits, products, etc.

It is difficult to evaluate the correctness of such an analysis, for there is no clearly defined standard of the extent of divergence in settlements which should be expected in the absence of a key-bargain wage pattern. In some years, and 1946 is the best example, there is no question but that there was key bargain-determined pattern. The pattern increase was 18.5 cents an hour, set by the Wage Stabilization Board. Sixteen of the 19 firms in the sample had settlements within half a cent of that figure. In 1950 the key settlement pattern was 10 or 11 cents, and 11 of the 19 firms were within half a cent of that figure. In 1953 the key figures were 7 to 8.5 cents, and 12 of 19 were within half a cent. In 1957, with a 12- or 13-cent pattern, only eight, or fewer than half of the companies, were within half a cent. Clearly, the widening pattern from a single figure to a range of a cent or a cent and a half and the decline in the number of firms within half a cent of the key pattern are indicative of a weakening in the linkage between firms. For the period 1946-57 as a whole, the median increase in the key wage pattern settlement was 129.2 cents. The increase in the median firm was 119.4 cents, and the interquartile range of individual firms' increases divided by the median was .179.

In some ways, especially if a table of firms, years, and increases is viewed, the closeness of the distribution, and hence the implied extent of pattern following, is relatively impressive. Yet it is difficult to say whether it is significant evidence because there is no acceptable nonpattern situation with which it can be compared. This point was recently clearly illustrated by Timothy W. McGuire and Leonard A. Rapping, who pointed out that the extent of deviation depends upon the industry characteristics and the degree of aggregation. Thus, for changes in hourly earnings in durable manufacturing between 1958 and 1963, the coefficient of variation (standard deviation divided by the arithmetic mean times 100) for four-digit industries was 18.7 percent, for three-digit industries 16.5 percent, and for two-digit industries only 13 percent. Among nondurable manufacturing industries the figures were 26.7 percent, 23.7 percent, and 18.5 percent. The latter two were quite close to those for the nonmanufacturing sector, which were 23.9 percent and 16.6 percent. These data provide the basis for an interesting, though not conclusive, test of the extent to which key wage patterns were followed in the years 1946-57 among the firms which Maher investigated.

There seems to be little question that some key wage patterns were followed right after World War II. Since it is generally thought that the degree of pattern following lessened over time, it should be expected that the degree of dispersion of negotiated settlements in the early years would be smaller than in the late 1950's and early 1960's. For the early years the inter-quartile range of settlements divided by the median was .179. For 1958-63 the coefficient of variation for increases in two-digit manufacturing industries' average hourly wages was .13. The ratio of these two measures of dispersion is .73--very close to .75, which is the ratio of those two measures in a normally distributed population. This is strongly suggestive that the dispersion pattern of the two periods is essentially the same. Granting their similarity leaves two possible interpretations: (a) that the following of the key wage pattern across industries which was observed in the immediate postwar years continued at least until 1963 or (b) that since the early period results are the same as those for 1958-63, when other evidence of key wage following is much weaker, the observed correspondence of results for 1946-57 largely represents suppressed inflation, catching up, or the normal flow of the economy rather than the outcome of some new sets of relationships.

The second principal examination of patterns of aggregate wage behavior came in August, 1962, when Eckstein and Wilson suggested that for the period December, 1948, to December, 1960, aggregate wage changes depended upon key industry settlements which were then extended throughout the economy in five wage rounds of unequal lengths. For example, round two extended from June, 1950, to June, 1951, but round four lasted from December, 1954, to December, 1958. Their analysis is filled with a rich and varied set of results. To the extent that it pertains to the issue of pattern following across industries, their views essentially rest upon their finding that changes in straight-time hourly earnings for most two-digit industries during the periods of the wage rounds are statistically more completely explained when group profit and unemployment levels are used than when specific industry profits and unemployment data are used. Within the key industries, largely durable manufacturing ones, the difference between the use of specific industry data and group data is only modest. Since the lengths of the wage rounds are impressionistically determined and the concept of industry unemployment rates is largely a meaningless one, the modest improvement in results from the use of group rather than specific industry data is not very meaningful. On the other hand, the results for the nonkey group, primarily nondurable manufacturing industries, are much more impressive. Using only specific industry profits and unemployment data within their postulated wage rounds, it was found that only for three industries out of 11 (textiles, lumber, and furniture) was there a statistically significant relationship between wage changes and changes in the industry variables. When the key wage settlement was used in conjunction with the nonkey industry variables, six industries contained significant relationships, and in eight out of the 11 cases the coefficient of the key wage change was statistically significant. This can be interpreted to mean that the movement in the key group's wages was significantly related to the movements in the wages of these eight industries. On the basis of these relationships it is appropriate to conclude that there was pattern following in this period, or at a minimum that one large segment of manufacturing was influenced by events in the other sector.

Given that one group of industries follows the lead of another, what determines whether an industry is a leader or a laggard? One could imagine a variety of classification schemes, such as concentration ratios or degree of union membership, but these were not used because the highly concentrated tobacco industry and the highly unionized petroleum industry were included in the follower group. Frank C. Ripley has shown that the principal difference between the two groups lies in the mean profit rate, which is significantly higher for the key group industries. It is also true that, except for a few of the key group industries, the volatility of the profit rates among the key group was greater than among nonkey industries. The value of the key bargain as a substitute for the traditional forces of labor demand and supply has been challenged recently by McGuire and Rapping, who argue that demand and supply variables are more important than is implied by supporters of the key bargain approach.[12] McGuire and Rapping's views are based upon estimated wage determination equations for two-digit manufacturing industries in a number of states. They found that coefficients for manufacturing wages by state were highly significant for all but one of the 19 industries. This result may be interpreted to mean that local conditions are an important determinant of wage changes. In their work they made use of a special spill-over variable, wage changes in the automobile or steel industry. This spill-over or key wage variable played its expected role, being more significant in the determination of wages in industries which are highly unionized. Unfortunately, data limitations are such that it is not possible to contrast the results of their demand-supply model with the results of a spill-over variable and a model like the Eckstein-Wilson-Ripley one, which uses profits, unemployment, and a spill-over variable.

Consequently, we are left with the results that (1) there appears to have been a decline over the postwar period in the degree to which the key bargain pattern is a meaningful explanation for the observed aggregate wage system, perhaps suggesting the return to influence of more traditional demand and supply variables, and (2) the high profits in some sectors of the economy spill over to influence wages in the less successful sectors of manufacturing.

Japan

For Japan there are the same three questions to be raised regarding pattern bargaining: the extent to which there is a pattern, who the leaders are, and what factors determine the initial decisions. As noted earlier, the years immediately after the war were ones of extreme flux, especially with regard to union and labor matters, and it is difficult to speak of any kind of a unified wage-setting pattern. The closest approximation would be the widespread establishment of the densan wage-payment system. Densan, literally "electric industry", was originally a demand of the Electrical Workers Union to transform the prewar wage structure, which had been based upon a very tiny standard wage and a number of special or bonus payments. The latter were considered to be given by the grace of the employer and consequently were not legally required to be paid. The desired change was to a system where the standard wage would cover minimum family living requirements. Bonus or extra payments, while not eliminated, would become a much smaller proportion of total income. In its computation of the standard wage, the union used official government figures on the cost of living and made use of elaborate statistical calculations. The densan system spread rapidly, and today the proportion of average monthly wages which are kihon (standard) is 80 percent. For the next several years union wage demands were closely geared to these calculations and were based upon cost-of-living changes. The demands were also widely decentralized, resting almost entirely upon the specific enterprise unions. This was because the union movement at the national level was intensely involved in political activities, and to the extent that it concentrated any efforts upon the specific employment concerns of the workers, these efforts were in support of opposition to mass discharges, which resulted primarily from the rationalization of the production process as the Japanese economy moved through reconstruction, the boom and recession of the Korean War, and its aftermath.

A new era in Japanese labor negotiations began on January 22, 1955, when the Sōhyō Spring Wage Hike Joint Council started its activities. This group, under the leadership of Ohta Kaoru, president of Gōkarōren (synthetic chemical workers), consisted of Gōkarōren and four other national unions, Tanrō (coal miners), Shitesusōren (private railway workers), Densan (electric power workers), and Kamiparōren (paper and pulp workers). The aim of the committee was, on the basis of a unified demand for wage increases on an industrial basis, to concentrate the efforts and strength of the unions. Following the establishment of the Spring Offense, Ohta challenged the leadership of Takano Minoru, then the General Secretary of Sōhyō. At the sixth annual convention in 1955 the Takano faction was defeated, and the Spring Wage Offensive became a key plank in the program of Sōhyō as led by Ohta. The number of unions and individuals who were involved in shuntō gradually increased, growing from 83 unions in 1955 to an average of about 460 after 1960.[13] The proportion of union members involved grew from 25.5 percent in 1956 to an average of over 50 percent in 1963-67.[14] In 1970 almost three out of every four union members participated. In 1961 Chūritsuroren joined the committee as an active participant. Unions of Dōmei continued to focus their bargaining activities in the fall, though a few of them conducted negotiations in the spring in de facto coordination with Sōhyō. In 1967 the bulk of Dōmei unions except Zensendōmei (textile workers) agreed to bargain in the spring at the same time as shuntō, but not in formal association. In 1968 Zensen was also engaged in active negotiation during the spring. Thus, one can characterize the Japanese scene now as one in which the unions engage in annual negotiations of a wage-round nature. One rare exception to the annual program was a three-year agreement signed in 1964 by the Kanegafuchi Spinning Workers. This agreement was under constant attack by Zensendōmei, and it was abrogated at the 1967 Kanegafuchi convention.

A somewhat clearer concept of what is involved in the organization of the Spring Wage Offensive may be obtained by a brief review of a typical year's proceedings. On November 15, 1966, the Sōhyō and Chūritsurōren Joint Spring Offensive Action Committee issued a white paper entitled "An Offensive to Initiate the Prospect of a High Wage Era by Fighting for High Wage Rates in a Period of Prosperity." It proposed an increase in wages of 10,000 yen ($27.78 a month, or about 30 percent). At the same time, it urged a vigorous drive for a statutory flat-rate national minimum wage, the extension of social security, tax reductions, opposition to the rise in prices of government-monopoly products, the restoration to government employees of the right to strike, and opposition to any rationalization which might be introduced in the wake of wage increases.

On January 17, Nikkeiren (Japan Federation of Employers' Associations) responded with its white paper, "The New State of Liberalization [of capital imports] and Wage Issues." It said that wages should be set on the basis of long-term prospects, and not on the expected prosperity of the spring of 1967.

In each shuntō, a "top batter" union is selected. This union begins negotiations first, and is expected to be the first to reach agreement; the hope is that the terms will be highly favorable and can be emulated. Thus, a union whose economic position is favorable and whose spirit is strong is selected. In 1967, such a union was Tekkōrōren (Federation of Iron and Steel Workers Unions). Tekkōrōren's February convention decided to demand 5,000 yen ($13.89) from major firms and 6,000 yen ($16.67) from minor ones, increased retirement pay, a boost of 35 percent in overtime rates, and the introduction of a minimum rate of 20,000 yen ($55.56). The demands would be submitted on March 6, the strike ballot would be held on April 6, management's offer would be received about April 10, and the target date for the completion of negotiations would be April 15, 1967.

Other unions then adjusted their demands and schedules, reflecting Tekkōrōren's leadership role, so that they could insist upon an equivalent settlement. The plan received something of a jolt when, on April 6, the employees of the Yawata Iron Works voted against giving national executives control of an industry-wide strike, thus making the proposed "united strike" impossible. The Joint Action Committee then directed other unions to be prepared to "struggle" without regard to the outcome in steel, since it was feared that the steel union's wage position was seriously weakened. All turned out well, however, since the steel management's offer was unexpectedly high (4,300 yen, or $11.94).

Evidence as to whether the institutional system of shuntō and its "top batter" have had a marked impact upon Japanese wage setting can be sought in two areas: the response of firms and unions to questions concerning influences on their wage decisions, and observed wage movements. Information concerning influences on wage determination is available from a recent study conducted at Keio University which utilized the responses of 630 companies and 675 unions.[15] Within the manufacturing sector there appear to be four important factors influencing the decision on regular wages: the company's own situation, the starting wage for new graduates, the cost of living, and the social standard. When the replies are divided according to the size of the firm, it appears that the larger the firm, the more important is its own position and the less meaningful is the starting wage in its decision process. The greater importance of market forces for the smaller firms is also evident in the fact that the preservation of the firm's current labor force is equally as important as the company's overall position as an influence on wage setting for those employing between 100 and 499 persons, but among firms employing 5,000 and more persons, the company's own position is 20 times as important as is the preservation of the existing labor force. The replies are largely the same when the question concerns bonus items, except that company position clearly becomes dominant and the starting wage becomes very important. Unions and companies are largely in agreement on the relative importance of different factors, except that the union places an important emphasis upon the "will" (the extent of their determination to obtain the union wage demand) of the union members, a factor to which firms attach almost no importance.

When they seek specific wage comparisons, both company and union pay primary attention to events within their own industry, though they find useful and instructive the decisions and events in other parts of the economy.[16] Among firms 11.8 percent and among unions 13.7 percent report that they use a fixed relationship between themselves and others to make their own decisions, while a little over an equivalent percentage say that events outside their own industry have no influence upon them. The important influences within the same industry are having the same union, profit levels, size of the firm, and degree of industrial competition. Influences from other industries stem largely from geographical proximity or a decision that a particular firm or industry is a useful model for wage decisions. Again, there are some differences by size of firm, principally that the use of a model company and/or industry is much more prevalent among larger (1,000 or more employees) firms than among smaller ones. This can be seen in the replies of both the companies and the unions.

On the basis of the above it seems reasonable to conclude that a form of pattern bargaining across industrial lines is influential among larger firms and that decisions made among the larger firms are transmitted down through the specific industry to the smaller firms. Consequently, at least in form, aggregate Japanese wage determination can be said to be in the nature of pattern bargaining.

Turning to the evidence concerning actual wage movements, it is necessary to decide whether wage changes are to be measured in percentage or in yen per month or per hour. The principal argument in favor of a percentage measurement is the relative price, an argument taken from traditional economic theory. Also, over longer periods and to some extent for comparisons between two very divergent circumstances, the avoidance of a fixed base may enable the analysis to sidestep many difficult problems. The rationale for the use of absolute wage increases is derived from the fact that this is what is important to the worker, both in terms of his making comparisons with the gains received by other workers and for his real consumption needs. An additional merit of the absolute yen approach is that it coincides with the most common formulation of demands by unions and the method of expressing the eventual settlement.

There are several data series which could be used: average monthly wages by industry, commonly used in Japan; an hourly rate obtained by dividing monthly wages by hours worked; or the increases obtained during each year's shuntō bargaining period. Each of these has its own advantages and disadvantages. The monthly or hourly figure is influenced by the degree of boom in the economy and its subsequent influence upon overtime hours and certain special payments. The structure of wages, with its emphasis upon such personal characteristics as level of education and age, means that average wages by industry are more susceptible to change due to shifts in the nature of the work force than would be true in the United States. The wage gains during shuntō contain both the increase in base rates as well as the periodic increase which is central to Japan's wage structure. The data are largely grouped by union rather than industry, and the industrial and historical coverage is limited. The grouping by union is not as serious as it may sound, because Japanese unions contain less industrial overlap at the two-digit level than do similar unions in the United States. However, the principal advantage of these data is that they represent the actual outcomes of a pattern bargaining situation, and for that reason they will be used.

If there is following of key wage patterns in Japan, an analysis of union increases over time could be expected to reveal (1) that the dispersion of settlements was declining over time because more and more unions were bargaining during the shuntō period, and (2) a stable relationship between settlements by the pattern leaders and the rest of the industries. For 1960-69 there are reasonably complete data on the level of shuntō settlements in 17 union-industrial groupings. These data show inter-quartile dispersion ranging from a high in 1963 of .51 to a low of .13 in 1967. The pattern appears to be a reasonably stable one, though the level of dispersion appears to be generally lower after 1964. Thus, for the 17 principal unions there appears to be but a modest pattern of increasing concentration of results since 1960. For all surveyed firms in general (see Table 20), there appears to have been a marked decline in dispersion of wage increases, especially since 1956-58, though it is possible that the increased size of the sample and the growing participation in shuntō, rather than a more fundamental movement, is what is being seen. It is also possible that the greater degree of inflation after 1960 may have an independent influence on money wage levels which will yield an appearance of pattern following which does not in fact exist. Yet there is no simple year-to-year relationship between dispersion and the rate of price increase in the preceding year and the dispersion of the shuntō results. The data on dispersion by size of firm suggest that it is among firms of 100-500 employees, and not among the larger firms, that a real decline in dispersion took place, perhaps indicative of a greater degree of pattern following among the smaller

TABLE 20

Shuntō Statistics, Japan, 1956-70

Year	Monthly Wage Increases Granted During Shuntō (yen)	Dispersion of Shuntō Settlement (by firm)
1956	1,063	.57
1957	1,518	.39
1958	1,050	.58
1959	1,281	.39
1960	1,792	.34
1961	2,970	.27
1962	2,515	.26
1963	2,237	.31
1964	3,305	.20
1965	3,014	.31
1966	3,273	.24
1967	4,214	.13
1968	5,213	.14
1969	6,768	--
1970	8,983	--

Note: Data are from tabulations of the Ministry of Labor. The number of firms included per year varies from 72 to 84 in 1956-59, from 159 to 163 in 1960-66, 157 in 1967, but only 149 in 1970.

Source: The figures for 1956-68 are in Furuya Kenichi, Nakamura Kōshi, and Suzuki Kōyū, Chingin Hendo Yoin no Kenkyū [Determinants of wage movements] (Tokyo: Keizai Kikaku Chō, 1969), p. 181.

firms, though the pressures of the tight labor market upon the smaller firms may also play a role.

Existence of a pattern is also given some support by an examination of the leading unions. On a random basis over a period of 10 years, each of 17 principal unions could be expected to be among the top five three times (measured in terms of highest wage increases). For the period 1960-69, 13 of the 17 unions are among the top five at least once, but only seven are there at least three times. Four unions--metal workers, synthetic chemical workers, petroleum workers, and electrical workers--appear among the top five between six and nine times, and thus can be considered pattern setters. The relationship of the median settlement among each year's top five to the median increase among all 17 was close to 20 percent greater through 1966, but in 1967-69 it was only about 10 percent greater. Thus, we have found a declining dispersion of bargaining outcomes and a reasonable relationship between pattern leader and follower. Upon the basis of this it can be concluded that the existence of pattern bargaining in Japan is an important factor in the wage-setting mechanism.

Additional evidence concerning the relationship among wage increases for these 17 union groupings may be found in the multiple regression analysis of their shuntō wage increases. To be consistent with the survey results, such an analysis would utilize data on profits, industrial concentration, and the price level and would be subdivided by size of firm. Unfortunately such a grouping is not possible, and perhaps the best approximation is the use of total industry profit rates, specific industry profit rates, the consumer price level, and unemployment, the data used in Sano Yōko's analysis of 13 industries in 1960-68. Her results were as follows:[17]

$$Y = 8.48 + 7.67X_1 + 1.32X_2 + 8.44X_3 - 497.4X_4$$

$$(6.35) \quad (1.37) \quad (0.20) \quad (6.66) \quad (163.3)$$

The regression coefficient, adjusted for degrees of freedom, was .862 and all three variables were significant. The coefficient of determination for prices was only about a third as important as the individual profit variable, which was only about half as important as all profits. The figures were .132, .323, .594, and -.142 for unemployment. The lesser importance of consumer prices here, as compared with the response of firms, may be due to the more rapid rate of consumer price increases in recent years.

Thus it can be seen that aggregate determination of regular wages in Japan in recent years has become more completely organized into the process of shuntō, which stresses the concepts of wage rounds, coordinated union bargaining demands, the use of inter-industry standards for wage setting, and the attempt to emulate a key bargain.

In addition to having a pattern bargaining structure, the important influences on wage setting as seen by unions and companies are the state of profits and other conditions of similar firms within their own industries, except for the very large firms, where the influences tend to run across industry lines. Lastly, the dispersion of bargained wage increases has tended to decrease over time, and the profit and price levels of the entire economy are significantly related to the wage decision in each industry.[18] Given these facts, the conclusion is that Japanese wages are the product of pattern bargaining where the key bargain is established among the largest firms during shuntō and then, largely during the same period, spread down through the various sizes of firms on an industry basis, a process which is strengthened by the enterprise union characteristic of Japanese unionism.

Comparative Pattern Bargaining

The Japanese and U. S. experiences with pattern bargaining contain differences and similarities. The Japanese system of bargaining is concentrated into short annual periods. Until 1968 there were two annual periods, spring and fall, but with Dōmei's shift to a spring schedule, there is now only one period. In Japan it is possible to identify the nominal wage leader, the "top batter" of the shuntō period, and to compare the wage gains of particular industries, or rather union negotiating groups, on an annual basis. Consequently it is possible to speak with relative assurance about a pattern's having been set which other unions and/or firms can attempt to emulate. And the experience of recent years is that among those bargaining during shuntō there has been increased emulation; in other words, there is increased evidence of pattern following.

In the United States there has been divergence of contract periods and an introduction of deferred compensation agreements. This has made the decision concerning the length of a wage round, as well as the tune to which negotiations are marching, much more difficult to determine. Also, beyond the key group there is evidence to suggest that pattern following has become weaker. An additional factor which may be relevant is that in the United States, collective agreements cover many more areas than do those in Japan, and consequently it is much more difficult to determine whether a pattern is observed or not.

A comparison of the two countries at this point shows that their patterns of experience differ markedly. In the United States, the trend has been from rather distinct annual wage rounds to a rather disjointed pattern with no clear-cut key bargains. In Japan the movement has been progressively toward an annual key bargain type of negotiation. The reasons for these differences are not immediately obvious, but it will be fruitful to speculate briefly upon the rationale. In general there are two broad areas in which the cause might lie: the nature of the economy, and the nature of the union-management relationship. The basic nature of the U. S. economy, especially since 1954, has been one of relative stability. In the 15 years 1954-69 the unemployment rate ranged between 3. 8 percent and 6. 8 percent with no particular trend; the greatest change within any two years has been 2. 5 percent, and in less than half of the year pairs is there a change which exceeds 1 percent. In Japan the maximum difference is essentially the same, 3. 2 percent (from a low of 2. 4 percent to a high of 5. 6 percent). The greatest difference between two adjacent years was somewhat smaller, 1. 7 percent, and in only two out of 15 of the years did it exceed 1 percent. In terms of productivity changes, the U. S. maximum year-to-year change was 5. 2 percent, but the more normal change has been around 1 to 3 percent, with 11 out of 17 year pairs falling in that range. In Japan the maximum is three times greater, 16. 5 percent, and about a quarter of the pairs exceed 10 percent. Turning to the consumer price index, in the United States after the immediate postwar years, the movements in the consumer price index have been both modest and relatively uniform, except for two periods. The first was the period of the Korean War, when the 1951 rate of increase--6. 7 percent--was eight times greater than the preceding year and 3. 5 times greater than the following year. The second major one was associated with Vietnam, though there was some inflation around 1957.

In Japan the movement of the price index has been much greater, both between years and over time. Thus, whereas the U. S. cost of living went from 92. 5 in 1952 to 127. 7 in 1969, the Japanese index went from 82. 6 to 164. 9. Even in 1965-69 Japanese prices rose almost 1. 5 times faster than those in the United States. Yet it must be noted that 1955, the initial period of shuntō, was a year of falling consumer prices and was followed by four years of relatively constant consumer prices.

Based upon the above, it is possible to argue that because there were not marked changes in these key series, cost of living and productivity, U. S. unions could make longer-term contracts with the relative assurance that through the use of deferred wage and fringe benefit increases they would adequately protect the interests of the workers. At the same time, management would be willing to agree to deferred increases, since they would be confident that the next few years would involve few major changes. The same cannot be said for the unions in Japan, where both the pace of productivity and the year-to-year differences in changes in prices and the forced draft economic growth policies of the government would make it much more difficult for both management and unions to make those decisions which would be most appropriate and would best represent their respective interests.

The material presented above is strong supporting evidence for the continuance of the divergent trends in the two countries, but it may not adequately explain the original decisions, especially in the United States, where the United Auto Workers and General Motors began to move away from the one-year contract as early as 1948, when they entered into a two-year agreement. Thus it is necessary to look into the nature of the contract and the bargaining procedure.

The U. S. union contract covers a multitude of employment terms in addition to the more basic items of wages and fringe benefits. Even for the latter there is a much more detailed and explicit agreement between the parties as to the structure of these wages and benefits than would be true of the Japanese negotiations, which are almost purely a question of average wage increases. Even the question of the internal distribution of wage increases in Japan is left largely to management. Consequently, the time and effort of both parties in preparing for annual negotiations and in carrying them out is often excessive for parties in the United States. This excessiveness seems not to be true for the Japanese, who even negotiate separately over the summer and end-of-year bonuses.

There are also rather basic differences in the nature of the basic union units and their relationships with management and their own members. In the United States the basic units, the local and the national union, have been largely self-sufficient and only tangentially concerned with matters which have not directly affected them. As a result, with few exceptions, there has been little incentive for inter-union cooperation, and those formal institutions devoted to cooperation--the AFL-CIO and such--have remained relatively powerless. In Japan, however, because of certain weaknesses of enterprise unionism in a context of familism or paternalism, the principal federations, Sōhyō and Dōmei, have played a much more important role in encouraging inter-union cooperation. The dominant position of these labor groups has been enhanced by their active role in political activities, and consequently they have been the natural point around which to rally for unified bargaining, timetables, and contract periods.

The character of the business may also be important. The typical large Japanese firm has a greater degree of reliance upon sales and purchases in international trade, with all the balance of payments problems this may entail. As a result of this international position, certain historical factors, and pressure from government policies designed to insure rapid growth, there seems to be a greater degree of cooperation among the large Japanese firms than is true in the United States. Additionally, industry-wide bargaining, let alone inter-industry bargaining, has in most industries been bitterly opposed by U. S. management.

It is also worthy of note that the union which pioneered the move toward an annual and unified bargaining round, Sōhyō, is heavily influenced by constituent unions made up of government employees. The annual government budget-setting mechanism, the unions' inability to strike, and their consequent reliance upon conciliation boards for their final wage increases have meant that these government unions could only very imperfectly survive without an annual wage demand.

Last and perhaps most important is the character of the local union. It is doubtful that the local could survive very well under a multi-year agreement. Thus, despite repeated calls by Nikkeiren for a longer contract period, it seems unlikely that they will be received with any favor by the unions, at least in the near future.

Thus, we conclude that the difference in the nature of wage rounds is primarily a result of the very different nature of the Japanese and American unions, the very different costs of negotiation for the parties, given the relative degrees of stability and instability in the two economies, and the much more comprehensive and complex nature of contracts resulting from collective bargaining in the United States.

Despite the quite different institutional approach to

aggregate wage setting, the factor which determines the extent of the real wage gains in both cases is profits. In Japan it appears that the overall industrial profit rate is equally as important as an industry's own profits in determining the size of the wage advance. In the United States the important element for the nonkey group industries is the wage advance in the key sector, which in turn depends upon profits both directly and in the factors which underlie the division of industries between the key and nonkey groups. That profits are equally important in both economies should come as no surprise, considering the similarities of technology and private enterprise character, but it does serve to underline how very different institutional arrangements may yield economic results which are remarkably similar.

In summary, aggregate wage determination in Japan has since 1955 gradually evolved into a classic, annual pattern-bargaining situation where there appears to be increasing emulation of the "top batter's" results and where industry and national profits provide the most important explanation for the level of wage advance in any given year. In the United States, the institutional form of pattern bargaining, which was evident right after World War II, has disintegrated; evidence of overt pattern following is sparse, but there are strong indications that profits and subsequent wage gains among leading industries do influence aggregate wages.

THE PHILLIPS CURVE

Writing in the centennial issue of Economica (1958), A. W. Phillips, then at the London School of Economics, advanced the hypothesis that the rate of change of money wages in the United Kingdom could be explained by the level and rate of change of unemployment, but that it required some modification in those years when there had been a rapid rise in import prices. This hypothesis, modified, expanded, and elaborated upon under the general name of the Phillips curve, has formed a major thrust of recent aggregate wage research, especially in the United States. Conceptually the formulation can be related to wage determination at the level of the individual firm, as in a simple excess-supply-of-labor model, with the measured unemployment rate serving as a measure of the excess supply of labor. Thus, in a sense it is a modern version of both a classic labor market and a Marxian one with the reserve army of the unemployed determining wage levels. Alternatively, it is possible to place the emphasis upon unemployment and additional variables, such as profit rates, as determiners of collective bargaining results, in which case the Phillips curve and pattern bargaining become very similar. Recently an additional elaboration has been suggested in which the emphasis has been placed upon expectations. In part these alternative formulations have resulted from the difficulties in obtaining satisfactory curves for the United States.

Phillips Curves in the United States

The U. S. economics literature is filled with Phillips curves of a bewildering variety of specification in terms of years, sources of data, forms of the equation, and the nature of the result. One of the more common approaches has been to use quarterly changes in average hourly earnings. Their use in opposition to median increases in new contracts has the advantage of taking account of the fact that there is no specific time of the year when most, or the more important, contracts are negotiated. It also allows for the factors of built-in wage increases and wage drift, and provides a large number of observations which may increase the accuracy of the statistical results. The chief disadvantage of the use of quarterly data is that it does not provide a very useful tie to the institutional mechanisms of actual wage determination.

In general the Phillips curve studies have dealt with the manufacturing sector and have used the general unemployment rate, profits, and the consumer price level to predict changes in average hourly earnings for the postwar period. Application to other types of wages and to disaggregated data has generally not been successful, because of data problems and serial correlation. Given the variety of models tested, variables and data used, and time periods covered, it is not possible to discuss the Phillips curve for the United States. Nevertheless, it is possible to illustrate the main thrust of this work by reference to one of the more widely known studies, that of George L. Perry.[19]

One of the principal formulations which Perry used contained data from the fourth quarter of 1947 to the third quarter of 1960 and used four variables. The variables were the cost of living lagged by one year, 1 minus the unemployment rate, a one-year lagged profit rate expressed as a percentage of stockholders' equity, and the change in the profit rate. The explanation of the variance, as measured by the squared partial correlation coefficients, was .508 for prices, .501 for unemployment, .456 for profits, and .316 for the change in profits. The importance of the variables is not constant; rather, the period seems to be divided into two separate parts: the first from the fourth quarter of 1947 to the second quarter of 1953, and the second from that quarter until 1960. The biggest change in the importance of the variables was in the value of consumer prices, which before 1953 had very little influence but which, after the second quarter of 1953, greatly increased their influence. There is almost as marked a change in the influence of the profit rate, though in this case its influence was reduced. In addition, the typical Phillips curve is quite nonlinear, especially for extreme values of unemployment, and compared with those estimated for England, the U.S. Phillips curve lies to the right and has a less well-defined statistical fit.[20] This last point and the changing importance of the variables reported by Perry are illustrative of the extreme instability of the U.S. Phillips curve over any but the shortest time periods.[21] The causes of this instability of results have been ascribed to a variety of factors: cost-push inflation, changes in labor market institutions, government policy (for example, wage-price guidelines), or the failure properly to account for industrial concentration, sectoral shifts in demand, the reestablishment of union-nonunion industrial wage differentials, etc.[22] Despite the fact that plausible explanations for the instability have been suggested, the exact identification and verification of these variables over any extended period remain to be accomplished.[23]

The net result of the above is the conclusion that there exists for some short-run periods a reasonably systematic nonlinear relation between the state of the economy as measured by unemployment rates and profits (productivity) and the rate of increase of real wages. The relationship is perhaps useful for econometric models, but largely fails to provide any greater understanding of the process of labor market operation and the process of wage determination than provided by the pattern bargaining analysis.

Phillips Curves in Japan

Formal Phillips curve analysis has not generated as much enthusiasm in Japan as it did in the United States.[24] There are a number of possible reasons for this. One of the most important is that in the United States, this type of analysis was seen as contributing to an understanding of, and perhaps solutions to, the seeming problem of inflation under conditions of less than full employment. And it was in this connection that it was initially introduced into elementary economics textbooks, rather than as an aid to the understanding of labor markets and wage decision mechanisms. In Japan, until 1960 there was a clear excess supply of labor and, with productivity increases dramatically outracing wage gains, the potential usefulness of this type of analysis was much less. Too, with Japan's different institutional arrangements, the expected impact of general unemployment upon the wage decisions of the modern sector of industry was negligible if not nonexistent.

The Phillips curve for Japan, estimated by Watanabe Tsunehiko, may be directly compared with the American situation.[25] More than most American authors, Watanabe was interested in the relationship between wage gains and subsequent inflation. As might have been expected, the unemployment rate was not systematically related to the movement of wages, though the index of unemployment calculated from unemployment compensation payment data did turn out to be significant. On the basis of the sign of his price variable, he concluded that there was not a simultaneous determination of wages and prices. Rather, it appeared that for the period 1955-62, the relationship between the cost of living index and money earnings was one of a successive determining system, with the pressure originating on the wage side. In other words, an excessive rise in money earnings in one year would lead to an increase in the cost of living, and this in turn would give rise to higher demands for money wages in the following year.

The potential of such a system for an ever-increasing wage and an ever-increasing rate of price inflation has not been realized. As can be seen in Table 15, the rate of increase in money wages was approximately 10 percent per year in every year from 1960-61 to 1965-66, and has been even higher since then. There has been more variation in the growth in consumer prices and productivity, so that the rate of real wage increase has had a more cyclical pattern. It is possible that this result, which is seemingly inconsistent with the implications of Watanabe's findings, may result from deflationary pressures associated with foreign exchange problems or, more likely, from the special properties of the period Watanabe studied. His period marked the end of a few years of relative price stability, the Jimmu boom, a strong growth in the heavy industry sector of manufacturing, and the shift of the economy from one of relative abundance of labor to one with some shortages. The usefulness of the Phillips curve approach for more recent years may be seen in an estimation of an equation using annual data for the years 1959-67.[26] Annual wage changes in manufacturing industries were related to changes in employment by industry (X_1), manufacturing profits (X_2) and profits by industry for two-digit manufacturing industries (X_3). Changes in employment by two-digit manufacturing industries were used in lieu of unemployment, since the unemployment rate moved within such a narrow range and the rate of unemployment compensation payments is conceptually weak. The resulting equation was

$$W = 3.24\,a_0 + 0.702\,X_1 + 0.0685\,X_2 + 2.19\,X_3$$

$$(1.40) \quad (0.208) \quad (0.0371) \quad (0.56)$$

with a correlation coefficient, corrected for degrees of freedom, of .625. The relative importance of the variables, as measured by squared partial correlation coefficients in their respective positions, was .33 for changes in employment by two-digit industry, .17 for average industrial profits, and .35 for profits of individual two-digit manufacturing industries. The importance of overall profits and individual industry profits is consistent with the earlier pattern bargaining results. Consequently, while certain aspects of the Japanese situation are consistent with a Phillips-type analysis, it does not appear to have added very much to an understanding of Japanese wage determination.

Comparative Phillips Curves

There is only a modest amount to compare between the United States and Japan, although we are fortunate that a recent article reports on exactly the same relationships for the United States that Watanabe used for Japan. From this, Charles Holt and Kyu Sik Lee concluded that, contrary to the finding for Japan, the concept of a successive determination of prices and money wages was not evident in the United States.[27] Another major difference was that the impact of the unemployment rate upon wages was five times more important in Japan than it was in the United States. In view of the much more limited mobility of regular Japanese workers among firms which can be considered wage setters, such a finding makes no sense. Holt and Lee suggest that it may have resulted from the use of linear equations on a highly nonlinear relationship. It is also possible that the growing coverage of the unemployment compensation system gave it a trend (see Table 19) which reflected more the changing nature of unemployment compensation than it did conditions in the labor market.

A comparison of the Perry and Sano results indicates that the relative importance of the profit and employment variables were approximately equal to each other in both economies, though the time periods were different, being the years before 1960 for America and largely after 1960 for Japan. The state of excess demand in the labor market was quite similar in these respective time periods. Thus, despite the decline in the importance of profits in the United States during the early 1960's, these results are highly suggestive of a similarly functioning wage determination under similar conditions of demand for labor in Japan and the United States.

LABOR SUPPLY

The pattern bargaining and Phillips curve types of analysis were introduced into wage analysis in part to account for the importance of demand-related factors (profits and productivity) without using marginal productivity analysis and in part as replacements for a historical emphasis upon labor supply as a principal factor in wage determination. Recently there has been a renewed interest in labor supply as a principal factor in aggregate wage determination. In part this reflects a development in the Phillips curve literature including the importance of employment growth, such as that reported above or the study of Simler and Tella.[28] This last study found that the use of a potential labor force concept, the inclusion of secondary workers attracted into the economy with expanding job opportunities, improved the results of Phillips curve analysis, especially in the 1960's. Here we are more interested in a hypothesis which places its emphasis upon labor supply, Charles L. Kindleberger's adaptation of W. Arthur Lewis' growth model to situations involving mature industrial economies.[29]

The Kindleberger proposal is quite straightforward. It says that if a country's growth is begun in periods when there is a relative abundance of labor, then growth will be rapid but real wage increases will be very modest. When, for whatever reason, the high elasticity of labor no longer applies and labor bottlenecks appear, the rate of real wage increase will rise, the amount of extra product which goes to profits will decline, and "super" growth will become a thing of the past. This is not a marginalist proposition; a country either has relative labor abundance or it doesn't, and the hypothesis has little to say about transition periods as one moves between excess and shortage.

The Kindleberger hypothesis implies that if either Japan or the United States experienced a period of relative labor surplus, then in that period there should have been a high rate of economic growth, modest increases in real wages, and no real improvement in the proportion of national product going to labor. In the case of Japan, there were relatively abundant supplies of labor before 1960. (See Table 18.) Between 1953 and 1960 the labor force grew by some 5.7 million persons, or a little above 1.85 percent per year. Labor force participation rates of both males and females stayed roughly constant, and average monthly hours grew from 194.4 to 202.7. During these years the unemployment rate from the labor force survey remained essentially constant, as did the rate of separation from manufacturing employment. Taken together, these data suggest that the labor market did not become tighter during this period. This is contradicted slightly by the unemployment rate for those covered under the unemployment compensation law, for their unemployment rate underwent a rather sharp decline, from 5.6 in 1954 and 1955 to 2.9 in 1960. Since, however, a large number of those receiving unemployment compensation are seasonal workers or women out of a job for family reasons, it may not be the most sensitive indicator of the true state of the labor market.

Then in 1960-61 the labor market in Japan began to become much tighter. This can be seen in a variety of data and the pronouncements of Japanese employers. The overall growth of the labor force from 1960 to 1969 was less than 6 million, a rate of 1.36 percent per year, almost one-third less than the rate for 1952-60. At the same time, hours worked declined and labor force participation for both males and females declined, resulting in about a 4.5 percent drop in gross labor force participation. The impact of this reduced elasticity in the labor force may be seen in the higher rate of separation in manufacturing, averaging 20 percent more in the years after 1960 than in the years before. The labor force survey unemployment rate was halved, but the unemployment compensation index of unemployment remained more or less unchanged until 1967, when it began to decline.

Real hourly wages (see Table 15) reacted according to expectations, rising more than 2 percent a year faster in 1961-69 than they had between 1952 and 1961. Employee compensation as a percentage of national income also experienced the bulk of its gain after 1960, going from 50.2 percent to 56.4 percent in 1966, but then down to 54.4 percent in 1968. In these years the growth in income going to private corporations leveled off and commenced a modest decline, from which it has since recovered.

The U.S. experience also is consistent with this theoretical view, though in terms of timing it was the exact opposite of Japan's; that is, growth after 1958-59 (until 1966) was accomplished under conditions of surplus labor. Between 1952 and 1958 adjusted real gross national product grew at only 2.8 percent per year. It is slightly larger, 3.6 percent per year, if the entire postwar period (1948-58) is considered. Yet after 1958 and until 1966, adjusted gross national product advanced at 4.1 percent per year. In other words, real growth was some 45 percent faster per year during the years after 1958 than it was during the years which preceded it. The importance of the surplus labor can perhaps be seen by the fact that between 1952 and 1959, the total labor force grew by 5.2 million persons, a rate of 0.9 percent per year. Between 1958 and 1969 the rate of total labor force growth was 1.7 percent per annum, a growth rate almost twice as large. That the increased rate produced a surplus until 1966 can be seen in the higher levels of unemployment and in the lower quit rate among workers in manufacturing. (See Table 19.)

Movements in employee compensation as a percentage of national income and in real wage gains were also consistent with the surplus labor view. There was essentially no relative gain in employee compensation after 1958 until Vietnam, whereas there had been some slight growth in the previous decade. Real wages also grew more slowly during the years after 1958 than during the years before, about 1.9 percent per year, compared with 2.8 percent. This conclusion concerning the role of surplus labor is also consistent with the finding that the incorporation of the concept of a labor reserve into the Phillips curve analysis improved its capacity to predict wages in the post-1960 period, and with a recent study in which special demand and supply relations for skilled workers played a dominant role.[30]

The super growth under conditions of the surplus labor hypothesis is consistent with certain wage developments in the two countries. Whether it is superior to either of the other constructs, pattern bargaining and Phillips curves, is not clear and probably impossible to tell, since there exists considerable overlap among them. Suffice it to say that conditions of labor supply play an important role in wage determination in the Japanese and American labor economies.

RECONCILIATION

Each of these three explanations of aggregate wage determination--pattern bargaining, Phillips curve, and labor supply--appears to have some merit. Yet to paraphrase the pig in 1984, which is more equal than the others? The alternative claims might be stilled by an elaborate and sophisticated statistical analysis, but this is unlikely.[31] The years since 1948 have been witness to a bewildering array of aggregate wage determination models and studies, some of which have been reported here, but there is still no widely accepted view of the relative importance of the variables. The reason for this lack of a unified view may be seen most clearly in Japan. Under the vigorous growth policy proposed and encouraged by the government, wages, productivity, prices, skyscrapers, and super tankers have sprouted at rates which truly bedazzle the spectators. In such a context the interrelatedness of variables in the wage determination process is not capable of separation. In the United States, the pace has been slower but probably equally complex.

The solution, provided there is one, would seem to lie in some combination of institutional and market variables, as two recent studies would seem to indicate. In the United States, Sara Behman has reported upon an analysis which incorporates union organization and concentration data into an excess-demand-for-labor analysis.[32] In Japan, Shimada Haruo has studied shuntō settlements in a model which allows for the shift in labor market conditions from surplus to relative shortage around 1960-61.[33] The authors report significant results, and in both cases the institutional and market variables played their expected roles. In the United States one implication was that productivity gains were more apt to go to workers in unionized and concentrated industries, while in Japan the tightening of the labor market around 1960-61 apparently shifted the wage equation upward, so that for any given level of profits, higher wage gains were granted after 1960-61 than before. Encouraging as these results are, they are not unexpected on the basis of earlier studies. Thus, they must be considered as only desirable first steps toward the development of a comprehensive model of wage determination.

WAGE-PRICE GUIDELINES

One of the principal policy problems associated with aggregate wage determination in most, if not all, industrialized countries has been the danger of excessive wage gains which in turn, or in concert, give rise to other economic difficulties. A common proposed solution to potential excess wage increases has been an income or a wage-price policy set forth and administered by the government. There has been a range of specific policies which have achieved divergent success in a number of countries. A coherent theory of the process of aggregate wage change and propagation throughout the economy has seldom accompanied these income-restraining policies, yet they are generally consistent with results obtained by the three forms of analysis which have been discussed. They merely require that variables like profits, productivity, demand and supply conditions for key classes of labor, and union monopoly power produce large wage gains in a few industrial sectors. These gains are then transmitted to other sectors with lower profits, smaller gains in productivity, etc., via institutional conduits, of which unions are usually thought to be the most important. Because the wage gains which are transmitted are inappropriate for the receiving firms, there is a resulting rise in unit costs followed by rising consumer prices. Since there is so much uncertainty over the initiating variable and over the exact institutional process of transmission, the typical government response has been to try (1) to control the size of wage gains in key situations in a manner similar to that recently used in the United States or (2) to control the increases in all cases, which was U. S. policy during World War II.

Wage-Price Guidelines in Japan

In Japan there has been no recent experience with an income or wage-price guidelines policy. The government has talked in vague terms about such a policy, and Nikkeiren (Employers Federation) has come out in favor of income restraint. The unions, predictably enough, have been vehemently opposed, pointing to how much lower their wages are than are wages abroad. Late in 1970 the Council of Economic Affairs, a consultative group to the government, set up a subcommittee on prices, incomes, and productivity, but the increasing interest in the concept does not seem to indicate any action in the near future. It is interesting, however, to speculate on the success of such policies. Earlier we concluded that pattern bargaining exists in Japan, institutionally in the form of shuntō and its "top batter" and empirically in the observed wage relationships. As a first approximation, then, if the government were able to limit the demands of the Joint Wage Council, and by implication the wages granted in the leading sectors during shuntō, the subsequent observed wage increases in the private sector should be smaller. Since wage increases in the public sector are by law keyed to those in the private sector, limitations on shuntō gains would tend to control the incomes of the vast majority of employed Japanese. Given the political situation, however, such a possibility seems to be quite remote. The principal trade union federations are closely allied--intertwined is perhaps a better word--with the opposition political parties. Thus it is highly unlikely that the unions would be willing to cooperate with the government in order to make an income policy succeed. An additional factor here is the role of the Central Labor Relations Commission, which mediates in many of the principal negotiations. As Ishikawa Kichiemon[34] has pointed out, the government would not have direct authority over members of the Commission, and consequently wage increase limitations would require either express legislation or special taxes, permission for which would be difficult to obtain from the Diet. Thus, apart from their role in the dialogue and political fencing between unions and companies, price and wage controls would seem to have a limited future in Japan.

Wage-Price Guidelines in the United States

While earlier Presidents had talked of a public interest in negotiations between major companies and unions and specifically had urged noninflationary settlements, it fell to President Kennedy and his Council of Economic Advisors to articulate a specific wage price guideline. The President's Economic Report 1962 stated:

> . . . the general guide for non-inflationary price behavior calls for price reduction if the industry's rate of productivity increase exceeds the overall rate--for this would mean declining unit labor costs; it calls for an appropriate increase in price if the opposite relationship prevails; and it calls for stable prices if the two rates of productivity increase are equal. These are advanced as general guideposts.[35]

There was no formal enforcement of either the wage or the price provisions, but vigorous informal measures were used: private discussions between the President and the parties, the threat of government action, the use of the effect of public knowledge, etc. Gradually, under the economic pressures of the growing war in Vietnam and individual rivalry among unions, the wage-price guidelines were reaffirmed in the 1968 President's Economic Report, although attempts to implement them were quietly dropped. During their brief existence they were lauded by supporters, damned by critics, and formed an intense subject of conversation among businessmen, politicians, and academics. Despite the torrent of words, it is very difficult to answer the question of whether the controls worked.

The most positive affirmative answer comes from George L. Perry.[36] He used his Phillips curve for 1947-60 to estimate what wages would have been between 1960 and the first quarter of 1966, given observed unemployment and profits. His results showed that, beginning in the third quarter of 1962, the equation consistently predicted higher wage changes than those actually observed, a process that ended in the first quarter of 1968. From this Perry concluded that a leftward shift in the Phillips curve had taken place and that its timing was consistent with the hypothesis that the cause of the shift had been the introduction of wage-price guidelines. To test this hypothesis further, he selected by an undefined method ("advice of experts") a group of "visible" manufacturing industries which he felt should have been more affected by the policy of wage restraint than the other, "invisible," industries. The industries selected as visible are largely the same ones which were identified by Eckstein and Wilson as key industries. Perry then compared the ratios of changes in wages for the two groups in the years 1954 to 1957 and 1963 to 1966. The results obtained were that in the visible industries the wage changes had slowed down relative to the invisible group. From this he concluded that the impact of the wage-price guidelines upon these industries caused their divergent behavior. One thing is quite clear: blue-collar wage gains in the period 1960 to 1965 or 1966 were not what would have been anticipated by most observers in 1960, but whether it was guidelines or some other change in the economy which produced the change is still not clear. Certain conclusions from earlier sections of this chapter are relevant.

The most fundamental problem is the instability of the estimated Phillips curves, since this means that what Perry observed may have been due to the guidelines or to other factors. Additionally, in the discussion of key bargaining it was concluded that the profit-induced wage gains in the key industries had a marked impact upon wages in the follower industries. While total manufacturing profits after taxes as a percentage of equity were little different in the two periods 1954-57 and 1963-66, being 11.43 percent and 12.08 percent, their distribution was quite different. In the first period (1954-57), the average profit of the key group was 12.3 percent, compared with 9.3 percent in the follower group. In 1963-66, the figures were 12.3 percent and 11.3 percent. Thus, an advocate of pattern bargaining might cite this change as the cause of the different wage patterns between the two groups. In fact, there is a highly significant (.71) rank-order correlation among two-digit manufacturing industries between their ratio of wage gains 1954-57/1963-66 and their ratio of average profits for the same periods. In other words, those industries with relative profit gains in 1963-66 over 1954-57 also tended to be the industries with a relative gain in the rate of wage advance. These results are consistent with the view that wage behavior in the early 1960's reflected the operation of real economic forces rather than public pronouncements,[37] except to the extent that the guidelines reduced manufacturing profits.

Changes in skill differentials, the catching up of union-nonunion wage differentials, and labor supply factors have also been suggested as explanations for the observed wage behavior.[38] Sara Behman suggested that a change in the demand condition for skilled craftsmen was important in explaining the slow-down in wage gains in the early 1960's and more recently has stressed the importance of the ratio of relative factor prices.[39] Simler and Tella proposed a revised Phillips curve which included a potential labor force concept.[40] A more extreme labor supply view can be obtained via the surplus labor hypothesis just discussed. This states that a period of relatively rapid economic growth, coupled with modest wage gains and no increase in labor's share of total product, is facilitated by an elastic labor supply. Since such a pattern of events began in the United States around 1958-60, it predates wage guidelines by several years.

Unfortunately, the true facts will probably never be known. What is clear is that wage gains in the key manufacturing industries during the early 1960's were not what was expected. Yet the key industries differ from the followers by more than wage behavior, for they are characterized largely by a greater degree of industrial concentration and union membership, by higher profit rates and capital labor ratios, and by being composed of larger and more technologically advanced companies. Consequently, it is extremely difficult to pinpoint the exact cause of divergent behavior.

SUMMARY

On the basis of a catalog of the facts of wage changes and their timing, it would not be unnatural to conclude that aggregate wage determination in Japan and the United States is quite different. U. S. pattern bargaining became less institutionalized with the passage of time, while Japan's became more formal. Japan's labor shortage came after 1960, while in the United States the shift around 1960 was from labor shortage to surplus. Wages and productivity have generally moved together in the United States, but in Japan productivity has outrun wages. Yet viewed in terms of the mechanism of wage setting and the importance of various factors, there tends to be a far greater degree of similarity between the two economies.

This can be seen more clearly if, as stressed earlier, the three approaches to aggregate wage determination which have been discussed are seen less as competitive and more as complementary views of the economy. The results which were reported suggest that wage changes depend upon the strength of the demand for labor associated with economic growth, the degree of elasticity in the supply of labor, and the role of imperfections, rigidities, or lags in the system. Pattern bargaining may then be seen as an approach which places its emphasis upon demand factors, profits or productivity, and a particular form of imperfection, wage spill-over.

The validity of this approach was observed in both countries. In Japan the profit record of the major industries has been an essential element in the rate of wage advance. The same was true in the United States. Wage decisions in the key U. S. industries then spread their influence throughout the economy. In Japan, follower firms and industries also looked to key wage decisions in making their own. With rapid growth continuing in Japan, it is not surprising that the correctness of the pattern bargaining view has appeared to increase while, with years (1958-66) of slack in the U. S. economy, the demise of this approach there is perhaps to be expected.

The rise to prominence of the Phillips curve, with its initial emphasis upon conditions of labor supply, as reflected in the unemployment rate, might be seen as a natural development. As it developed in the United States, it came to incorporate the demand influences of pattern bargaining through the inclusion of profits or productivity. The particular transmission mechanism and the reason that the curve lay so far to the right were largely left unexplained. This lack of explanation would be consistent with the failure of the easily identifiable "wage rounds" of the immediate postwar years to be maintained. An excess supply of labor (only partly measured by the unemployment rate) has had an impact upon both economies, though it would appear that the interests and concerns of the employed workers are more important in determining Japanese and U. S. managements' response. This means that profits and productivity play a larger role than does unhired labor in influencing the course of the two labor economies.

It seems probable, at least on the experience of the postwar years, that cyclical and secular changes will mean that elements of demand, supply, and imperfection will in certain circumstances play a more important role than they will at others. In such circumstances it is to be expected that not only will certain variables appear to be more meaningful in certain periods, but that forms of analysis will tend to place their emphasis upon different variables, depending upon the circumstances. The fact that the time sequence of events in Japan and the United States has been quite distinct has given the appearance of wide differences. In years when the economic circumstances have been the same, the responses of the economies have been remarkably similar, as have been the labor market mechanisms. On balance, then, we obtain the general conclusion that the mechanisms of aggregate wage determination in Japan and the United States are fundamentally similar.

NOTES

1. This emphasis upon manufacturing may be unfortunate, for in 1969 only 26.8 percent of Japanese employment and in 1969 only 26.4 percent of U. S. employment was in manufacturing.

2. The reader interested in a more technical review of some of the U. S. experience might consult Richard Perlman, Labor Theory (New York: John Wiley and Sons, Inc., 1969), pp. 143-66, 199-232.

3. A brief summary of the principal economic policies of the occupation will be found in Kozo Yamamura, Economic Policy in Postwar Japan (Berkeley: University of California Press, 1967), Chs. 1, 2.

4. Data are taken from G. C. Allen, Japan's Economic Expansion (London: Oxford University Press, 1965), pp. 266, 280.

5. Kazushi Ohkawa and Henry Rosovsky, "Postwar Japanese Growth in Historical Perspective: A Second Look," a chapter in Lawrence Klein and Kazushi Ohkawa, eds., Economic Growth: The Japanese Experience Since the Meiji Era (Homewood, Ill.: Richard D. Irwin, 1968), p. 7.

6. H. Gregg Lewis, "The Effects of Unions on Industrial Wage Differentials," in Universities National Bureau Committee for Economic Research, Aspects of Labor Economics (Princeton: Princeton University Press, 1962), p. 338.

7. Since April 25, 1949, the foreign exchange rate has been $1=360 yen, and it is often convenient to think of 1,000 yen as being equal to $3.

8. George Seltzer, "Pattern Bargaining and the United Steel Workers," Journal of Political Economy, LIX (August, 1951), 322-23.

9. Harold M. Levinson, "Pattern Bargaining: A Case Study of the Automobile Workers," The Quarterly Journal of Economics, LXXIV (May, 1960), 296-317; George Seltzer, "The United Steel Workers and Nationwide Bargaining," Monthly Labor Review, LXXXIV (February, 1961), 129-36.

10. Yōko Sano and Toshiaki Izeki, Labor and Product Markets as Wage Determiners: A Local Market Study, Keio University Institute of Management and Labor Studies (English) 18 (September, 1966).

11. John E. Maher, "The Wage Pattern in the United States 1946-1957," Industrial and Labor Relations Review, XV (October, 1961), 3-20; Otto Eckstein and Thomas A. Wilson, "The Determination of Money Wages in American Industry," Quarterly Journal of Economics, LXXVI (August, 1962), 379-414; Frank C. Ripley, "An Analysis of the Eckstein-Wilson Wage Determination Model," ibid., LXXX (February, 1966), 121-36.

12. Timothy W. McGuire and Leonard A. Rapping, "The Role of Market Variables and Key Bargains in the Manufacturing Wage Determination Process," Journal of Political Economy, LXXVI (September-October, 1968), 1015-36.

13. "A Decade of the Spring Offensive," Japan Labor Bulletin, IV (May, 1965), 4; and private calculations by the Japan Institution of Labor.

14. Sano Yōko, Koike Kazuo, Ishido Hideo, Izeki Toshiaki, and Shimeda Haruo, "Chingin Hakyū no Kōzō to Mekanizumu" [The structure of wage spill-over], Sangyō Kenkyū [Review of industry and labor] (December, 1968), p. 46.

15. Ibid., Chs. 3-7.

16. Senior managers in a recent Nikkeiren survey also reported that they were heavily influenced by the decisions of other firms in the area of wages advances. The Oriental Economist, XXXVII (October, 1969), 45.

17. Sano Yōko, Chingin Kettei no Ketryō Bunseki [The measurement and analysis of wage determination] (Tokyo: Tōyō Keizai Shinhō Kai, 1969), pp. 144-46.

18. Senior managers, perhaps not unexpectedly, report that the wage increases granted during the shuntō periods are excessive in terms of the state of the economy. This is based upon replies to Nikkeiren questionnaires.

19. George L. Perry, Unemployment, Money Wage Rates, and Inflation (Cambridge, Mass.: M.I.T. Press, 1966), p. 50.

20. Perlman, *op. cit.*, pp. 212, 218-19.

21. A recent book review contained the following evaluation: "Our final caution . . . authors of Phillips Curves would do well to label them conspicuously, *'Unstable. Apply with extreme care'*." Albert Rees and Mary T. Hamilton, "The Wage-Price Productivity Perplex," *Journal of Political Economy*, LXXV (February, 1967), 70.

22. On this point see Adrian W. Throop, "The Union-Non-union Wage Differential and Cost-Push Inflation," *American Economic Review*, LVIII (March, 1968), 79-99.

23. For a number of citations to what has been done, see Edmund S. Phelps, "Money-Wage Dynamics and Labor-Market Equilibrium," *Journal of Political Economy*, LXXVI (July-August, 1968), 709-11.

24. Some of these are discussed in Sano Yokō, "Waga Kuni Chingin Kittei Kōzō no Keiryō Bunseki (=)" [A quantitative analysis of wage determination in Japan (2)], *Mita Gakkai Zasshi* [Mita journal of economics] (May, 1968), pp. 51-80.

25. Tsunehiko Watanabe, "Price Changes and the Rate of Change of Money Wage Earnings in Japan 1955-1962," *Quarterly Journal of Economics*, LXXX (February, 1966), 31-47.

26. Sano, "Waga Kuni Chingin . . . ," pp. 67-73.

27. Charles C. Holt and Kyu Sik Lee, "Price Changes and the Rate of Change of Money Wage Earnings in the Light of American Data," *Quarterly Journal of Economics*, LXXXI (May, 1967), 347-50.

28. N. J. Simler and Alfred Tella, "Labor Reserves and the Phillips Curve," *Review of Economics and Statistics*, L (February, 1968), 32-49.

29. Charles P. Kindleberger, *Europe's Postwar Growth* (Cambridge, Mass.: Harvard University Press, 1967), Ch. 1.

30. Sara Behman, "Wage Determination Process in United States Manufacturing," *Quarterly Journal of Economics*, LXXXII (February, 1968), 117-42.

31. Data limitations will be one problem.

32. Sara Behman, "Wage Changes and Relative Factor Prices in Manufacturing," Review of Economics and Statistics, LI (August, 1969), 227-38.

33. Shimada Haruo, "Waga Kuni Chingin Kattei Kikō no Keiryō Bunseki (-)" [A quantitative analysis of wage determination in Japan (1)], Mita Gakkai Zasshi [Mita journal of economics], LXI (May, 1968), 34-64; and "A Quantitative Analysis of Negotiated Wage Settlements in Japan," Keio Economic Studies, VI, 1 (1969), 55-81.

34. Kichiemon Ishikawa, "The Rule of Government in Labor Relations in Japan," Labor Relations in the Asian Countries, Japan Institute of Labor, Proceedings of the Second International Conference on Industrial Relations (Tokyo, 1967), pp. 137-44.

35. Economic Report of the President, 1962, (Washington, D.C., 1962), p. 189.

36. George L. Perry, "Wages and Guideposts," American Economic Review, LVII (September, 1967), 75-82.

37. A similar view has been expressed by John T. Dunlop in his "Guideposts, Wages and Collective Bargaining," in George P. Shultz and Robert Z. Aliber, eds., Guidelines, Informal Controls, and the Market Place (Chicago: University of Chicago Press, 1966), p. 84.

38. Paul S. Anderson, Michael L. Wachter, Adrian W. Throop, and George L. Perry, "Wages and the Guideposts: Comments and Reply," American Economic Review, LIX (June, 1969), 351-70.

39. Behman, "Wage Determination . . .," pp. 117-42; and "Wage Changes . . .," p. 235.

40. Simler and Tella, op. cit., pp. 32-47.

CHAPTER 4

WAGE DIFFERENTIALS

The multitude of forces whose interplay determines the wages which are actually received by any specific employee or group are almost too numerous to name. There are influences related to types of occupation, the character of the industry, and geographical location, even including the exact location of the employer within a city. There are the special attributes of the employing firm, such as size, and the personal characteristics of the individual, such as age, level of education, and prior work experience. Unfortunately, too, other aspects, such as color of skin, religion, national origin, etc., are used as the basis upon which employers discriminate in determining wages. This chapter examines only a few of these forces, hopefully the most important ones, and certainly those which have been most widely discussed in Japan and the United States. It will be only partially possible to follow the most desirable practice and focus upon the same type of differentials in both countries because, as described in Chapter 2, the institutional functioning of the labor markets has been quite distinct and, as a natural consequence of these institutional differences, the governmental data collection systems have concentrated upon alternative dimensions of the employment relationship. In addition, the interests and concerns in 20th century Japan and the United States have placed different emphases on growth and equity. This has meant that scholars and governments have asked different questions and collected dissimilar data for the two economies.

The employment practice in the larger and more modern sectors of Japanese industry, business, and government has been to hire regular employees upon graduation from school, and to provide continuous employment until retirement at 55-57 years of age. Over these years of employment individual wages move upward along a maturity curve whose initial position and slope depend largely upon the individual's educational level. With rising levels of general wages, these maturity curves are periodically shifted upward and in some instances have their slopes modified. As a consequence of this employment and wage pattern, differences in age or length of service and level of educational attainment have been the principal wage differentials which have been noted, watched, and analyzed in the postwar period. A second widely discussed differential relates to variations by size of firm, which seems to be related to the degree of modernization in the industries. Historically, in the 1920's and 1930's, much less complete data on internal wage structures and differences in size of firm were collected. The primary emphasis then was on average wages by industry. As a consequence, this chapter is concerned principally with internal wage differentials in the postwar years and with industrial wage differentials over a longer period.

The folklore of the U. S. economy is that, as in an earlier and more craft-centered day, people are hired to fill a particular occupational position. Consequently, it is believed that occupational wage differentials are the most important ones. The postwar growth in the importance and prevalence of internal promotion, on-the-job training, etc., has not dimmed this concern with and interest in occupational differences, which will be given a primary emphasis here. Some additional data will allow a modest discussion of size of firm and wage differences to provide some comparison with the Japanese situation.

The discussion of the patterns of wage differentials and the factors associated with their change rests upon certain theoretical constructs, and it will be useful to begin with a very brief discussion of these before proceeding to an analysis of the data.

THEORIES OF WAGE DIFFERENTIALS

The basic concepts in the analysis of wage differences are largely taken directly from the writings of Adam Smith. In The Wealth of Nations, Smith pointed out that the wages of skilled craftsmen should exceed those of the unskilled in order to compensate for the time and expense spent in learning the craft.[1] Such a pure skill differential, in conjunction with others, such as those associated with danger or unpleasant working conditions, probability of success, constancy of employment, etc., has been gathered into a class of differentials termed "compensating." This means that, relative to a "standard job," each job will be characterized by factors which are variously viewed by the average workman as being either more or less desirable. Under such a situation the observed wage differentials among jobs will depend upon the characteristics of the available employment and the tastes and skills of the workers who are available. If there are a large number of men who enjoy working underwater (divers), but only a few jobs, there will be no differential, or a negative one for underwater work. Conversely, if there are a number of diving jobs to fill and few potential employees, then the differential for diving would have to be large in order to induce other workers to overcome their distaste and work underwater. Since labor in Smith's era tended to be viewed, and not to unreasonably, as largely homogeneous in taste and ability, it was expected that the wages of labor would tend toward equality for the great majority of jobs.

But wages did not tend toward equality; rather, they continued to demonstrate that great diversity which characterizes them today. To explain this, James Mill formulated the concept of the noncompeting group, which emphasized that a variety of barriers and restrictions to worker mobility exist and that in the short run these restrictions may give rise to large wage differentials which would not exist in a frictionless economy. Such a concept was useful in explaining the seeming paradox of brutish labor. It was noted that, relative to the number of brutish jobs, the supply of persons who could compete for brutish labor but could not compete for other, more desirable types of employment was large relative to the number of openings available. Thus, competition for the brutish jobs drove down wages for this type of work. The concept of noncompeting groups is similar to that of an economic rent, which is often used to explain the high wages received by truly unique individuals like Babe Ruth or Taiho (a Sumō). Economic rent is also a useful construct with which to handle less unusual individuals. For example, the wages of the skilled workman can be divided into a pure return to skill (a compensating differential) and rental elements associated with the fact that more parents did not provide their sons with such training, or that only a given number of new members were accepted into the union.

An additional factor used to try to explain why diversity persisted was Marshall's contribution of the concept of efficiency wages, which was a straightforward adaptation of the newly developed concepts of marginal productivity. Since the contribution of a worker to the value of the final product might vary in different employments, it was only wages adjusted for these differential contributions which should be expected to tend toward equality. One other important concept which served to explain certain areas where efficiency wages did not appear to tend toward equality was also discussed by Marshall. This was the fact that over a period of several generations the pure skill differential did not approach the discounted cost of obtaining training.

The explanation was that wage levels would reflect both short-term and long-term barriers to the mobility of labor. If unskilled parents did not recognize the value of training for their children, then the supply of skilled workers in the next generation would be too small to reduce the pure skill differential to equality with the discounted cost of the training required to become a skilled workman.

Since Marshall's time there has been little change in the basic concepts used in the analysis of wage differentials, and many studies have been devoted to a discussion of particular types of differentials and their size over time. There has been some greater elaboration of the factors associated with continuing high returns to skill, including high rates of time discount upon the part of the worker or his parents, and a shortage of the capital needed to pay for the initial cost of the training. This has been part of a much broader consideration of the role of investment in education, which has been a major emphasis of postwar labor economics.

There has also been an increased emphasis upon imperfections in the labor market, especially in terms of information available to both demander and seller of labor and the role of barriers of racial discrimination. The principal modern emphasis has, however, been less on the explanation of static wage differentials and much more on an analysis of the change or lack of change in the size of particular differentials over time.

A Theory of Occupational Wage Differentials

What changes in occupational wages in the United States should be expected over the 20th century? A standard analysis would suggest that there has been a great increase in the supply of skilled individuals, due to increases in education; an increase in the number of semi-skilled jobs; and a great deal of replacement of human skill and judgment by machine skill and judgment. The former additions to the supply of unskilled workers in the form of immigrants have declined, though the movement of labor off the farm into other sectors of the economy has continued. On balance, there would appear to have been a net increase in the supply of skilled workers relative to the demand for such skills. Consequently the long-term trend in the skilled/unskilled ratio would be expected to have declined. Other changes over these years in the degree of unionization, geographical patterns, or sex and color discrimination could have reversed these trends, but it is commonly accepted that they did not do so. Progress in closing the gap in wage levels between skills has not been steady, and difficulties associated with the business cycle have intruded upon the smooth adjustment of these forces of relative supply and demand.

The intrusion of the business cycle raises the question of how cycles and the allied forces of war and depression would affect the long-term adjustment in differentials. To the extent that a particular cycle was concentrated among firms employing a particular type of labor, the ratio might go either up or down, depending upon which sector was affected and whether expansion or contraction was involved. The defense industry during World War II produced standard items on a large scale, but during the "Cold War" production has been on a smaller scale, with a steady stream of new and more sophisticated weapons. Thus the ratio of engineers' salaries to production workers' wages could have been expected to contract during World War II and expand during the "Cold War." Under the more normal assumption of neutral distributional impacts, a ratio invariant with the business cycle might be expected. This would be consistent only with no substitution of labor between the two skill groups. With substitution, during a downturn the employer would try to substitute higher-quality labor for lower-graded skilled workers to do the unskilled work. This might be accomplished with no relative movement in hourly wage rate. In such a case, unemployment would be concentrated among the unskilled, and wage ratios for the skilled and unskilled, measured in annual incomes, would widen.

Once the world of perfect competition and knowledge is left behind, there are other factors which must be considered. Skilled employees, especially those with some experience within the firm, may be a scarce resource difficult to replace during the next expansion of the business cycle. Thus the firm may retain these skilled employees at their old wage categories even though these may exceed their current marginal contribution to the firm's output. These extra costs will be offset against the savings in costs of hiring and training new employees during the next upturn. It is probable that in such a situation a widening of occupational rates will be observed, the firm retaining the skilled at their old rates while allowing the unskilled wage rate to fall to market levels.

The case of an upturn with a generalized strong demand for labor is more difficult to describe. Again abstracting from distributional effects, equal increases in demand might be expected to produce equal increases in wages along supply curves whose elasticities were the same. There are, however, a number of reasons for thinking that the elasticities will not be the same. The supply of skilled laborers can be augmented from that of the unskilled through training, redesign of jobs, etc. The supply of unskilled can be augmented only from those not in the labor force. In a developed economy the short-run elasticity of labor from outside the labor force will probably be less than the elasticity of supply from unskilled to skilled employment.

Under conditions of increased demand, the higher costs of labor will induce the employer to redesign jobs for more complete concentration of the truly skilled tasks among a smaller group of employees. Instead of employing more skilled workers or completely training unskilled workers, the employer could take the more capable unskilled, give them limited training, and place them in a position formerly occupied by a more thoroughly trained employee. If this policy is followed, then the average capability level of the skilled category has been lowered and the supply of those persons in jobs labeled "skilled" has increased. Since data are collected by job title more than by job content, the observed result will be a declining ratio of wages between skilled and unskilled.[2]

The combination of short-run and long-run factors discussed above leads to an expectation of a continuous downward trend in the U. S. wage ratio between skills, a downward trend that would have occasionally been slowed or accelerated by an excess supply of or demand for labor. A similar expectation would seem to apply to Japan, with one qualification. It is possible that since Japan is at an earlier stage in her economic development, the demand for skilled workers may have outpaced the ability of the economy to supply them, thus leading to a widening of the skill ratio. This may have occurred, for Koji Taira, who has made an exhaustive study of Japanese wage differentials, concluded that the secular trend of occupational wage differentials before 1940 was one of widening.[3]

Inflation and Equity

During periods of rapid inflation, many of which have been associated with wartime situations of an excess demand for labor, rapid narrowings of observed wage differentials have occurred. This happened during the U. S. Civil War in both North and South, during World War I in the United States, and during the great inflation in Germany in the 1920's. An "inflation" hypothesis for shifting wage differentials has been drawn from these experiences.[4] The hypothesis states that the wages of the lower-paid workers are raised proportionately more than those whose wages are higher, on the equitable grounds of maintaining standards of living. The concept of equity is also a basic principle in the job cluster and wage contour analysis initially sketched out by John Dunlop.[5]

The concept of the job cluster states that within any firm there are only a few jobs, known as key jobs, which, in terms of their skills and characteristics or their being direct entry jobs into which newly hired workers are placed, have close ties to jobs in other firms in the labor market. Within the plant or office, jobs which, in terms of content, promotion ladder, or physical proximity of work station, share characteristics with key jobs become tied to them. This means that the relative wage shifts of the tied jobs move more in tune with the wage of the key job than they do with general labor market conditions. A good example of a key job would be that of tool and die maker, a job which probably serves both as an entry job and is one which would be found in a number of different plants and industries. Market conditions for tool and die makers would be important in determining tool and die wages, but the jobs tied to tool and die that are filled largely by internal promotion and have no direct counterparts outside the firm would not be dependent upon market forces; rather, they would be dependent upon what happened in tool and die wages. In part this merely reflects the needs of the firms and unions to have a standardized wage structure.

The concept of a wage contour is largely an extension of job clusters to inter-industrial wages. It states that when an occupation is associated with low-wage workers in one industry but high-wage workers in another, then it is the wages of the associated jobs rather than the occupation's own intrinsic characteristics which are most important in determining what the wage level will be. A clear example, taken from Dunlop, is the truck driver who in association with low-paid laundry workers receives lower wages than does his counterpart who works with highly paid newspaper employees. In the context of this book the job cluster is an example of the equity concept within the firm, and the wage contour represents equity between firms and among industries.

These concepts of job clusters, wage contours, and the role of equity in wage determination are very similar to the key bargain concept in pattern-bargaining aggregate wage determination which was discussed in Chapter 3.

Occupation or Industry?

The recognition that wages vary widely across industries for seemingly similar types of work is suggestive that industrial wage differentials may be of greater importance than occupational ones in explaining the pattern of wages. In the United States, differences in the average wages of various industries commonly have been seen as the product of three types of subdifferentials: the average level of skill required, supply factors associated with geographical differences or percentage of females in the labor force, etc., and certain imperfections associated with product market competition or unionization. For example, the 1969 difference of $1.64 in the average wage of workers in the petroleum and apparel industries ($4.01-$2.37) reflected a higher average level of skill, a greater concentration in urban areas, a smaller number of female employees, and a more concentrated product market in petroleum than in apparel. The usual assumption has generally been that skill differences were the dominant long-run factor in determining the observed pattern of industrial wages, for in the short run any number of factors may prevent the observed wage pattern from being in equilibrium.

Viewed in a contrary manner, however, there are three factors which give rise to the very strong suspicion that it is industrial, and not occupational, forces which stamp the pattern of industrial wages. One is the fact that the Japanese economy also exhibits large and continuing industrial wage differentials within an institutional labor market and an internal wage structure which place little, if any, emphasis upon occupational categories. The second is that for occupational differences to be the heart of industrial wage difference would require that industries use occupations which are quite similar. Yet the available evidence is that there is very little occupational overlap. Third, if industrial differentials are composed of occupational differences and if the latter move in response to excess supply and demand for the various categories of labor, then industrial wage levels ought to move in sympathy with movements in employment. Yet it is becoming increasingly clear that this has not been true in recent years in the United States and other advanced industrial nations.[6] The same conclusion emerges from studies of many European labor markets.

The above may overstate the case, for the stress on occupations may exclude the relevant similarities of skill or ability. Yet in economics where mobility, especially at older ages, is modest and where most training is obtained on the job, the lack of extensive occupational overlap among industries weakens the labor market pressures upon the wage determination decisions in the various industries.

These three concepts, the shift in long run occupation requirements, the role of equity, and industrial differences, form the basis of our evaluation of the movement in wage differentials in the two countries during this century.

WAGE DIFFERENTIALS IN THE UNITED STATES

The principal concern in the United States has been the pace of occupational wage differentials. The broad sweep of these may be seen in Tables 21 and 22. Two things in the Table 21 series stand out: the secular decline of 81 percent over the 55-year period and the extent to which the declines are concentrated in two or possibly three periods before 1947 and then a continuous but slight downward slide after 1947. During the World War I years there was a precipitous decline of 36 points in the five years from 1916 to 1920. Close to half of that drop was recouped during the boom years in the 1920's, so that there was a net drop of 22 points in the pre-Great Depression era. The second major narrowing was in the years 1940 to 1947, when a drop of 27 points was registered. Between 1935 and 1938 there was a 11-point decline which might be considered as a third period. In summary, during 17 years, or one-third of the period, there was a gross decline of 74 percentage points in the skilled/unskilled wage difference. During the other two-thirds of the years there was essential stability in the ratio before 1948 and a steady but modest decline after that.

TABLE 21

Skilled/Unskilled Wage Differentials, United States
1914-69

Year	Skill Margin	Year	Skill Margin	Year	Skill Margin
1914	213	1933	194	1952	147
1915	212	1934	189	1953	144
1916	212	1935	191	1954	143
1917	202	1936	186	1955	142
1918	194	1937	183	1956	140
1919	192	1938	180	1957	139
1920	176	1939	180	1958	138
1921	178	1940	179	1959	136
1922	185	1941	177	1960	135
1923	192	1942	170	1961	134
1924	192	1943	169	1962	134
1925	192	1944	168	1963	134
1926	188	1945	164	1964	133
1927	191	1946	156	1965	132
1928	190	1947	152	1966	132
1929	190	1948	149	1967	132
1930	188	1949	150	1968	133
1931	190	1950	148	1969	132
1932	190	1951	147		

Note: The skill margin is the ratio of union wage scales of journeymen to that of laborers and helpers in the building trades.

Sources: Arthur Rose, "Wage Differentials in the Building Trades," Monthly Labor Review, XCII (October, 1969), 16; Handbook of Labor Statistics 1970, p. 185.

TABLE 22

Skilled/Unskilled Wage Differentials, Nonelectrical Machinery Industry, United States, 1945-68 (1958-59=100)

Year	Tool and Die Makers	Production Workers	Laborers and Materials Handlers
1945	48.4	45.0	40.7
1946	56.6	53.8	51.0
1947	61.0	59.0	55.1
1948	65.3	64.1	60.8
1949	66.5	65.1	62.5
1950	--	--	--
1951	70.0	70.0	67.4
1952	73.5	73.8	72.0
1953	77.9	78.7	77.1
1954	82.7	82.6	80.7
1955	85.1	85.2	83.7
1956	89.2	89.3	86.7
1957	--	--	--
1958	98.0	98.4	97.7
1959	102.0	101.6	102.3
1960	105.9	105.8	105.7
1961	109.7	109.0	109.9
1962	112.7	112.1	112.5
1963	115.4	115.1	115.8
1964	119.2	118.2	119.6
1965	122.4	121.1	122.0
1966	127.8	125.8	125.9
1968	149.5	142.9	142.6

Source: Handbook of Labor Statistics 1970, p. 190.

In the construction trades (see Table 22) the post-1948 period appears quite distinct from the early years because of the slow but steady downward drift in differentials. This series probably overstates the degree of decline, for in the machinery industry the ratio between tool and die makers and production workers has remained constant since 1951 and, for laborers, since 1953. There were declining skill ratios for these two occupations in 1945-51 and 1945-53 respectively.

Consequently, any wage difference hypothesis which is to be applicable to the 20th century must utilize an explanatory variable which is operational only in these selected periods before 1947, or it must contain some sort of threshold limitation which in practice makes it operational only in these times.

A basic and widely discussed hypothesis used to explain the long-term decline in skill ratios is that it represents a relative increase in the supply of skilled labor. The principal problem with this hypothesis is one of timing, since the declines in the skill ratios came only in specific year intervals and the increase in the supply was fairly continuous. One measure of increased skill, an increasingly educated labor force as measured by the ratio of secondary school students to elementary school students, grew rapidly in all decades from 1910 to 1940. The median for years of education of the younger members of the labor force has continued to grow both absolutely and relative to older workers since World War II. It is estimated that in 1975, for males 25 to 34 years of age, the median education will be 12.6 years, compared with 11.4 years for those 55 to 64. Measuring high school completion, the estimate for 1975 is that 69.6 percent of the younger men and 45.9 percent of the older ones will have completed high school. It is possible that there has been some complex shift in the demand for skilled labor which has made it fail to keep pace with the growth in supply during only the special periods, yet there is no evidence to suggest this. There is also the difficulty of suggesting why two war periods and that of partial recovery from the worst depression in American history should be ones which are characterized by a slow growth in the demand for skilled labor.

Melvin Reder, in his pioneering discussion of this paradox, suggests an explanation for the observed pattern.[7] His hypothesis is that in times of excess demand for labor, as during the two wars, when the preponderance of the decline in the skill margin took place, the employer conserved on labor costs either by partial training or by upgrading the best of the unskilled so that they were doing work which previously had been done only by skilled employees. During the remainder of the excess demand years, by observation, experience, and "just picking it up," the upgraded worker became a skilled worker. The result was that the supply of skilled workers underwent a permanent shift upward, and consequently there was little if any backsliding in the skill margin in more normal times.

It is a reasonable and realistic hypothesis. The wartime years were ones of very tight labor markets. The unemployment rate, at best an imperfect measure of labor market tightness, which was 14.3 percent in 1915, had fallen to 2.1 percent in 1918. The 14.6 percent unemployment rate of 1940 was down to 1.6 percent in 1943. Also, the hypothesized process of obtaining skills is consistent with much of the available evidence on skill acquisition. A recent study of tool and die makers in Massachusetts reported that about 15 percent of the men in this highly skilled occupation had "just picked it up," and even the men with some basic training from a vocational school or apprenticeship had obtained much of the actual training necessary to becoming a competent craftsman on the job.[8] There are, however, certain difficulties with this approach to an explanation. Between 1918 and 1920 the unemployment rate more than doubled (2.1 percent to 5.8 percent), yet the skill margin continued to fall, going from 194 to 176. Again, in the World War II period the unemployment rate rose from its 1943 low of 1.6 percent to 5.3 percent in 1946, yet the skill margin kept falling, this time from 169 to 156.

Another characteristic of these two wartime periods, with their rapid declines in skill margins, was inflation. Consumer prices, which had been 35.7 in 1914 (1957 = 100) had doubled to 71.3 in 1920. In World War II the rise was more modest, going from 49.8 in 1940 to 79.5 in 1947. It is possible that it was the concern for equity, prompted by inflation, which allowed the wages of the more poorly paid workers to rise faster than those of the more highly skilled and better-paid workers. One test of the relative merits of the inflation-equity hypothesis in comparison with the excess-demand-for-labor hypothesis would be to examine year-to-year changes in the skill margin to see if they are more highly correlated with year-to-year changes in the excess demand for labor or in price increases. This was done in an earlier article.[9] During both wars the rank-order correlations between changes in unemployment and changes in the skill margin are insignificant: .11 in World War I and -.40 in World War II. The correlations for inflation and skill ratio changes are much better--.85 and .78--both of which are significant at the 5 percent level. Additional evidence may be obtained from the Civil War experience of the North, where again inflation, and not excess demand for labor, appears to be the most important causal factor in explaining a skill margin which declined from 171 in 1861 to 147 in 1864.

Even if it is granted that the equity hypothesis is the correct one,[10] it is still necessary to explain why after World War I the skill margin should partly rebound, but not rebound after World War II. The same question also plagues the excess demand-learning hypothesis of Reder.

In the context of the equity hypothesis, there are two factors which probably account for the different postwar experiences. The first is the fact that there was a postwar depression and price decline in the early 1920's, an event which did not follow World War II. The second factor is unionization. In the nonunion atmosphere of the 1920's and with a reasonably loose labor market caused by renewed immigration, depression in the farm sector, and falling prices, it is not surprising that there was some movement in the skill margin back toward an earlier relationship. In the late 1940's unions were well organized. Their internal and politically motivated greater interest in the well-being of the less skilled and lower-wage groups, combined with a natural tendency not to open up the Pandora's box of reestablishing prewar wage relationships, suggests that no reversal in the skill margin was to be expected.

In the years since 1945 the collection of data on the labor economy has greatly increased, and some of these data, as they relate to occupational wages, may serve further to illuminate the forces which control wage differentials. Reference has already been made to the data for the machinery industry. (See Table 22.) Another source of extensive occupational wage data has been the Occupational Wage Survey conducted in a number of cities. Early in the postwar era the Department of Labor began collecting occupational wage data in various cities. While this data has been useful in the analysis of the wage patterns of particular cities over time and for comparisons of geographical differences or national trends, it has been less useful for the pure analysis of skill differentials. This results from the variable size of each year's sample of cities and the fact that each city is surveyed in a different month and not always the same month each year. Given the sampling problem and the general lack of a trend in occupational differentials, it is not surprising that these city data present a complex picture.

In the decade 1951-61 there was a tendency for skilled wages to advance more rapidly in 11 of the 16 larger cities, yet if the measurement is between 1952 or 1953 and 1964, the movement was toward narrowing, with 11 cities out of 17 exhibiting this type of movement. Inclusion of some smaller geographical areas in the latter comparison resulted in finding that 29 areas had narrowed differentials, 14 had widened, and seven were constant. It is not possible to explain away this paradoxical result. The most likely explanation lies in the different composition of the samples. If the results of the two studies are arranged in a common table, it can be seen that, for those cities which are included in both periods, seven of the 11 have consistent results. That is, they either widen or narrow in both periods. A second factor is that, with few exceptions, none of the cities exhibits major changes. In the first period no more than five of the cities had changes in excess of 5 percent, and in the second only three diverged by more than 5 percent. On balance it would appear that there has been a constancy of occupational wages in the years since 1950. This view is also reinforced by data for the production workers and tool and die workers in the machinery industry, measured on a city basis. In the cities used in the studies there was a widening in 10 and a narrowing in seven in that industry for the period 1958-66. A Bureau of Labor Statistics study which compared 1961-62 with 1953 also found that there had been a consistency in the occupational differentials.[11]

WAGE DIFFERENTIALS IN JAPAN

Unlike the United States, where the traditional questions about wage differentials have been set within a context of decline and stability in wage differentials, the basic problem in Japan has been to provide a satisfactory explanation of the emergence of substantial differentials in the 1920's. Related questions are the reestablishment of differentials following World War II and their seeming decline in the more recent years.

A supplementary problem is the seeming largeness of the Japanese differentials when they are compared with those in the United States. In 1963 Japanese manufacturing establishments with 1,000 or more employees paid average wages which were 166 percent of those paid by establishments with 10-19 employees. In the United States the similar 1963 ratio was 155 percent. Within Japanese manufacturing in 1968, wages in iron and steel were 240 percent of those in the lowest manufacturing industry, apparel. In the United States in 1969 the wages of the highest industry, petroleum, were only 174 percent of those in the lowest, apparel.[12]

The Emergence of Differentials

Various possible interpretations have been given to the emergence of substantial wage differentials, especially establishment-size ones. One long-term student of the Japanese economy, G. C. Allen, offered the following:

> One may conclude then that the disparities in wages for plants of different sizes are due, first, to the existence of two distinct labor markets in Japan, separated by institutional arrangements which preclude mobility between them, and secondly, to the more highly competitive conditions that prevail in the product-markets of the small firms as compared with those of the large firm.[13]

An elaboration of one possible institutional mechanism associated with the large establishment difference has been given by Kozo Yamamura:

> The large firms had begun to modernize rapidly during World War One. As a consequence, large firms enjoyed sharp increases in the productivity of labor and were able to "skim" the top of the labor market by offering slightly higher wages than those offered by smaller firms.[14]

Yet the above provides little in the way of a basis upon which to expect the development of substantial differentials. One such rationale is provided by Ohkawa Kazushi and Henry Rosovsky. They view the formation of wage differentials as only another aspect of the general phenomenon of economic dualism which they call differential structure. This economic dualism implies differing levels of productivity and capital intensity between the modern and traditional sectors, and rapid growth in the advanced sector and lagging growth in the traditional sector. In Japan this process of differential structure in wages began near the end of the Meiji era and became a powerful influence at the end of World War I. Ohkawa and Rosovsky thus conclude:

> Real wages in modern industry rose in spite of unlimited or highly flexible labor supplies. Modern enterprise increasingly needed a reliable, committed, and above all trained labor force and this suggests why the wage differentials increased despite the validity of the two-sector labor-surplus model.[15]

While the above is quite reasonable, it requires for validation a more detailed explanation of how the significant differentials came into being and the relative magnitudes of the different forces. Hugh Patrick has suggested that the differentials were produced by "a combination of World War One boom-induced disequilibria, subsequent deflationary expectations about price movements, and a downward stickiness of money wages."[16] A somewhat similar position has been taken by Odaka Konosuke, who has argued that the wages in the traditional sector are pushed up relative to those in the modern sector during long periods of expansion, but that during long periods of downturn, traditional-sector wages are pulled down while those in the modern sector remain at the original high levels.[17] This, of course, leads to a widening in the wage differentials.

There is still an essential ingredient lacking. That ingredient is some explanation of the internal dynamics or institutional arrangement which would explain why the modern-sector firms pay much higher wages than would seem to be required by labor market conditions. One hypothesis has been suggested by Solomon Levine. His explanation concerns the emergence of the nenkō system in connection with training within industry, the response of the large firms to their twin needs: skilled workers and a way to reduce the power of the oyakata.[18] The basic problem of the large modern firms, as described in Chapter 1, was to find a way to insure that employees were provided with the required training. The solution was to incorporate the oyakata and his more traditionally oriented wage and status system into the operation of the firm at the production worker level. In so doing the internal labor markets of the firms were largely isolated from the free play of competitive forces in the external labor market, except perhaps at the level of new graduates' wages. In cutting itself off from the external market, a firm also tended to make internal criteria and economic events of prime importance in determining wage policy. We have, then, two hypotheses, one laying stress upon the normal factors of demand and supply in the labor market and the other placing a greater emphasis upon internal institutional factors. The market hypothesis is essentially the same as that presented for American occupations, except that for Japan in the 1920's it is hypothesized that the demand for skilled labor rose more quickly than did the supply, while a surplus farm labor force maintained an excess supply of unskilled factory labor. The internal institutional hypothesis is not quite the same as the equity hypothesis used for the United States. It is, however, rather similar in that it stresses the importance of forces internal to the firm as opposed to external forces in the establishment of wage patterns.

English-language discussions of the formation of wage differentials in Japan have tended to stress the basic movements of the demand and supply of labor.[19] A number of Japanese economists, however, have discussed a variety of characteristics which separate large and small enterprises and which are said to be related to the wage differentials.[20] These include imperfections in the labor market associated with lifetime employment, different capital-labor ratios associated with capital concentration, a lack of product market competition, etc. In the context of this chapter these explanations are largely modifications of the demand and supply hypothesis. They suggest that demand and supply conditions in the various markets lacked an equilibrating mechanism between large and small firms, or between the traditional and advanced sectors of the economy. Alternatively, the equilibrating mechanism may have worked, but only with lengthy lags. These explanations also contain two weaknesses. They tend, as Shinohara Miyohei has written,[21] to be "truncated," in that they consider the problem as arising out of a particular imperfection or an interaction in only a single market rather than realizing that the problem to be explained involves interactions among all markets and that if imperfections are involved, there are probably several different kinds which act to reinforce each other. The other shortcoming is that the various hypotheses do not satisfactorily explain the large size of the differentials.

Table 23 presents wage differentials by size of establishment for 1909, 1914, 1932, and selected postwar years. There

TABLE 23

Size-of-Firm Wage Differentials, Japan, 1909-67

Size	1909	1914	1932	1951	1955	1960	1965	1967
5-9	103	107	80	86	93	79	--	--
10-19	100	100	100	100	100	100	100	100
20-29	--	--	115	110	--	--	--	110
50-99	100	96	125	130	131	137	118	113
100-199	--	--	130	149	--	--	--	119
100-499	102	97	--	--	165	151	133	--
500-999	98	106	--	208	204	188	150	144
1,000 +	104	117	--	232	234	240	180	171

Sources: Columns 1 and 2 are estimates by Umemura Mataji and Atsushi Nakamura, based upon data in Nōshōmushō Kōjōtōkei sōhyō [Summary of factory statistics], also reported in Shōwa Dojinkai, Waga Kuni Chingin Kōzō no shiteki kōsatsu [Historical analysis of the Japanese wage structure], p. 471.

Column 3 is from Koji Taira, "The Dynamics of Japanese Wage Differentials, 1881-1959" (unpublished Ph. D. dissertation, Department of Economics, Stanford University, 1961), p. 75.

Column 4 is from Tsunehiko Watanabe, "Industrialization, Technological Progress and Dual Structure," in Lawrence C. Klein and Kazushi Ohkawa, Economic Growth: The Japanese Experience Since the Meiji Era (Homewood, Ill.: Richard D. Irwin, Inc., 1968), p. 125.

Columns 5-7 are from Economic Planning Agency, Economic Survey of Japan, 1967-68 (Tokyo: The Japan Times, 1968), p. 118.

Column 8 is from Kōgyō Tōkei Hyō, 1967 [Census of manufacturers], II, 495.

is some evidence of a growth in the size of differentials by size of establishment between 1909 and 1914, with wages in the 500-999 class going from 96 percent to 105 percent of those in the 10-30 class, while wages in the 1,000+ class went from 103 percent to 116 percent of the wages in the 10-30 employee class. What is abundantly clear is that sometime between 1914 and 1951 major changes in the differences by size of establishment took place. We know that in general, differentials in 1951 represented a return to those in the prewar years, and so it seems probable that significant differentials by size of establishment also emerged in the 1920's or 1930's.

Tables 24 and 25 present certain reconstructed basic series for the economy of Japan in the inter-war period. From Table 25 it would appear that the differential between low-skilled manufacturing wages and agricultural wages, as measured by male earnings in textiles and agricultural pursuits, emerged in three periods: 1919-21, 1925-26, and then powerfully in 1929-32. The male machinery worker and metal-worker wages do not begin to show a difference from textile wages until after 1932, a factor which may have been related to the rapid growth in military expenditures which began in 1930, when military expenditures as a proportion of net domestic product began to increase again after the declines of the 1920's.

An examination of the pattern of differentials between average wages in the low-wage and high-wage sectors of manufacturing suggests that the basic differential was established from 1924 and 1930.[22] Additional evidence for this comes from an examination of the coefficients of variation for 75 manufacturing industries. These coefficients ranged between .21 and .25 in the years 1921 through 1928, but jumped to between .30 and .36 during 1929-36. The meaning of the particular years when the differentials were first established and the significance for the two hypotheses may be more clearly understood after a brief overview of the Japanese economy of the 1920's and early 1930's.

The literature commonly refers to the 1920's as a period of lagging or faltering growth. The growth in real net domestic product between 1910 and 1920 was 61.5 percent, and for 1930 to 1940 it was 72.1 percent, yet for the years 1920-30 it was only 33.4 percent, or about half as fast. In addition to the low absolute level of growth, growth in the 1920's was characterized by considerable fluctuation. The absolute decline in domestic product in 1920 was followed by a short boom, the Tokyo-Yokohama earthquake of 1923 was followed by a second

TABLE 24

Manufacturing Statistics, Japan, 1919-39
(1934-36 prices)

Year	Production per Worker (yen)	Employment (thousands)	Wages (yen/day) All	Male	Annual Rates of Change in Net Domestic Product Manufacturing	All
1919	492	1808	.92	1.26	--	--
1920	464	1758	.90	1.26	-9.1	-2.8
1921	502	1888	1.16	1.61	9.8	5.4
1922	514	1871	1.16	1.64	4.3	3.1
1923	472	1939	1.11	1.59	-7.5	3.2
1924	495	1968	1.11	1.62	6.9	8.2
1925	533	1996	1.08	1.57	9.1	3.9
1926	597	2062	1.15	1.69	13.4	2.3
1927	635	2083	1.16	1.74	7.6	2.7
1928	646	2133	1.24	1.76	2.9	3.5
1929	698	2056	1.25	1.88	5.6	-0.1
1930	704	1875	1.29	1.96	5.6	-3.7
1931	829	1842	1.36	2.07	10.6	5.1
1932	858	1921	1.34	2.08	7.9	9.4
1933	789	2102	1.34	2.07	-2.5	9.8
1934	813	2392	1.37	2.07	14.8	3.4
1935	852	2620	1.33	1.98	11.2	6.5
1936	925	2864	1.32	1.91	6.9	8.6
1937	818	3253	1.31	1.85	-8.7	6.2
1938	1009	3590	--	--	28.2	10.7
1939	1254	4354	--	--	30.3	--

Source: Data are from Hugh T. Patrick, "Some Aspects of the Interwar Economy," a paper presented to the Sixth Seminar Conference on Modern Japan, Puerto Rico, January, 1968, pp. 8, 11, 20, 21. Much of the underlying data is the 13-volume series Kazushi Ohkawa, Miyohei Shinohara, and Mataji Umemura, Estimates of Long Term Economic Statistics of Japan Since 1968 (Tokyo: Tōyō Keizai Shimbunsha, 1967-69).

TABLE 25

Wage Ratios, Japan, 1919-38
(real wages, 1934-36 prices)

Year	Textiles (m) / Agriculture (m)	Textile (f) / Agriculture (f)	Textiles (m) / Textiles (f)	Machinery (m) / Textiles (m)	Metal (m) / Textiles (m)
1919	0.80	0.74	1.55	1.80	1.40
1920	0.82	0.73	1.58	1.67	1.28
1921	1.01	0.82	1.66	1.55	1.49
1922	0.98	0.78	1.61	1.64	1.57
1923	0.98	0.74	1.67	1.70	1.65
1924	1.04	0.76	1.71	1.72	1.69
1925	1.02	0.76	1.69	1.74	1.67
1926	1.10	0.82	1.69	1.77	1.68
1927	1.03	0.70	1.76	1.78	1.74
1928	1.06	0.77	1.80	1.84	1.78
1929	1.09	0.72	1.88	1.88	1.87
1930	1.21	0.79	2.05	1.84	1.86
1931	1.45	0.89	2.19	1.79	1.84
1932	1.63	0.98	2.31	1.90	1.87
1933	1.54	0.92	2.27	2.00	1.92
1934	1.51	0.89	2.18	1.97	2.00
1935	1.42	0.88	2.05	1.91	2.00
1936	1.32	0.85	1.98	1.89	1.99
1937	1.22	0.76	1.97	1.85	2.02
1938	1.06	0.66	2.04	1.71	1.96

Source: Data are from Hugh T. Patrick, "Some Aspects of the Inter-war Economy," a paper presented to the Sixth Seminar Conference on Modern Japan, Puerto Rico, January, 1968, p. 24. Much of the underlying data is the 13-volume series Kazushi Ohkawa, Miyohei Shinohara, and Mataji Umemura, Estimates of Long Term Economic Statistics of Japan Since 1968 (Tokyo: Tōyō Keizai Shimbunsha, 1967-69).

short-lived boom, and 1929-30 witnessed yet another absolute decline in net output. The record in agriculture was even worse than that of the economy as a whole. As a result of faltering growth, personal consumption per worker and per capita rose moderately, increasing but 5 percent between 1922 and 1928 and then losing almost all of that gain between 1928 and 1932.

Measured in terms of output, the performance of the manufacturing sector was considerably better. The growth rate for 1925 to 1930 was 7.0 percent. It was 8.2 percent for 1930-35 and 11.0 percent for 1935-40. Much of the latter was, of course, associated with the China incident and preparation for war. The cotton textile industry came into full flower, and there was continued diversification into iron, steel, chemicals, and machinery. As an absorber of labor, manufacturing played a much less significant role in the 1920's than it had previously or than it was to in the 1930's. Employment in manufacturing in the 1920's absorbed only 11 percent of the increase in the labor force, but 74 percent of the increase in the labor force in the 1930's was absorbed by manufacturing.[23]

Wage Differentials in the 1920's

It is generally accepted that the Japanese economy's rapid growth during the World War I era, especially in the modern sector, led to a relative labor shortage and an increase in wages. The fact that major wage differentials developed during the depressed era of the 1920's which followed make it tempting to elaborate a business cycle explanation similar to that discussed earlier. Applied to Japan it would be as follows: During a long period of downturn in the growth rate of the economy, the expansion of the modern industrial sector was unable to absorb the influx of new workers and persons desiring to move out of what in the 1920's was an increasingly backward agriculture. Despite the greater relative supply of labor in the capital-intensive modern sector, wages did not decline. Among small employers and in the area of self-employment outside of agriculture, the increased supply of labor resulted in falling wages as would be expected.[24] That wages were not equally depressed in the modern sector has been explained variously: (a) the oligopolistic nature of the firms, (b) the need of the larger firms to maintain or obtain skilled manpower, and (c) the influence of lagged relationships.

There are a number of elements which give support to a business cycle hypothesis, especially if the years from 1919 to 1932 are viewed as a whole. This can be seen in Table 25, where the ratio of male wages in textiles to male wages in agriculture moves from .80 to 1.63 between 1919 and 1932, or in the ratio of male wages in metals and textiles, where the expansion of the ratio is from 1.28 in 1920 to 1.92 in 1933. Certain regional data shown in Table 26 suggest that these business cycle factors were highly influential. The wage ratios shown are the average wages for two of the principal employers in the Kita Kyūshū area divided by the average wages of two skilled groups in city employment whose skills were most comparable to the skills which the companies used. The data suffer the weakness of regionalism and limited sample size, but have the advantage of being consistent annual observations. In the business cycle trough around 1905 and at the peak in 1919, these ratios may be observed to move in conformity with the business cycle hypothesis: the more flexible small-employer wages rose more rapidly and fell more precipitously.

While the wage differential pattern of the 1920's as a whole is consistent with a business cycle hypothesis, the year-to-year fluctuations suggest the alternative possibility that other factors were at work. In Table 25 it can be seen that the differential between wages in manufacturing and agriculture grew in 1920-22 and 1925-26. Rather than representing downturns in manufacturing, these were periods when the rates of growth in net product in manufacturing were much greater than for the economy as a whole. (See Table 24.) The same relationship between rapid growth in manufacturing output and an expanding wage differential also holds for 1929-31. The pattern was broken after 1931, for manufacturing wages continued to pull away from agriculture even though growth in manufacturing output was not outstandingly rapid in comparison with the entire economy. There is also a similar pattern in the regional data after 1925. (See Table 26.) It will be noted that although output per worker in manufacturing is growing modestly after 1925, an increasing wage differential begins to form for iron and steel around 1926 and for shipyards around 1928. These differentials, especially for iron and steel, continued to grow into 1934 or 1935.[25] On the basis of the above, the conclusion is drawn that the rise of significant wage differentials during the last half of the decade of the 1920's cannot be adequately explained by the business cycle hypothesis.

A related hypothesis which has often been suggested is that of a skilled worker shortage. This states that the

TABLE 26

Iron and Shipbuilding Wage Ratios, Japan, 1898-1936

Year	Long-Swing Periodization	Yawata Iron & Steel Iron Molders	Nagasaki Shipyard Blacksmiths
1898	Peak	--	.928
1899		--	.976
1900		--	1.053
1901		--	.989
1902		.980	1.013
1903		1.056	1.024
1904		1.042	1.054
1905	Trough	.782	.931
1906		.929	.907
1907		.794	.768
1908		.817	.858
1909		.844	.767
1910		.858	.819
1911		.902	.831
1912		.889	.839
1913		.878	.864
1914		.883	.942
1915		.861	.984
1916		.835	.819
1917		.622	.785
1918		.462	.713
1919	Peak	.690	.700
1920		.887	.759
1921		1.143	.980
1922		1.283	1.155
1923		1.207	.934
1924		1.157	.882
1925		1.140	.930
1926		1.125	1.006
1927		1.139	.971
1928		1.289	.974
1929		1.327	1.006
1930		1.363	1.135
1931	Trough	1.394	1.086
1932		1.561	1.191
1933		1.731	1.178
1934		1.793	1.159
1935		1.779	1.112
1936		1.714	1.125

Note: The iron molders and blacksmith wages are for cities in Fukuoka prefecture. The company wages are those for the Yawata Iron and Steel Company and the Nagasaki Shipbuilding Yard.

Source: This is a reproduction of Table 3-7, "Selected Wage Ratios, 1898-1936," from Konosuke Odaka, "Historical Developments in the Wage Differential Structure" (unpublished, July, 1967).

qualitative and quantitative growth of modern-sector firms was sufficiently large, even though manufacturing in general was not expanding rapidly, that firms faced problems in the retention and development of skilled workers. The efforts of the firms to deal with the shortage of skilled workers led to the development of significant wage differentials. If the skilled worker theory is correct, it should be possible to observe differential patterns in the wages or labor turnover of skilled workers relative to unskilled workers. To date, however, such patterns do not appear to be in evidence, with the exception of 1927-28, the years in which the wage differentials became significant. It is possible that even during a period of general decline some firms or industries had to pay higher wages in order to attract workers, but the evidence does not appear to indicate that this occurred.[26]

Wage and employment data for 40 occupations in 1924 and 1933 indicate a widening of differentials, with the coefficients of variation going from .195 in 1924 to .232 in 1933; but there is no relationship between expanding occupational employment and the increase in wages, nor do those occupations with the highest initial wages (the most skilled?) experience the largest wage gain.[27] It is possible that it was not so much the need to attract skilled workers as it was management's desire to retain its key employees which led to the growth of the wage differentials, but again the evidence is not very supportive. The monthly rate of separations in manufacturing did decline from an average of 5.6 percent in the five years 1920-25 to 3.9 percent in 1934-36, but the basic occurrence of the decline was in 1925, several years before the development of wage differentials, which probably reflects the fact that the earlier data refer to all factories employing over 15 workers, whereas after 1924 they refer only to factories employing at least 50 workers.[28] Nor does the proportion of workers with more than five years of service show any dramatic increase, though it does move up from 38.4 percent in 1924 to 46.6 percent in 1933. Such a movement is quite consistent with employee reaction to the depressed conditions of the time and the lack of opportunities elsewhere, coupled with the relatively favored position of the manufacturing worker--all of which would have tended to produce the same result.

A lack of potential high-quality employees does not appear to have been a problem either, especially during years of declining employment. Male and female graduates of upper elementary schools numbered about 300,000 in 1918. The graduation rate rose rather steadily to 500,000 per year in

1930. The majority of these were available to industry, since there were only 60,000 middle school graduates a year in 1930. Since manufacturing employment was only about 2,000,000, experienced an annual turnover rate of 50 percent, and could draw upon more than one-third of a million new compulsory school (upper elementary) graduates annually from 1918 to 1930, it would have been quite easy for the manufacturing sector to have had very high ratios of compulsory school graduates to total production employment if they had needed the skills. In fact, in 1933 only 37.5 percent of the production employees in machinery and 39.2 percent in metals were compulsory school graduates. Yet in the more traditional areas of lumber the ratio was 49 percent, food and liquor 51.3 percent, and textile mills 66.3 percent, the last no doubt a result of the high proportion of females employed in that industry.

The significant wage differentials emerged in the last half of the 1920's and early 1930's. During these years the rate of durable capital formation was modest and employment in manufacturing was stable or declining. On an intra-industry, occupation, and firm basis, there is little evidence of any association of employment and wage changes which would indicate a consistency with theoretical expectations if the economy were experiencing a shortage of skilled or high-quality labor. Consequently, the skill shortage hypothesis must be rejected.

An Equity Hypothesis

In connection with the United States it was suggested that most of the wage differentials were more responsive to equity considerations than they had been to even rather large shifts in demand and supply. The level of value added per employee or the profits of the firm, in conjunction with the need to attract and to hold key employees, sets the level of key wages, while considerations of internal equity determine wages for the remainder of the employees. The essence of this approach is the suggestion that regardless of how cheaply the employer may be capable of obtaining his labor, if his value added or profits are high, equity (or fears of poor work habits, sabotage, etc.) will cause him to pay a wage which is above the minimum supply price. The strength of this equity force may be partially hidden because the employer, faced with the equity need to pay higher wages, will often artificially set employment standards which give the illusion that the high wages result from the employment of high-quality labor.

In the United States it is usually thought that unions have played an important role in making the equity wage viable throughout manufacturing. The union movement in Japan in the 1920's and 1930's was clearly too small, both in numbers and in influence, to have performed this role by itself. Rather than the union, the crucial institution in Japan was the nenkō system of wage payment, which stressed an equity relationship. The evidence strongly suggests that nenkō and equity influenced the wage structure even though many regular workers were not included under nenkō, nor were additional numbers of temporary workers.

The ratio of annual output per worker in manufacturing to the male daily wage declined from 390 in 1919 to a low of 296 in 1923. It then rose slowly and (except for a relapse to 360 in 1930) steadily to 412 in 1932. These figures suggest that the increase in the manufacturing wage relative to agriculture in the late 1920's and early 1930's was justified by productivity. Additional evidence for the role of equity in distributing the gain in productivity may be found in Table 27, which presents some selected wage differentials. The higher wages for primary metal and machinery employees, compared with those in textiles and food, in 1927 may be thought to indicate skill or size-of-firm differences. The relative wage movements between 1927 and 1933 for these industries, wages in metals and machinery going from 180 percent of the textile wage to 205 percent of it, is consistent with the gains-in-productivity hypothesis. What is more interesting is that women's wages in these industries experienced a similar (actually greater) increase, with those in primary metals going from 127 percent to 172 percent of textile wages and those in machinery going from 146 percent to 207 percent. Since it seems unlikely that there was at this time an increase in the relative demand for female labor in these heavy industries, it appears logical to conclude that male wages acted as a key wage determinant for women's wages. Basically the same arguments apply to the data for male and female wages by age. Wages for males over the age of 35 increased from 55 percent to 68 percent more than those for men aged 20-25.[29] This could be attributed to their greater skills, but more probably it stems from the greater use of the nenkō system. Since women were not covered by nenkō, it is difficult to understand the corresponding movement in their wages except as a result of pattern-following stemming from equity considerations.

TABLE 27

Indexes of Selected Wage Differentials, Japan, 1927, 1933, 1936

	1927	1933
Males		
Textile spinning	100.0	100.0
Food	131.0	138.5
Primary metals	183.1	210.3
Machinery	184.5	205.1
Chemicals	141.5	141.0
Females		
Textile spinning	100.0	100.0
Food	100.0	118.5
Primary metals	127.4	172.2
Machinery	146.4	207.4
Chemicals	110.7	144.4
Males		1936
Age 18-20	71.8	65.0*
20-25	100.0	100.0
25-30	68.9	123.9
30-35	142.9	145.4
35-40	153.1	161.3
40-50	158.8	176.7
Females		
Age 18-20	90.2	86.0
20-25	100.0	100.0*
25-30	100.0	109.7
30-35	101.9	115.2
35-40	101.0	116.5
40-50	99.0	119.5

*16-20 years of age.

Source: Rokuro Hotani and Takashi Hayashi, "The Evolution of Wage Structure in Japan," Industrial and Labor Relations Review, XV (October, 1961), 60, 63.

Postwar Wage Differentials

The much richer source of data on postwar wages raises questions concerning the most meaningful system of measurement. The importance of specific characteristics, such as industry, size of firm, and sex, could be estimated by constructing a standard population or by an analysis of variance. A third alternative--the one adopted--is to examine the differentials as they exist in the raw data. This has the advantages of ease of calculation and a close tie to reality.

Table 28 presents the basic differentials by size of firm for 1968. There it will be noted that while the average wage of employees in establishments of 1,000 and more is 35 percent greater than the average wage of those employed in establishments of 30-99, the differentials are most pronounced for older men and for the lower education levels. Table 23 indicates that the basic pattern for the postwar period (after 1951) has been one of a slight decline in differentials up to 1955. This was followed by increases in differentials until 1960, after which they declined again. The dispersion of average wages in manufacturing industries indicates a similar time pattern, widening from 1954 to 1960 and then contracting.

The most common explanation for the widening pattern between 1954-55 and 1959-60 is that it resulted from the extraordinarily rapid growth in the economy, especially in the heavy and chemical sectors of manufacturing. The basis of this expansion was probably the rapid increase in productivity, both absolutely and relative to wage payments. In 1954 value added per employee in manufacturing firms employing more than 1,000 was 104 percent greater than that of those in firms employing 30-99, and wages were 93 percent greater. These expanded to 157 percent and 93 percent, respectively, in 1960.

After 1960 the major indicators suggest a modest decline in wage and productivity differentials. The 1,000+ establishments' productivity advantage over firms with 30-99 employees dropped from 138 percent larger in 1960 to 110 percent, and in wages the decline was from 93 percent greater to 53 percent. These levels are all lower than in 1954, as was the dispersion of average wages by manufacturing industry. A labor shortage, the existence of which is often measured by the ratio of job seekers to job openings, is a common explanation for the narrowing of differentials after 1960.

There are several difficulties with the labor shortage

TABLE 28

Representative Manufacturing Wage Differentials, Japan, 1968

Characteristic	Size of Establishment (no. of employees) 30-99	100-499	500-999	1,000+
All employees	100	104	113	135
Male employees	100	103	107	121
Male middle school graduates, wage earners	100	103	110	131
Male high school graduates, salaried	100	96	99	110
Male university graduates, salaried	100	96	97	115
Males 18-19 years	100	98	103	113
Males 30-34 years	100	105	108	114
Males 50-59 years	100	112	130	167

Note: Manufacturing wage is monthly contract cash earning.

Source: Ministry of Labor, "Basic Survey of Wage Structure," Japan's Labor Statistics (Tokyo, 1970), pp. 82, 86-87.

hypothesis. One is whether there was a real labor shortage before 1968 or 1969. A second is finding an appropriate mechanism which would serve to translate the "labor shortage" into declining wage differentials. A labor shortage is widely discussed by management organizations and in the business press. Apart from new school graduates, a labor force pressure upon wages is difficult to document. The survey unemployment rate was halved between 1955 and 1961 and then remained virtually unchanged. The level of unemployment suggested by the ratio of unemployment compensation claimants to those eligible rose from its lows in 1960 and 1961, only to decline again in 1967-69. Currently the number of job applicants, excluding new school graduates, is approximately equal to the number of job openings, though in some areas and for those under 35-40 years of age there are more jobs than applicants. The placement rate of the employment offices has declined from about 17 percent in 1960-61 to 14.4 percent in 1969. Thus it would appear that the "shortage" is confined largely to certain segments of the labor force.

A common explanation of the mechanism which translates the "labor shortage" into narrowed wage differentials is that competitive pressures on the entry-level jobs (new school graduates) do not generate pressure for higher wages in the internal labor markets within the firm. The employers with the larger wage differences between entry-level and upper-level jobs can more easily resist the upward pressure on wages, and as a consequence the average wage level of high-wage firms rises less rapidly than does the level in low-wage firms, resulting in a compression of the wage scale. Alternatively, since starting wages are a greater fraction of final wages[30] in the smaller firm than in the larger firm, disproportionately large wage increases for new graduates tend to reduce the age and length of service differentials, especially in smaller firms.[31]

The principal weaknesses in these explanations are their failures to relate the dynamic movement in wage differentials to the rationale for the initial wage differences. If the high-wage firms can more easily restrict internal market pressure under conditions of a labor shortage, why didn't they do so under conditions of surplus? Alternatively viewed, if the nenkō wage curve of the firm under surplus labor was a rational lifetime income designed to attract the needed quality of employees, what happened to make a less desirable relative lifetime income sufficient for the firm's quality of labor needs under the conditions of "labor shortage"? Before attempting to answer, it would be helpful to know in somewhat greater detail exactly which differentials changed.

Wage structure data for 1958 and 1965 were used.[32] Both years were ones in which the economy experienced modest slowdowns which should reduce the problem of a stage of the business cycle bias in the comparison of two years. As can be seen in Tables 29 and 30, the basic trend has been one of narrowing, but the degree of narrowing varied greatly. In Table 29 the industrial dispersion of wages for 40-49-year-old middle school-educated production workers in firms of 10-99 employees hardly changed, going from .190 to .186, while for 18-19-year-old middle school-educated production workers in 1,000+ employee firms it went from .202 to .085. In Table 30 the college to high school wage ratio for 30-34-year-olds declined up to 1964 and since has remained constant. At younger ages the decline has been more continual; for the older employees the timing has been somewhat different, but the direction has been toward narrowing.

In an effort to determine the extent to which these changes in wage differentials could be explained on the basis of changes in other variables in the economy, the changes in four wage differentials were regressed against five potentially explanatory variables.[33] The results were not impressive, largely because 13 of the 19 two-digit manufacturing industries ranked among the first five industries in terms of wage gains for at least one of the five employee groups, but only three industries--chemicals, textiles, and lumber-- were represented among the first five as many as three times. When all of the differentials were combined into an average and the regression analysis was repeated, there was some slight improvement. These results suggested that lessened inter-industry wage differentials were positively associated with growth in total employment, an increase in the proportion of nonproduction workers, but negatively associated with increasing union contract coverage and with increasing profits. A similar reduction in the influence of unionization and productivity has been reported by Tuvia Blumenthal, using an analysis of variance approach for the years 1958 and 1964.[34]

Are any firm conclusions to be drawn from the above? Perhaps not, but some tentative ones do seem reasonable. The period 1958-65 was one of decreasing wage differentials, but no consistent and uniform pattern was evident. Second, it was a period during which smaller establishments with lower levels of absolute productivity improved their productivity relative to that of the larger firms. Third, the

TABLE 29

Dispersion of Monthly Wages in Manufacturing, Japan, 1958 and 1965

Wage Category	1958	1965
Male college graduates, age 40-49, in nonproduction work, firms of 10-99 employees	.147	.217
Same, except high school graduates	.152	.124
Same, except middle school graduates and production workers	.190	.186
Male college graduates, age 40-49, nonproduction workers, firms of 1,000+ employees	.164	.112
Same, except high school graduates	.114	.127
Same, except middle school graduates and production workers	.245	.179
Male high school graduates, age 18-19, nonproduction workers, firms of 1,000+ employees	.179	.048
Same, except middle school graduates and production workers	.202	.085

Note: Dispersion is the interquartile range divided by the median. The observations are over the two-digit manufacturing industries.

Source: Ministry of Labor, *Chingin Kōzō Kihon Chōsa*, 1958, and *Chingin Kōzō Kihon Tōkei Chōsa*, 1965 [Basic survey of wage structure].

TABLE 30

Selected Wage Differentials, Japan, 1954-69

		1954	1961	1964	1969
Ratio of male university graduate wages to high school graduate wages					
Age	20-24	115.9	115.0	111.5	106.2
	30-34	125.4	118.9	115.3	116.5
	40-49	156.4	140.1	145.6	140.5
Index of male wages in manufacturing, by age (20.24=100)					
Firms Employing 1,000+					
Age	18-19	70.5	76.7	76.7	79.8*
	30-34	172	188	171	156
	40-49	222	261	240	211
Firms Employing 10-29					
Age	18-19	75.8	77.1	76.7	75.8
	30-34	151	140	134	140
	40-49	159	151	141	141

* 1968.

Source: Ministry of Labor, Chingin Kōzō Tōkei Chōsa [Basic Survey of Wage Structure]. The title varies slightly in different years.

increased dispersion of wages for college-educated workers in smaller firms (see Table 29), the smaller decrease in the college to high school wage differential for older workers (see Table 30), and the increase in the value of higher education measured by analysis of variance[35] all suggest that technological changes increased the value to the firm of the college-educated worker. Lastly, these years have been marked by a labor shortage which has been dramatized by stories of Tokyo companies flying in new recruits from southern Kyūshū. The shortage has been concentrated chiefly among new school graduates, and even there more among middle school graduates, whose numbers have been declining. With the exception of the shortage of new school graduates, the other factors mentioned above have made their principal wage impact upon internal wage structures. In other words, the consequence of their impact is to cause firms to readjust intra-firm wage relationships with reference to internal or external standards. Even the significance of the shortage of new school graduates is more in terms of readjustments in internal wage relationships rather than as a symbol of a general shortage of labor.

The process was as follows: Initially the lifetime earnings in both large and small firms (traditional or modern industries) reflected their relative profitability-productivity situation. In the case of the large-modern sector, the lifetime earnings involved low beginning wages which rose rapidly over years of service. Conversely, in the small-traditional sector wages progressed only moderately with years of service. Recently the shortage of new school graduates has resulted in rapid increases in the starting wage, increases which had to be matched for the older workers in the small-traditional sector in order to maintain internal wage equity. In the large-modern sector a decline in the profit-productivity position relative to small firms and traditional industries resulted in a reduction of lifetime earnings in these firms relative to the lower wage groups. This reduction took the form of allowing the starting wage ratio between themselves and the small-traditional sector to approach parity while maintaining much wider differentials at older ages.

The rising productivity in the smaller and more traditional sectors, in combination with the labor shortage among new school graduates, has been the impetus to change, but with the exception of starting wages, the changing pattern of differentials has been determined largely by the needs of the internal labor market, where equity considerations have clearly played a significant role.[36]

Occupational Wage Movements

The internal structure of the Japanese firm has made little use of occupational titles and work assignments. Consequently, only limited data on occupational wages have been collected, and even fewer instances of analytical work are available. One recent analysis did make use of data on chauffeurs and kanji (ideograph) typists, but the emphasis was upon the importance of certain factors in the one-digit industrial wage structure.[37] The study found that there were relatively large differences in the wages received by workers in these occupations, depending upon which industry they were in. The range in 1961 for chauffeurs was from 101 yen per hour in construction to 154 yen per hour in utilities, while for kanji typists the range was from 64 yen per hour to 100 yen per hour, again for the same two general industries.

Relatively extensive occupational data published for the years 1956 and 1964 included 150 manufacturing occupations which were common to both years. Monthly wage increases over the eight-year period ranged between 50 percent and 100 percent, and employment changes ranged from a 6.3-fold increase in the number of female watch and clock assemblers to a decline of 80 percent in the number of male paper-cutting machine operators. Movements in occupational employment were not, however, particularly associated with wage movements. This was true both for manufacturing as a whole and for particular industries which were represented by a reasonable number of occupations. These results are also consistent with and provide support for the view that occupational wage data provide little insight into the Japanese economy.

The Impact of the Union on Occupational Wage Differentials

It is difficult to relate the role of the union to wage differentials. First, it is necessary to distinguish between inter-industry wage levels and occupational wages within industries. It is generally believed that the union impact upon the former has been significant but modest. The most careful and complete analysis of the unions' impact on inter-industry wages was published by Gregg Lewis in 1963.[38] He concluded that probably an increase of 10 to 15 percent was the maximum influence of unionization some 15 years after World War II. In other words, the most highly organized and effective unions had achieved wages for their members which were up to 15 percent higher than those workers would have received in the absence of unions.[39] The highest differential for union member wages over nonunion member wages has varied from near zero in the inflation of 1947-48 to perhaps 25 percent in the largely nonunion depression years of 1932-33. Since those industries that are highly unionized tend also to be those with high average wages, it is doubtful that unionization has had much of an impact upon the industrial wage rankings. The usual view of union impact upon inter-occupational differentials has been that it has been quite modest. The view is based upon the fact that there are such great differences among industries that there has been no real motivation for unions to have a wage differential policy. Secondly, there have been no policy decisions at the federation level in favor of some particular pattern of differentials such as has been characteristic of some of the Scandinavian federations, which have adopted policies in favor of a reduction in wage differentials.

This is not to say that unions have had no role. Certainly in some industries, such as meat packing, steel, autos, and bituminous coal, geographical differentials within the unionized sector have been reduced as a direct result of union policy. Within the firm the union's role is more difficult to assess. Robert MacDonald, in his extensive study of collective bargaining in the auto industry, concluded that the union's influence upon personal differentials coincided with management's own decisions in the same direction.[40] In terms of relative hourly earnings, it would appear that the union may have increased the compression of semi-skilled and unskilled job rates, with lesser impact upon the highly skilled. Thus in 1957 with a laborer or material handler's wage equal to 100, assemblers received 105 and punch press operators 106. Yet in 1922 the punch press operators' wage index had been 144 and the assemblers' 134 and 131, compared with the laborers' and handlers' 100. Yet the tool and die worker, whose wages had been 55 percent greater than the laborer's in 1922, had seen his wages decline to where they were 36 percent greater than the laborer's. Since at least part of this decline would seem to be related to the general decline in skilled wages over the last 50 years, the independent influence of the union would seem to be quite minor. This is also the conclusion which George Delehanty and George Hildebrand reached in their recent study.[41]

Unlike the United States, where significant percentages of the manufacturing labor force are organized, only 37 percent of the workers in Japanese manufacturing are organized, though this is almost twice as great as the organization rate in the next most highly organized sector. The low rate reflects the failure of unions to organize in the smaller firms, where in 1969 the organization rate was 4 percent, as compared with 63 percent in firms employing more than 500 workers. There is some variation by manufacturing industry in the percentage of union members who are covered by contracts, but it is not very great. The role of the union in industrial wage differentials is not clear, but at best is probably quite small. The study of kanji typists and chauffeurs cited earlier concluded that union organization was significant in determining wage levels at the one-digit industry level, and Baba Masao, in his study of changing labor shares in income distribution, reported a measurably weak significance for the degree of union organization.[42] Apart from its questionable influence on industrial differentials, it would appear that it had no role whatsoever on intra-enterprise wage distributions because of the nature of the Japanese union (discussed in Chapter 1) and the fact that all collective bargaining concerns the average wage advance and not a set of specific wages, as is the case in the United States.

Here the inter-country comparison seems to be quite straightforward: the role of the union has been such that it has not affected the internal distribution of wages, at least among union members.

Wage Differences by Size of Establishment

There is little in the way of systematic data on wage differences by size of establishment in the United States.[43] The basic pattern for these differentials from the 1963 Census of Manufacturers is shown in Table 31 in conjunction with similar Japanese data. What is shown is that for firms employing between 10 and 249 employees there is little in the way of wage differences. Above 250 employees some large differences are apparent. There is, however, great divergence by two-digit manufacturing industry. In textiles, wages are highest in the 10-19 employee group and vary between 88 percent and 94 percent of that level for all larger groups. Yet in lumber and in ordnance the wages of the 20-49 group are 13 percent and 15 percent greater than in the 10-19 group. In general, those industries which have high differentials for smaller groups have even higher ones for the largest groups, though

TABLE 31

Size-of-Establishment Wage Differentials
in Manufacturing,
United States and Japan

Size (employees)	Japan (1965)	United States (1963)
10-19	100	100
50-99	118	103
100-249	--	106
250-499	--	110
100-499	133	--
500-999	150	119
1000+	180	146*

* This is the median value for the two figures, 134 for those employing 1000-2499 and 154 for those with 2500 and more.

Sources: Japan (cf. source for Table 23); United States, Census of Business 1963, I, Table III.

the rank-order correlation between the size of the differential for the 500-999 group and the 1000+ group is only .67. There does not appear to be any clear-cut criterion that would suggest which industries will have large wage differentials by size of establishment, there being no simple correlation between that and either average wages or value added per worker. The only hint of a pattern is that industries which are symbolic of the machine age--primary metals, fabricated metals, machinery, electrical machinery, transportation equipment, and instruments--seem to exhibit rapid and continuous increases in wage differentials beyond the 250-499 group.

Compared with those of Japan (see Table 31), the U. S. differentials are considerably smaller, though significant differences do not appear except above 500 employees. The U. S. differentials have changed hardly at all during the postwar years, whereas the Japanese ones have been substantially reduced. Thus, continued reduction of size of firm differentials in Japan would bring the two countries into even greater similarity.

COMPARATIVE WAGE DIFFERENTIALS

A first impression is that the wage differential experiences of Japan and the United States have been opposite. In the United States it has been occupational differences and their decline which have formed a staple subject of examination and discussion. In Japan this role has been played by differentials by size of firm and their increase in the 1920's and 1950's, and modest decline in the 1960's. The closest similarity has been that some of the largest and most interesting changes in differentials took place during the 1920's, when data were much less carefully and completely collected.

One of the biggest differences between the United States and Japan has been in the frequency with which significant changes in differentials have been observed. Especially in the postwar years the U. S. differentials have been more stable than the Japanese. There are two possible explanations. One is that size of firm differentials are probably inherently less stable than occupational or industrial ones. The second and more meaningful one is the greater youthfulness of the Japanese economy. The U. S. economy is now a mature economy which has largely expanded along already well-defined paths. Japan, during the postwar years, has just been developing her manufacturing economy along modern lines, and consequently it is perhaps to be expected that some industries or segments would be the first to grow and that a more stable pattern of wage differentials will emerge during the 1970's. This latter suggestion is essentially an extension of Taira Koji's explanation for the apparent stability of Japanese differentials during the first 80 years of her modern economic history, whereas during these same years U. S. differentials were compressing.[44]

The theories which have been used for the principal analytical explanations have tended to be the same: straightforward neoclassical demand and supply analysis with but very slight modification in terms of recognition (1) that labor quality is important and (2) that most firms prefer to retain most employees rather than to hire employees at a daily auction. There has not been much in the way of systematic analysis of the impact of the two internal wage-setting systems, nenkō in Japan and job evaluation and career ladders in the United States, on wage differentials.

The application of a labor shortage hypothesis as the principal explanation for changing wage differentials produces a reasonable consistency with the observed pattern of wage differentials in the two countries. For Japan this meant a widening of differentials in the 1920's because of a shortage of key workers and a narrowing in the 1960's because of a general shortage of labor. For the United States it meant a narrowing due to a relative shortage of unskilled workers in the very tight labor markets of the two world wars. The business cycle hypothesis that differentials will expand in downturns and contract during expansions appears to have been somewhat more noticeable in Japan than in the United States.[45] To the extent that this is true, it would appear to result from a greater flexibility of reported wages in Japan and the fact that in Japan it was a smaller segment of the economy in which it was rational to maintain an excessive labor force during downturns in order to reduce costs of new hiring during the following upswing.

In both economies the traditional skill surplus or shortage hypothesis has failed to provide a really good explanation for the observed pattern of events. There have been too many problems of timing. There has been no stability in the degree of change in the differential, which has resulted from any given shortage or surplus. Also, the expected relationships between specific changes in wages and employments which should follow from such a theory have too often been nonexistent. These failures suggest the need for the use of an alternative hypothesis.

The alternative hypothesis which has been suggested for Japan and the United States was the equity hypothesis, which argues that standards of appropriateness and internal considerations are the factors which are most important in determining most short-run changes in wage differentials.

There are certain differences, however, in the meaning of equity in the two economies. In the United States the "orbits of coercive comparison" involve the ties between key jobs and those in their orbit, ties between key jobs within the same firm, and ties between companies either in well-established industries or within the local labor market. Examples abound. Two of them are the historical parity between municipal police and fire departments and the fact that entry-level job rates in highly unionized industries have moved in parity with other wages within those industries instead of with conditions in the labor market.[46] In these comparisons three factors are dominant in the establishment of equity: similarity of work, historical relationships, and similarity of work location. Family considerations--age, education, etc.--except to the extent that they are related to the type of work which is being done, are not deemed relevant.

In Japan there exists a somewhat different basis for equity. The strongest relationship is in terms of historical relationships between persons, which may include educational differences unrelated to the job being performed. Family considerations are thought to be an appropriate element in wage setting, as shown by the fact that 91 percent of the Japanese workers included in a recent survey approved of the use of such a factor.[47] In Japan the similarity of employer or place of employment is not a strong factor in the determination of equity. Regular employees of a firm receive substantially more than do temporary employees or the employees of subcontractors working at the principal job site. Paying temporary employees less than regular employees was approved of by 58 percent of the Japanese workers in the cited survey, but only 27 percent of the American workers.[48]

Despite the differences in the concept of equity, its force in the establishment of wage differentials seems evident in both economies, especially within the firm. Perhaps because the institutional arrangements within Japanese and American firms are more divergent than is true of the arrangement for aggregate wage settlement, even though the labor shortage and equity hypotheses are equally useful in both economies, one is left with the feeling that there is somewhat more dissimilarity here than in other aspects of the two economies.

NOTES

1. Adam Smith, Wealth of Nations, Harvard Classics ed. (New York: P. F. Collier and Son, 1910), Book I, Chapter 10, p. 106.

2. In such a situation it would be possible for the observed skill ratio to fall but for the skill ratio based upon job content to have risen. Such a situation seems to have existed during the American Civil War, when the median wage ratio for machinists and laborers fell but the dispersion of wages for both groups widened. Robert Evans, Jr., "Wage Differentials, Excess Demand for Labor, and Inflation: A Note," The Review of Economics and Statistics, XLV (February, 1963), 95.

3. Koji Taira, "The Dynamics of Japanese Wage Differentials, 1881-1959" (unpublished Ph. D. dissertation, Department of Economics, Stanford University, 1961), p. 59.

4. One of the earliest proponents was Wesley C. Mitchell, in A History of the Greenbacks (Chicago: University of Chicago Press, 1903), p. 303.

5. John T. Dunlop, "The Task of Contemporary Wage Theory," in George W. Taylor and Frank C. Pierson, eds., New Concepts in Wage Determination (New York: McGraw Hill, 1957), pp. 117-39.

6. The bivariate correlation coefficients between percentage changes in gross hourly earning and in employment do not in any of the subperiods between 1948 and 1960 reveal evidence of a systematic relationship between changes in earnings and in employment in 57 industries drawn from the Department of Labor's employment and earnings bulletins. Lloyd Ulman, "Labor Mobility and the Industrial Wage Structure in the Postwar United States," The Quarterly Journal of Economics, LXXIX (February, 1965), 78-79.

7. Melvin W. Reder, "The Theory of Occupational Wage Differentials," American Economic Review, XLV (December, 1955), 838-40.

8. Morris A. Horowitz and Irwin L. Herrnstadt, "The Training and Education of Tool and Die Makers," Proceedings of the Industrial Relations Research Association, 1967 (May, 1968), pp. 15-24.

9. Evans, op. cit., pp. 95-98.

10. A British publication reaches a similar conclusion concerning the role of inflation in wage narrowing and the equity considerations which underlie it. Guy Routh, Occupation and Pay in Great Britain 1909-1960 (Cambridge: Cambridge University Press, 1965), pp. 150-51. However, many American economists would not agree with such a conclusion. For a strong defense of the competitive hypothesis, the reader should consult Melvin W. Reder, "Wage Structure Theory and Measurement," in Universities National Bureau Committee for Economic Research, Aspects of Labor Economics (Princeton: Princeton University Press, 1962), pp. 257-311. The movements of wage differentials are also discussed in Richard Perlman, Labor Theory (New York: John Wiley and Sons, Inc., 1969), pp. 79-123.

11. The data from the two studies are found in Martin Segal, "Occupational Wage Differentials in Major Cities During the 1950's," in Mark Perlman, ed., Human Resources in the Urban Economy (Baltimore: Resources for the Future and Johns Hopkins Press, 1963), pp. 195-207; and George H. Hildebrand and George E. Delehanty, "Wage Levels and Differentials," in Robert A. Gordon and Margaret S. Gordon, eds., Prosperity and Unemployment (New York: John Wiley and Sons, Inc., 1966), pp. 265-96. The Bureau of Labor Statistics study was Donald J. Blackmore, "Occupational Wage Relationships in Metropolitan Areas, 1961-1962," Monthly Labor Review, LXXXVI (December, 1963), 1426-31.

12. Taira, op. cit., p. 59, notes that the absolute skill differentials in prewar Japan were lower than in the United States.

13. G. C. Allen, Japan's Economic Expansion (London: Oxford University Press, 1965), pp. 218-19.

14. Kozo Yamamura, "Wage Structure and Economic Growth in Postwar Japan," Industrial and Labor Relations Review, XIX (October, 1965), 60.

15. Kazushi Ohkawa and Henry Rosovsky, "Postwar Japanese Growth in Historical Perspective: A Second Look," in Lawrence C. Klein and Kazushi Ohkawa, Economic Growth: The Japanese Experience Since the Meiji Era (Homewood, Ill.: Richard D. Irwin, Inc., 1968), p. 30.

16. Hugh T. Patrick, "Some Aspects of the Interwar Economy" (paper presented at the Sixth Conference on Modern Japan, San Juan, Puerto Rico, January 2-7, 1968), p. 7.

17. Konosuke Odaka, "Historical Developments in the Wage Differential Structure," (unpublished paper, July, 1967), p. 32. Some of the material in this paper appears under the title "A History of Money Wages in the Northern Kyūshū Industrial Area 1898-1939," Hitotsubashi Journal of Economics, VIII (February, 1968), 71-100. See also his "A Study of Employment and Wage-Differential Structure in Japan" (unpublished Ph. D. dissertation, University of California, University Microfilms, 1969), Chapter 3.

18. Solomon B. Levine, "Labor Markets and Collective Bargaining in Japan," in William W. Lockwood, ed., The

State and Economic Enterprise in Japan (Princeton: Princeton University Press, 1965), pp. 641-51.

19. "One feels that Japanese development has been neoclassical throughout." Koji Taira, Economic Development and the Labor Market in Japan (New York: Columbia University Press, 1970), p. 75.

20. See the excellent discussion of some of these in Miyohei Shinohara, "Formation and Transition of the Dual Economy in Japan," Hitotsubashi Journal of Economics, VIII (February, 1968), 11-38.

21. Ibid., pp. 7, 21.

22. The composition and selection rationale for the low-wage and high-wage sectors are discussed in Chapter 5.

23. These paragraphs draw heavily upon Patrick, op. cit.

24. This is Taira's view. He considers the years 1924-34 as a period of widening differentials. Economic Development . . ., pp. 61-63.

25. This latter emphasis represents an interpretation of these two wage ratio series, which is not the same as that of the developer of the series, Odaka.

26. The average gain in employment between 1924 and 1930 for 19 manufacturing industries was .022 percent (median .13 percent), and money wage declines averaged 19 percent (median 16 percent). The largest wage and employment increase occurred in petroleum, but across all 19 industries there is no association between changes in wages and employment.

Data are available on the average wages and employment for 33 large firms in Tokyo (500+ employees) for 1925 and 1933. The rank-order correlation between changes in employment and changes in average wages turns out to be an insignificant -.10. Since during these years many firms underwent declines in employment, it is possible that increased average wages due to the retention of higher-paid employees in the 17 firms with declining employment confound these results. This is not the case, for the correlation between growing employment and changing wages for the 16 firms with expanding employment is an insignificant -.20. These data are from Sano Yōko, "Dainiji Taisenzen niokeru Kibobetsu Chingin Kukusa Shiryō," [Data on wage differentials by size of firm before World War Two], Keio University Institute of Management and Labor Studies Series No. 25 (Japanese) (1961-62), pp. 116-21.

27. For the sample of 40 occupations as a whole there is a modest rank-order correlation (.29), significant at the 5 percent level, between the level of the initial wage and the degree of wage change. This could be interpreted as evidence of skilled (higher) wages rising most rapidly. However, it is probably more accurate to consider it a reflection of interindustry effects. This is because for the four industries which are represented by at least four occupations, only for food is there a significant link between the initial wage and the degree of positive wage change. In fact, two of the four industries had negative relationships. The data are from Odaka, _op. cit._, pp. 73-75.

28. Taira, _Economic Development . . ._, p. 155.

29. Data for male white-collar wages also indicate a widening by age during this period. Magota Ryohei, "Nenkō Chinginren no Shiten" [A view of the Nenkō wage system], in Shinohara Miyohei and Funehashi Naomichi, eds., _Nihongata Chinein Kōzō no Kenkyū_ [Research on the structure of Japanese wages] (Tokyo: Rōdō Hōgaku Kenkyūsho, 1961), p. 291.

30. In 1968 the 50-59-year-old male employee in manufacturing firms of 30-99 employees received 86 percent more than the 18-19-year-old male. For firms employing 1,000 or more, the figure was 178 percent.

31. Haruo Shimado, "A Quantitative Analysis of Negotiated Wage Increases in Japan," _Keio Economic Studies_, VI, 1 (1969), 58.

32. At the time this part of the research was begun, 1965 was the last complete year and 1958 was the earliest year for which comparable data were available.

33. The five wage differentials were those for old (40-49) and young (18-19) high school-educated nonproduction workers,

old college-educated nonproduction workers, and old and young middle school-educated production workers. The wage data were for establishments employing more than 1,000 in 19 two-digit manufacturing industries. The independent variables used were changes in the degree of union contract coverage, the ratio of nonproduction workers to total employment, which was used as a proxy for levels of technology, the ratio of female employment to total employment, the level of profits, and value added per employee. With the exception of the regression for old production workers, which had an r^2 of .68, the correlations were very low and the independent variables were not significant. Combining all of the differentials provided some slight improvement, an adjusted-for-degrees-of-freedom multiple correlation coefficient of .50, and standard errors for four variables were less than half the value of their coefficients. Yet the results should be classed as suggestive rather than significant.

34. Tuvia Blumenthal, "Scarcity of Labor and Wage Differentials in the Japanese Economy 1958-1964," Economic Development and Cultural Change, XVII (October, 1968), 26.

35. Ibid., pp. 20-21.

36. The interested reader is referred to two recent discussions which stress slightly different views. Odaka Konosuke, "Rōdō Shijō no Jukyū Chēsei Kinō to Chingin Kōzoku," [Toward a theory of wage differential structure] Keizai Kenkyū [Economic Review], XIX (April, 1968), 168-72; and Umemura Mataji, "Nenkō Chingin ni suite" [Some notes on wage structure], ibid., XVIII (April, 1967), 160-63.

37. Yōko Sano, "An Analysis of Industrial Wage Differentials," Keio Economic Studies, IV (1966-67), 29-43.

38. H. Gregg Lewis, Unionism and Relative Wages in the United States (Chicago: University of Chicago Press, 1963), pp. 5, 45.

39. This estimate concerns increases relative to other industries and says nothing about the possibility that unions may have increased all wages as against profits, rents, etc.

40. Robert M. MacDonald, Collective Bargaining in the Automobile Industry (New Haven: Yale University Press, 1963), pp. 131, 138.

41. George H. Hildebrand and George E. Delehanty, "Wage Levels and Differentials," in Robert A. Gordon and Margaret S. Gordon, eds., Prosperity and Unemployment (New York: John Wiley and Sons, 1966), pp. 265-301.

42. Masao Baba, "Economic Growth, Labor Unions, and Income Distribution," in Ryūtaro Komiya, ed., Postwar Economic Growth in Japan (Berkeley: University of California Press, 1966), pp. 137-54. See also Taira, Economic Development . . ., pp. 198-203.

43. One recent exception is Richard Lester, "Pay Differentials by Size of Establishment," Industrial Relations, VII (October, 1967), 57-67.

44. Taira, "The Dynamics . . . ," p. 218.

45. Ibid., pp. 99, 218.

46. Hildebrand and Delehanty, op. cit., pp. 265-301.

47. A recent survey of 1,042 Americans and 958 Japanese in eight major unionized companies probed worker attitudes on a number of industrial relations issues. The results were reported in Arthur M. Whitehill, Jr., and Shin-ichi Takezawa, The Other Worker (Honolulu: East-West Center Press, 1968), p. 249.

48. Ibid., p. 220.

CHAPTER

5

LOW-WAGE INDUSTRIES IN JAPAN AND THE UNITED STATES

The recent upsurge of interest and concern in the United States over poverty and the problems of individuals and families caught up in it has served to focus attention upon a related situation, the complex of firms and employees who constitute the low-wage sector of the U.S. economy.[1] While there has not been a similar upsurge of concern in Japan, the recent years of relative affluence and international complaints of unfair competitive advantage due to low wages directed at Japan have generated some interest in low wages among influential segments of Japan's government and business circles.[2]

The object of this chapter is threefold. It seeks to present those attributes of firms, products, and geographical areas which are extensively involved in the low-wage sectors of the two countries. Then, by an examination of certain hypotheses concerning the causes of low wages, it seeks to deepen and extend our understanding of the low-wage problem in these countries, and lastly, by comparing two economies which are characterized by both a number of similarities and differences, it hopes to make possible a broader understanding of the general problem of low wages in modern industrial societies than would be possible by an examination of the experience of only a single country.

Abstracting from the problems of an inadequate level of overall demand, which may lead to a country's producing at less than its potential gross national product, it is possible to identify three broad hypotheses concerning the nature of the low-wage problem. The first two deal with structural problems of supply and demand, which are at least conceptually susceptible to correction by policy operations that would allow the individual firm or person to make full use of the situation or abilities. In short, they stress inequalities of opportunity. Hypothesis III deals with both demand and supply elements, but contrary to the first two it suggests that the nature of the low-wage problem is rooted in natural inequalities and cannot be solved by working only with the firms or persons involved. Alternatively stated, even with equal opportunity there will be inequality of results. The specific natures of the three hypotheses are given below.

HYPOTHESIS I: In the diagnosis of poverty-level incomes of employed persons, personal influences such as poor health, low intelligence, poor education, and lack of ambition, resulting in low personal productivity, are dominant causes.

HYPOTHESIS II: The causes of poverty-wage employment are found principally in the institutions and forces in the market place which keep wage rewards below marginal productivities and which inhibit the growth of personal productivity to its full potential.

HYPOTHESIS III: The earnings distribution depends upon endowments of abilities, tastes, and various assets. So long as these are unequal, the earnings distribution will also be unequal. A relatively "low-wage" sector will then persist as a result of "natural" inequality. Consequently, all persons can achieve a minimum absolute income standard only by a system of subsidies and/or as the entire income distribution moves to higher levels.

Inadequate incomes, of course, stem from causal factors related to more than one of these broad propositions. Low personal productivity may be due to lack of strength, poor health, or inadequate education. Market imperfections, of which poor information, classical monopsony in the labor market, and racial discrimination are examples, are more serious to those who have low personal productivity. In most cases they are reflected in employment and labor relations policies of individual employers. Inflexible hiring standards, eagerness to substitute capital for "low-quality" workers whatever the current cost ratios, and an understandable reluctance of employers to bear risks of employing disadvantaged workers (such as released and paroled criminals or the physically handicapped) are some examples. Certain anti-union philosophies or racial and religious preferences also belong in this class.

Two separate time patterns of inadequate incomes may also prevail. One is a full-time, full-year effort which for combinations of the reasons described yields only a poverty-level income. The other may have either part-time or part-year characteristics. Here, even though hourly wage rates or marginal rates of return on capital are adequate, the annual earnings remain below the poverty level unless other returns are obtained through holding two jobs or dovetailing with other seasonal occupations.

Within the general category of market imperfections, but deserving separate notice, might be a set of forces that could be described as wage-setting mechanisms. It is possible that the complex linkages throughout the economy that are supposed to ensure movement toward equilibrium in all labor markets have gaps. In the language of current quantitative research on wage behavior, there may be different Phillips curves (relationships between wage changes and unemployment rates with other variables) for different sectors of the labor market. There is no immediately apparent theoretical basis for distinguishing these sectors, but the old concept of "noncompeting groups" and the more recent notion of "wage contours" clearly suggest the phenomenon.

A DEFINITION OF LOW-WAGE INDUSTRIES IN THE UNITED STATES

Before the attributes of low-wage industries can be studied, certain standards by which these industries can be identified must be developed and accepted. For the purposes of an initial report, an industry was classed as being "low-wage" if nonsupervisory employees received average straight-time hourly earnings of $2.20 an hour or less in 1964. The standard was developed in the following way. It started with the popular but arbitrary determination that a family income of $3,000 or less was a poverty income. Using this, a low-wage recipient was defined as a male full-time employee who received wages which, on an annual basis, totaled $3,000 or less. It was recognized that, because of differences in costs of living and the possibility of multiple-earner families, this was not an ideal measure. Yet there appeared to be no straightforward method of adjustment for that. In any case, the results which are of interest and the conclusions drawn are not likely to be unduly biased by a failure to make adjustments for these problems.

The standard of $3,000 in wages applied to year-round firms meant an hourly wage of $1.50 ($3,000/2,000 hours), which thus became the standard for low-wage employment. Since distributions of earnings are seldom available by industry, it then became necessary to make two additional determinations. One involved an estimate of the proportion of an industry's employment which must have been at $1.50 or less in order for the industry to have been classed as low-wage. The second involved estimating that proportion from data on average earnings. Since approximately 20 percent of all family incomes were below the poverty limit of $3,000 when it was chosen, it was decided to use a 20 percent level for the lower limit of employees receiving $1.50 an hour or less in order for an industry to be classed in the low-wage category. When it was necessary to use a distribution standard for data prior to 1963, as with the 1960 census materials, the percentage of families with income below $3,000 as given in the Current Population Reports of the Bureau of the Census for that year was used.

The average wage level for low-wage industries was obtained in the following way. The _Secretary of Labor's 1964 Report to Congress on the Minimum Wage_ contains data on average straight-time earnings and percentage distributions of earnings for 14 approximately two-digit manufacturing industries. Plotting the percentage of employees earning $1.50 an hour or less against the average hourly earnings yields a reasonably good straight-line relationship. These data from the _Secretary's Report_ suggest that at an industry average straight-time wage of $2.00 an hour the probability was very high that at least 20 percent of an industry's nonsupervisory employees received $1.50 an hour or less. Consequently $2.00 an hour for straight-time earnings in 1964 was chosen as the low-wage limit.[3]

Since most data on industry wage rates are expressed in terms of gross hourly earnings, it was necessary to add $.20 an hour to the $2.00 to obtain the poverty limit of $2.20 an hour for 1964. The $.20 figure comes from the fact that in March, 1964, when the _Secretary's Report_ listed a straight-time average wage in manufacturing of $2.33 an hour, the

Economic Report of the President, 1965 listed a gross hourly average wage of $2.54 an hour for manufacturing. The poverty level wages for 1958 were obtained by subtracting from $2.20 the cents per hour increases between that year and 1964, as reported in the Economic Report of the President, 1965.

A DEFINITION OF LOW-WAGE INDUSTRIES IN JAPAN

In discussing low wages in Japan, it would have been desirable to use definitions that were equivalent to those used for the United States. One possibility would have been to have used a yen rate that would be equivalent to the $2.12 which was used for 1963. At the fixed exchange rate of 360 yen to the dollar, this would have yielded a monthly income of approximately 120,000 yen, a figure far in excess of the average wage in manufacturing. Indeed, it exceeds the highest wage for the highest wage class in the highest-wage industry. Even if dollars were to have been converted into yen at a rate of 200 to the dollar, a figure which may have approximately expressed the real purchasing power of the yen, the income standard would be close to 68,000 yen a month, which still exceeded the average wage in the highest-wage manufacturing industry.

There are three major reasons why a straightforward conversion of the dollar standard into yen could not be used. Since many consumption items--housing and medical services, for example--do not move in international trade and because persons of different cultural backgrounds facing divergent relative price ratios will consume dissimilar bundles of consumption goods, an exactly equivalent purchasing power exchange rate is impossible to calculate.[4] Also, the typical Japanese employee may receive more of his total compensation in fringe benefits than does his American counterpart. In 1964 employers spent 6.7 percent of cash earnings on benefits such as dwellings, medical facilities, etc., a practice which has few counterparts in American industrial relations practice. The third factor is that per capita income in Japan was only about one-third that in the United States, which meant that absolute levels of poverty were inappropriate standards.

Among the alternatives,[5] the one chosen was to use the ratio of 86.5 percent of average industry wages as the low-wage cutoff. This was the proportion which was used in the

United States in making inter-temporal comparisons. This yielded a monthly wage of 28,000 yen, which was just above the income level of the 20th percentile family.

There are obvious advantages and disadvantages associated with the choice of any of the alternatives given above. Since in Japan, as compared with the United States, the distribution of income is not the same, the self-employed constitute a larger share of the work force, the ratio of fringe benefits to wages is larger, and the general level of income is lower, any attempt to base the selection of the low-wage sector in Japan on income distributions was hazardous at best. Therefore, the last method was selected primarily because it was the same system used with U.S. data in moving away from the base year of 1963. In addition, it largely avoids difficulties of fringe benefits to earnings differences and the conversion of dollars into yen. And finally, it is simple and easy to apply.

The use of this system does involve certain assumptions, and it is well to make them explicit. It assumes that a quasi-relative measure of poverty is most appropriate. Such a system allows the absolute level of poverty income to rise with national income growth, but unlike a strictly relative system, it is possible for poverty to be eliminated by making the difference between median income and the lowest income very small.

LOW-WAGE INDUSTRIES

The industries which will be discussed are limited to those in manufacturing. This is unfortunate, but unavoidable. The study from which the U.S. material was taken contained some information on the trade and service sectors, but only very limited data were available. These data could not be duplicated for Japan, nor did they provide any insights which were not evident from the other material. Consequently this chapter deals only with manufacturing.

U.S. Manufacturing in 1963

In 1963 a manufacturing industry with gross hourly earnings for nonsupervisory employees of $2.12 or less was included in the low-wage category. Using this standard in conjunction with <u>Employment and Earnings Statistics for the</u>

United States, 1909-1964 yielded 33 three-digit low-wage industries. (See Table 32.) Of these, 23 are in the nondurable goods sector of manufacturing. While they are distributed among 11 of the 21 two-digit industries, the majority of the employees in the three-digit low-wage sectors were in seven two-digit industries. One-third or more of workers in these seven industries were in the low-wage three-digit subsectors. These seven classes and their percentages of employment in the low-wage subsectors were as follows: lumber and wood products, 60 percent; furniture and fixtures, 72 percent; miscellaneous manufacturing, 49 percent; textile mill products, 100 percent; apparel and allied products, 100 percent; rubber and miscellaneous products, 38 percent; and leather and leather products, 91 percent. In addition, food and kindred products, tobacco, electrical machinery, and instruments and related products had at least one low-wage three-digit component. For purposes of this chapter these first seven (the industries in which more than one-third of the employees were employed in subdivisions which paid low wages) have been identified as the low-wage two-digit manufacturing industries.

In 1958 a manufacturing industry with gross hourly earnings for production workers of $1.86 an hour or less was included in the low-wage category. Using this standard, obtained by extrapolating backward from the low-wage standard of $2.20 for 1964, in conjunction with the Census of Manufacturers, 1958, 38 low-wage industries were obtained. These 38 three-digit manufacturing industries included 10 which consist of only a single four-digit industry. These low-wage industries are given in Table 33. The list provides a few surprises. The most notable absence is the miscellaneous plastic products industry (307). This industry, which was on the low-wage border in 1963, had a 1958 average wage which placed it $.04 outside the low-wage category. Only 38 of the 142 relevant three-digit manufacturing industries were in the low-wage category. The use of U.S. averages for this determination may tend to understate the size of the problem. Looking at the average earnings of three-digit industries as they were reported for the individual states, it will be found that 111 of the 142 industries paid low wages in at least one state, and 45 paid low wages in 10 or more states. There was considerable overlap between the 38 low-wage industries based on national earnings and the 45 low-wage ones based on state data. On a combined, adjusted-for-overlap basis, the two methods of determination yielded a total of 56 low-wage industries.

The proportion of a state's three-digit manufacturing

TABLE 32

Low-Wage Manufacturing Industries, United States, 1963 and 1969

Industry Code No.	Title	Average Wage 1963	Average Wage 1969	Average Employment (thousands) 1963	Average Employment (thousands) 1969
242	Sawmills and Planing Mills	1.88	2.62	254.3	231.8
244	Wooden Containers	1.68	2.28	36.1	37.5
249	Miscellaneous Wood Products	1.83	2.43	63.0	87.3
251	Household Furniture	1.89	2.48	279.8	346.9
253,9	Other Furniture and Fixtures	2.07	--	42.4	--
325	Structural Clay Products	--	2.69	--	64.5
365	Radio and T.V. Receiving Equipment	--	2.69	--	154.6
367	Electronic Components and Accessories	2.09	2.68	262.4	410.1
384	Medical Instruments and Supplies	--	2.73	--	76.9
385	Ophthalmic Goods	--	2.74	--	32.4
387	Watches and Clocks	2.11	2.55	29.3	36.4
394	Toys, Amusement, and Sporting Goods	1.88	2.39	102.7	126.1
395	Pens, Pencils, Office, and Art Material	1.95	2.64	31.5	34.0
396	Costume Jewelry, Buttons, and Notions	1.86	2.45	54.5	61.7
203	Canned and Preserved Food, Except Meat	1.97	2.50	247.3	282.6
207	Confectionery and Related Products	1.97	2.58	76.3	85.3
212	Cigars	1.60	2.07	22.7	19.5
221	Cotton Broad Woven Fabrics	1.67	2.34	229.1	226.4
222	Silk and Synthetic Broad Woven	1.74	2.40	84.8	101.5

(continued)

TABLE 32 (continued)

Industry Code No.	Title	Average Wage 1963	Average Wage 1969	Average Employment (thousands) 1963	Average Employment (thousands) 1969
223	Weaving and Finishing Broad Woolens	1.83	2.41	50.4	44.0
224	Narrow Fabrics and Small Wares	1.74	2.32	27.8	31.7
225	Knitting	1.64	2.26	216.0	245.1
226	Finishing Textile, Except Wool and Knit	1.89	2.26	75.2	83.9
227	Floor Covering	1.79	2.42	37.4	54.2
228	Yarn and Thread	1.57	2.19	101.4	121.8
229	Miscellaneous Textile Goods	1.96	2.58	66.8	78.7
231	Men's and Boys' Suits and Coats	2.04	--	114.5	--
232	Men's and Boys' Furnishings	1.46	2.00	326.4	372.6
233	Women's, Misses' and Juniors' Outerwear	1.92	2.47	392.3	430.5
234	Women's and Children's Undergarments	1.55	2.11	116.7	125.4
235	Hats, Caps, and Millinery	1.83	2.17	33.0	20.5
236	Girls' and Children's Outerwear	1.55	2.13	76.7	79.6
237, 8	Fur Goods and Miscellaneous Apparel	1.80	2.44	73.3	78.2
239	Miscellaneous Fabricated Textile Products	1.77	2.41	151.6	174.2
302	Rubber Footwear	--	2.68	--	25.6
307	Miscellaneous Plastic Products	2.12	2.66	157.0	279.4
314	Footwear, Except Rubber	1.71	2.31	233.2	226.8
312, 313, 315-17, 319	Other Leather Products	1.71	2.31	86.3	89.2

Note: Wages are production worker gross hourly earnings, and employment is total employment.

Source: U.S. Bureau of Labor Statistics, Employment and Earnings Statistics for the United States, 1909-1964, Bulletin No. 1312-2. Also Employment and Earnings, XVI (March, 1970).

TABLE 33

Low-Wage Manufacturing Industries, United States, 1958 and 1963

Code	Title	Production Worker Average Hourly Earnings	
		1958	1963
203	Canned and Frozen Foods	$1.56	$1.85
207	Confectionery and Related Products	1.67	1.99
212	Cigars	1.40	1.65
213	Chewing and Smoking Tobacco	1.75	2.05
214	Tobacco Stemming	1.30	1.53
221	Weaving Mills, Cotton	1.46	1.71
222	Weaving Mills, Synthetics	1.55	1.79
223	Weaving Mills, Wool	1.69	1.88
224	Narrow Fabric Mills	1.43	1.80
225	Knitting Mills	1.49	1.68
226	Textile Finishing	1.77	2.03
227	Floor Coverings	1.63	1.80
228	Yarn and Thread Mills	1.39	1.60
229	Miscellaneous Textiles	1.75	2.07
231	Men's and Boys' Suits	1.75	2.00
232	Men's and Boys' Furnishings	1.29	1.46
233	Women's and Misses' Outerwear	1.61	1.77
234	Women's and Misses' Undergarments	1.37	1.57
235	Millinery, Hats, and Caps	1.72	1.90
236	Children's Outerwear	1.40	1.59
238	Miscellaneous Apparel	1.45	1.65
239	Fabricated Textiles NEC	1.55	1.78
241	Logging Camps	1.79	2.07

(continued)

TABLE 33 (continued)

Code	Title	Production Worker Average Hourly Earnings 1958	1963
242	Sawmills and Planing Mills	$1.59	$1.88
244	Wooden Containers	1.46	1.66
249	Miscellaneous Wood Products	1.62	1.84
251	Household Furniture	1.69	1.88
253	Public Building Furniture	--	2.15
259	Furniture and Fixtures NEC	--	2.17
277	Greeting Cards	1.79	2.06
286	Gum and Wood Chemicals	--	2.15
287	Agricultural Chemicals	1.83	2.10
307	Plastic Products	--	2.13
313	Footwear, Cut Stock	1.55	1.72
314	Footwear, Except Rubber	1.56	1.76
315	Leather Gloves	1.38	1.59
316	Luggage	1.60	1.76
317	Purses and Small Leather Goods	1.47	1.67
319	Leather NEC	1.50	1.61
325	Structural Clay Products	--	2.19
328	Cut Stone and Stone Products	--	2.16
379	Transportation Equipment NEC	--	2.15
385	Ophthalmic Goods	--	2.10
394	Toys and Sporting Goods	1.68	1.81
395	Office Supplies	1.80	2.06
396	Costume Jewelry	1.55	1.82

Note: Three-digit industries whose production workers received an average wage of $1.86 and $2.19 an hour or less are included.

Source: U.S. Department of Commerce, Bureau of the Census, 1958 Census of Manufacturers, 1963 Census of Manufacturers.

industries which had low wages ranged from Alaska's zero to South Carolina's 88 percent. The median for all the 50 states was 39 percent. Grouping the continental states into the nine proposed census regions yielded median figures ranging from the Far Western states' low 14 percent to the South Atlantic states' high of 75 percent. The median for the nine groups was 36 percent, essentially the U.S. median. The geographical distribution was about the same as that determined from data on the low-wage occupations. The adequate wage states were those in the Plains, the Midwest, the Far West, and the Middle Atlantic area. Rocky Mountain states comprised the median group, while New England and the three Southern state groupings were the low-wage states. The composition of the low-wage sector, while not stagnant, has been fairly stable. Two of 1963's 33 low-wage industries--watches and clocks and miscellaneous plastic products--would have been excluded had 1958 wages been used, while four currently excluded industries--other furniture and fixtures, optical and ophthalmic products, miscellaneous foods and kindred products, and agricultural chemicals--would have been included by the use of 1958 wage relationships.

The Department of Labor's three-digit data for 1969 (see Table 32) indicate that the changes in the low-wage sector between 1963 and 1969 were the addition of five industries and the removal of two. The data in the _1963 Census of Manufacturers_ (see Table 33) indicate an addition of eight industries. In both cases many of the new additions had been just outside in 1958 or 1963 and are now just inside the low-wage line.

For 1969 the low-wage standard for production workers was $2.76 an hour. Seven two-digit manufacturing industries--lumber, furniture, miscellaneous, tobacco, textile, apparel, and leather--would on this basis be included in the low-wage group. This is unchanged from 1963. The list includes tobacco, which has not been classed as a low-wage industry, and it excludes rubber and plastics, which were considered to be in that group. This, too, is unchanged since 1963. The apparent paradox results from the original decision that the low-wage composition would be made on the basis of employment in low-wage three-digit industries. This means that miscellaneous plastics, with over 40 percent of employment in rubber and plastics and a wage just under the poverty limit, caused this industry to be included. The very low wage in cigars, with only 27 percent of employment, in conjunction with wages just above the poverty line in the rest of tobacco left that industry outside, but with a very low average wage. Consideration was given to making an adjustment in the decision rule to eliminate this anomaly, but this did not seem to be consistent with intellectual honesty and was not done.

Low-Wage Manufacturing Industries in Japan

The 86.5 percent of average wages as a standard for inclusion in the low-wage category could be applied to two-digit manufacturing industries, using either those firms employing five or more regular workers or those employing 30 or more regular workers. Both of these sets of data are taken from the Monthly Labor Force Survey of the Ministry of Labor. It could also be applied to three-digit industries employing 10 or more regular employees, as drawn from the Census of Manufacturers.

The Census of Manufacturers for 1963 reported data on 143 three-digit industries. Forty-two of these, or 29 percent, were classed as low-wage. (See Table 34.) The proportion of low-wage three-digit industries in any two-digit industry ranged between zero in nine of the 21 two-digit industries to all six in the apparel industry. An examination of the Ministry of Labor data indicated that most industries were either clearly in or out of the low-wage category. The questionable ones were food, paper, rubber, and leather. Looking at the three-digit data for these four clearly placed food into and leather out of the low-wage group, for the former had a very high percentage of employment in low-wage three-digit subgroups, and the latter a very low percentage. The difficult decisions involved rubber and paper, both with about 40 percent of their employment in low-wage subgroups. It was finally decided to include rubber but to exclude paper. The basis for this was that the two-digit wage for rubber barely exceeded the 86.5 percent standard, while the wages in paper clearly were in excess--indeed, they were higher than a few of the industries which were clearly not low-wage.

For Japan, like the United States, there were seven low-wage two-digit manufacturing industries: food, textiles, apparel, lumber, furniture, rubber, and miscellaneous. The overlap with those selected in the United States is almost complete, except that leather was included in the United States and excluded in Japan. The exact opposite held true for food. It was included in Japan but excluded in the United States. Tobacco, which created such a paradox in the United States, was excluded from consideration because it is a government monopoly.

TABLE 34

Low-Wage Manufacturing Industries, Japan, 1963 and 1967

SIC Code	Industry	Annual Cash Earnings/ Regular Employee (1,000 yen)	
		1963	1967
182	Seafood Products	196	295
183	Canned and Preserved Fruits	173	265
187	Bakery and Confectionery Products	241	366
192	Misc. Food Preparations and Kindred Products	251	376
201	Reeling, Scouring, and Combing Plants	198	319
202	Yarn	243	342
203	Thread Mills	203	315
204	Broad Woven Fabric Mills	210	330
205	Knitting Mills	217	316
207	Rope and Netting	214	341
208	Embroidery	214	332
209	Misc. Textiles	243	369
211	Men's, Youths' and Boys' Suits	189	280
212	Men's Work Clothing	197	286
213	Headgear	277	396
214	Furs	226	390
215	Misc. Apparel, including Japanese	226	324
219	Misc. Fabricated Textiles	235	330
221	Sawmills and Planing Mills	229	354
223	Wooden Containers	265	391
224	Footwear (wooden) except Leather and Rubber	182	264
229	Misc. Wooden Products	236	352

(continued)

TABLE 34 (continued)

SIC Code	Industry	Annual Cash Earnings/ Regular Employee (1,000 yen)	
		1963	1967
231	Furniture	278	--
232	Religious Furniture	241	373
233	Fusama and Shōji	283	405
244	Paper for Office, School, and Daily Use	278	--
245	Paper Containers	256	--
282	Rubber Footwear and Plastics	230	368
284	Rubbish Rubber	273	--*
295	Leather Gloves	216	289
297	Handbags	265	376
299	Misc. Leather	275	--
303	Structural Clay Products	225	351
304	Pottery and Related Products	246	382
352	Public Electric Appliances	277	--
353	Electric Bulbs	259	--
357	Electronic and Communication Equipment	--	402
376	Glasses	277	403
391	Precious Metals	260	--
393	Toys and Sporting Goods	237	379
395	Costume Jewelry	248	--
397	Lacquered Ware	202	307
398-99	Misc. Manufactures NEC	254	403

*Absorbed into 2894.

Note: Industries paying less than 284,000 yen a year in 1963 and 408,000 yen a year in 1967 are classed as low-wage.

Source: Kōgyō Tōkei Hyō [Census of manufacturers], 1963, 1967.

An extensive analysis of geographical differences in low wages was not undertaken. Two industries, textiles and chemicals, were selected as representative of the two categories, and prefectural wages were examined. For chemicals, two out of the 44 prefectures reporting, Nara and Yamanashi, had low wages. In textiles, six of the 46 prefectures paid wages above the low-wage standard: Tokyo, Gifu, Kyoto, Osaka, Wakayama, and Shimane. As might be suggested by the above list, wages in the low-wage textile industry tended to be above the standard in the major urban areas. Thus, in the seven major industrial areas--Tokyo, Yokahama, Nagoya, Kyoto, Osaka, Kobe, and Kita-Kyūshū--only in Kita-Kyūshū were textile wages in the low-wage category.

On a cross-sectional basis there were a number of differences between the low-wage and the nonlow-wage industries.[6] (See Table 35.) There it can be seen that the proportion of production employees who were women was much higher in the low-wage group--49.7 percent--than in the others, where it was only 21.3 percent. In addition, the low-wage group worked in establishments which on the average were half as large--39 employees to 69 employees--and had but half the tangible fixed assets to work with--111,000 yen per employee to 203,000 yen. In terms of value added per employee, the ratio was close to two-thirds--637,000 yen to 999,000 yen--but when wages per employee were subtracted, the ratio returned closer to half. As can be seen in Table 35, there has been little change in the pattern since 1963.

The Anatomy of Low-Wage Relationships

What causes some industries to pay low wages? The economist's reply is that the answer lies within the determination of demand and supply schedules for labor in these industries. Under the general heading of demand would be included factors associated with the demand for the industry's final products, the technological relationships between the various factors of production, and the quantity, quality, and price of cooperating factors of production, especially physical capital. Within the category of supply would be the quality and quantity of labor offered to the industry at various wage rates and the alternatives available to those workers. These factors should be considered at a point in time and as they change over time. Thus, to answer the question of what distinguishes the low-wage industry from the rest of industry, it is desirable to

TABLE 35

Cross-Sectional Characteristics of Low-Wage and Nonlow-Wage Industries, Japan, 1963 and 1967 (based upon medians)

	Low		Nonlow	
	1963	1967	1963	1967
Women Production Workers / All Regular Production Workers (percent)	49.7	48.0	21.3	25.4
Value Added per Person Employed (thousand yen)	637	968	999	1,557
Value Added per Person Employed Less Wages per Person (thousand yen)	358	554	648	1,033
Average No. of Persons Employed per Establishment	39	39	69	77
Tangible Fixed Assets per Person Employed (thousand yen)	111	151	203	284
Ratio of Wages in Highest-Wage Size Class to Those in Lowest-Wage Size Class	1.30	1.27	1.45	1.38

Source: Kōgyō Tōkei Hyō [Census of manufacturers] and Labor Year Book.

examine available data on as many of the factors discussed above as possible. The examination can proceed in two ways: factor by factor or by multiple analysis using an appropriate statistical technique.[7] The advantage of the latter is that it underlines the inter-relation of the various factors and many even exclude from consideration a factor which appears important when it stands alone. The principal advantage of examining each component separately is that it provides a clearer insight into the various mechanisms which are involved in establishing distinctions between low-wage and high-wage industries in two countries. The clear insights provided by an examination of each factor, coupled with the relatively low levels of explanatory power of the multiple analyses, were the basis for the emphasis which this chapter gives to the component approach.[8]

Increases in Hourly Earnings in the United States

One of the principal dynamic differences was the slow rate of growth of average hourly earnings by the low-wage group. The gain in average hourly earnings for manufacturing as a whole in the period 1958-63 was 17 percent. The gain in the 33 low-wage industries was only 13.6 percent for the same period. The slow growth of wages among the low-wage industries is placed in a sharper perspective when it is contrasted with the experience of the 13 three-digit industries which had average wages which placed them just above the poverty class ($2.13 to $2.28 per hour in 1963). The 13 had an average increase of 15.8 percent. Despite the fact that wages moved more slowly, there were not marked differences in the growth of employment between low-wage and other manufacturing industries. Employment in low-wage three-digit industries in the durable sector of manufacturing grew by an average of 7.3 percent for the period 1958-63, while all durable employment rose by 9 percent. Among the nondurables the figures were 2.9 percent for the low-wage industries and 4 percent for all nondurables. Between 1963 and 1969 the median wage increase in the three-digit low-wage group was 35 percent, which was equal to the average gain for all manufacturing. Employment among these industries rose about 16.5 percent, which was also similar to the experience of all manufacturing.

Most of the published data on other characteristics of the manufacturing sector were available for two-digit rather than three-digit aggregations. The lower-than-average rate of wage increases noted for the three-digit firms was also observable for the seven two-digit low-wage manufacturing industries. The median increase in earnings for these seven in the period 1958-63 was 13 percent, while the median increase for the other 14 two-digit industries was 16.5 percent. The failure of the low-wage group to maintain its relative wage position appears to be a continuation of a longer-term trend. For the years 1953-63 the median increase in earnings among the seven low-wage industries was only 30 percent, as compared with a median of 45.5 for the rest of manufacturing industries.

Contrary to behavior at the three-digit level, however, there was a noticeable difference between the employment growth of the seven low-wage industries and the remainder of manufacturing. The median growth in employment for the period 1958-63 was 4 percent among the low-wage group, compared with the rest of manufacturing's median increase of 7 percent. Despite the combination of lagging employment and lagging wages, it is doubtful if one is the cause of the other, for the short-term correlation between employment and earnings is typically quite low. Between 1958 and 1963 the rank-order correlation between changes in employment and changes in wages among the nonlow-wage industries was -.38, which is insignificant.[9]

Wage Increases in Japan

Contrary to the experience in the United States, the rate of wage increases among the low-wage industries has been quite respectable. Between 1958 and 1964 the all-manufacturing total wage rose by 83 percent. (The median industry increase was 89.5 percent.) The median increase for the low-wage two-digit industries was 119 percent, compared with only 75 percent for the nonlow-wage industries. The same pattern--a more rapid rise in wages for the low-wage group--was also true over the longer period 1954-64, though here the differences were much less startling. It can be argued that such figures give a false impression of the situation because during these years, especially after 1958, there was a decrease in manufacturing wage differentials by size of firm, sex, and age. Since in the structure of employment the low-wage industries have younger workers, more women, and are smaller, their faster growth rate in wages may only reflect these other changes. Thus it would be desirable if estimates which are closer to a pure industry effect could be obtained. This is especially true because in the United States there do not appear to have been comparable movements in the size of establishment, sex, and age differentials in that period.

Two sets of data provide some insight into the importance of size of firm or industry characteristics. One is industry data by size of firm, and the other is highly detailed employee data by industry and size of firm. In 1964, for establishments employing 500 or more employees, the eight lowest-paying industries included the seven industries which have been identified here as the low-wage ones. The same was true in the employment class 100-499. In the 30-39 employee group, the lowest six industries were all among the low-wage ones, but the rubber industry paid wages at about the median. Turning to the data on specific groups of employees, white-collar male high school graduates 40-49 years of age in firms employing between 10 and 99 in the low-wage industries experienced wage increases between 1958 and 1965 of 87 percent, compared with a gain of 90 percent for the same type of employees in the nonlow-wage industries. Similar results are obtained for blue-collar middle school graduates of the same ages. In firms employing 1,000 and more, the magnitude of the wage increases for workers with these characteristics was smaller. Among white-collar workers the nonlow-wage gain exceeded the low-wage gain, 58 percent to 48 percent, but for the blue-collar workers it was reversed, 86 percent in the low-wage and 44 percent in the nonlow-wage industries. The conclusion can be drawn that the low-wage industries tend to be low-wage at all size categories but that much of their apparent rapid wage gain between 1958 and 1965 was probably attributable to changes in wage structure which were not closely related to industry characteristics.

The years 1955-65 were ones during which the number of employees in manufacturing grew quite rapidly, a growth in which the low-wage group fully participated. The greatest growth between 1955 and 1964 was in furniture, with 280 percent, and the lowest was 25 percent in textiles. The median of the seven was 170 percent, which was much greater than the overall average of 115 percent. The differential in employment growth was less between 1960 and 1965, and it slowed down even more to 1968. The gains were 35 percent to 26 percent for 1960 and 1965 and 3.5 percent and 3.4 percent between 1965 and 1968, but still in favor of the low-wage sector.

There are some inter-country differences in observed employment and wage patterns. In the United States the low-wage industries lagged behind the high-wage sector in wage growth during most of the postwar period, a position that was only partially redressed in 1963-69. In Japan, however, the wage levels of the low-wage industries gained upon the rest of industry between 1958 and 1965 and have run about even since then.

A similar reversal of experience is observed for employment. In Japan the low-wage group expanded relative to the rest of industry, but in the United States it did not. While there is no clear explanation for these differing experiences, the total growth in employment in manufacturing in the two economies was quite dissimilar. In Japan employment rose from 5.7 million in 1950 to 13.5 million in 1969, with the greatest growth, almost 2.5 million jobs, coming in 1955-60. This was also the period when most of the faster growth of employment in the low-wage sector took place. In the United States between 1958 and 1963, there was only a gain of 1,000,000 workers in manufacturing, from 15.9 to 16.9 million employees. The years 1963-1969 tripled that growth in manufacturing, 3.1 million new employees. And during these latter years the low-wage three-digit industries expanded at a slightly slower rate than did all manufacturing. At the two-digit level the rate of employment advance of low-wage industries lagged behind all manufacturing. Wage increases (median) for the three-digit low-wage group exceeded the all-manufacturing average. This was also true for the two-digit group. These results suggest that periods of major expansion in manufacturing employment will lead to both an enlargement in the number of persons employed in the low-wage sector and a modest decline in the extent to which they are low-wage industries.

Productivity in the United States

Another major attribute of industry behavior, commonly accepted as having a major role in dynamic wage movements, is productivity change. It is not possible to trace the disappointing wage gains among the low-wage firms to their failure to maintain productivity increases consistent with gains in the rest of manufacturing. Using the ratio of Federal Reserve Board Production Index divided by total employment as the measure of productivity, the seven low-wage industries had a median increase in productivity of 26 percent for the period 1958-63 and about half that (11 percent) between 1963 and 1969. In the remainder of manufacturing, less ordnance, the median increase was 25 percent, and it was 16 percent in the second period, 1963-1969. The experience of the 1958-63 period was consistent with the postwar period in general to that time, during which gains in productivity among the low-wage sector appear to have been somewhat greater than those for the remainder of manufacturing. Thus, the relative wage declines in the low-wage sector cannot be explained, until after 1963, by the failure to achieve gains in productivity.

There are several possible explanations for this combination of slow employment and average earnings growth, and the high rate of productivity change. If the industries are producing a declining proportion of total output, then their employment will tend to consist of a greater proportion of more skilled and senior workers than would be true of all manufacturing. The consequent decline in the number of firms and plants would see the "best practice" plants retained. Employers would not have to maintain a wage position in order to attract new entrants and could trade wage gains for the maintenance of employment when negotiating with their unions. A short-run alternative explanation would be that these industries had previously been operating below capacity and now were closer to an optimum capacity position. These industries may have acquired better management or experienced other changes, one of whose impacts has been to raise productivity.

Despite the fact that the low-wage sectors have increased their productivity in line with the rest of manufacturing, the sector's absolute productivity is significantly lower than that of the rest of manufacturing. Data in the _1968 Survey of Manufactures_ indicate that the range of value added per production worker man-hour in manufacturing was from $5.07 in apparel to $27.35 in petroleum. The median was $10.08. Among the industries in the low-wage sector, the range was only from $5.07 to $7.72, with a median of $5.97. In the other industries the range was $8.87 to $27.35, with a median of $12.00. Since wages and salaries are the largest single component of value added, it may be more meaningful to use figures on value added less payroll, divided by production worker man-hours. Using these data, the range of value added for all manufacturing was from $2.93 to $23.25. For the low-wage sector the range was $2.93 to $4.93, with a median of $3.43. The other industries had a range of $5.64 to $23.25, with a median of $8.40. Using either set of data, it can be seen that the absolute productivity of the median nonlow-wage industry exceeded that of the most productive low-wage industry. These figures suggest that the solution of the low-wage problem must deal with these low productivities and whatever factor or factors lie behind them.

Productivity in Japan

The labor productivity figures which are prepared by the Japan Productivity Center on an industrial basis do not include the full range of the manufacturing sector, and only four of the seven low-wage industries are included in the 13 private enterprise two-digit industries for which data were published. As a sample of the productivity picture for all of manufacturing, however, it painted a very bleak picture of the low-wage sector. The median industry in 1955 produced at 72 percent of its 1960 productivity level, yet all of the low-wage industries produced at higher levels, indicating a lower rate of growth in productivity during 1955-60. The next five years were equally bleak. The median increase in productivity was 46.8 percent, while the median of the four low-wage industries was 9 percent. This bleakness finds support in an estimate of the degree of disembodied technical progress in 14 manufacturing industries.[10] With the average annual rate in manufacturing being 6.4 percent, the median for the five low-wage industries included was only 4.4 percent, compared with an 8.7 percent rate for the nonlow-wage industries.

A somewhat more optimistic view may be obtained by an examination of the growth in value added by industry. Between 1954 and 1963 value added per worker in manufacturing grew 2.3 times, 2.2 times in the nonlow-wage. Between 1963 and 1967 the increase was 1.62 for all manufacturing and 1.48 for the low-wage group.

The difference in the productivity relationships between Japan and the United States is perhaps the most interesting and provocative difference in the low-wage area. In the United States the rate at which productivity increases have taken place in the low-wage and nonlow-wage sectors has been essentially equal, though in recent years the increases in the low-wage group have been exceeded by those in the nonlow-wage sector. In Japan, however, there is some evidence to indicate that productivity gains in the low-wage industries have been much lower than those for all industry during the entire postwar period, a point of particular importance, given the role of growth in value added in raising some three-digit industries out of the mire of poor wages.

Exploitation

It may be useful to examine certain alternative explanations for low wages, both of which are related to exploitation. One hypothesis is that employers have a position of monopsony relative to the employees. The second is that in the absence of sufficient unionization, employers in these areas have lacked the incentive to be as capable and vigorous in their operations as their more unionized counterparts. Limited data are available with which to test these two hypotheses. The first implies that the return upon capital invested in the low-wage industries should exceed that obtained on capital invested in the rest of manufacturing. The second hypothesis implies (1) that the low-wage sectors are less well organized than other industries and (2) that wage gains within the organized portions of the low-wage sector would be comparable with those obtained by unions elsewhere.

Profits in the United States

Exploitation does not seem to be a very powerful explanation for low wages in manufacturing. George Stigler's study of capital and the return to capital in manufacturing provides figures on rates of return on capital for most of the two-digit industries for the years 1948 to 1957.[11] In these years the average rate of return on capital in manufacturing varied between a low of 6.04 percent in 1954 and a high of 9.69 percent in 1950. The median return for the 10 years was 7.33 percent. Among the low-wage industries the range of the medians was from 4.32 percent in 1953 to 8.83 percent in 1950. The median of these medians was 5.75 percent, or 1.58 percent lower than that for all of manufacturing. In no year was the return of the low-wage industries in excess of the average return. The closest was in 1950, when the difference was only .86 percent. Nor do the individual industries, except for lumber, fare any better. In seven of the 10 years the rate of return on capital in the lumber industry exceeded the average for all manufacturing. Two of the rest, rubber and textiles, each had one year when their rates of return exceeded the average. The others were always below the average.

The profit picture can be brought somewhat up to date by using averages of the quarterly after-tax income as a percent of stockholders' equity reported jointly by the Federal Trade Commission and the Securities and Exchange Commission for

1957 through 1968.[12] For all manufacturing (except newspapers) these average returns ranged between a high of 13.1 percent in 1966 and a low of 8.6 percent in 1958. The medians of the 20 manufacturing industries (miscellaneous manufacturing is combined with ordnance) range from 8.2 percent to 13.9 percent. As in the earlier period, the median return for the low-wage industries is less than the average for all manufacturing except in 1966-67 and less than the median of the 20 industries. The median rate for all the industries for the eight years 1957-64 was 9.0 percent and 11.6 percent for 1964-68. Among those with low wages it was 7.5 percent and 11.2 percent. The difference in the rate of return favored the nonlow-wage industries by about 2.5 percent in the first period and 1 percent in the second. The failure of the profit takers (successfully) to exploit the workers is placed in sharp relief by a comparison in each year of the median return to the nonlow-wage group with the high value for any of the low-wage industries. In seven of the 12 years the highest profit rate of a member of the low-wage group exceeded the median of the other industries. As in the earlier period, the individual industries have poor records, except for the rubber industry, whose profit rate exceeded the median for all the industries in 10 of the 12 years. Similar results are obtained when profits per employee in the low-wage sector are compared with those in the rest of manufacturing. For example, in 1961-62, the median profit per employee for 30 three-digit low-wage industries was $499. The 68 nonlow-wage three-digit industries had a median profit per employee of $1,177.

Profits in Japan

Only very limited data on profits are available. One widely used source, the Shuyō Kigyō Keiei Bunseki (Analysis of the management of principal firms) of the Bank of Japan, includes only two of the low-wage industries, and even one of them, textiles, presents certain problems because it includes synthetic textiles which are more usually included in the chemical industry. Some additional data are available in the Bank of Japan's reports on medium-size and small industries. Even there, only five of the seven low-wage industries are represented. The general pattern of profits per employee in large-scale (more than 300 employees) and modest-scale (50-299 employees) firms is that between 1956 and 1964 the larger ones earned 3 to 3.5 times higher profits than did the smaller ones.[13] Given the disproportionate representation of the smaller firms in the low-wage industry category, the expectation would be that profits would be lower than for the nonlow-wage industries. The one exception is the food industry, which is more profitable than the average manufacturing industry. Even among small firms, however, the low-wage industries earn smaller profits per employee. The nine-year annual average profits per employee for the 50-299 employee firms was 76,000 yen. Yet the median for the five low-wage industries was 51,000, or only two-thirds as great. Consequently, in Japan, as in the United States, the conclusion must be that the low-wage workers are not being exploited by their employers, whose profits are tiny.

In the United States it was clear that the profit position of the low-wage industries was significantly below that of the nonlow-wage. From this followed the conclusion that not only workers, but also capitalists, suffer the curse of the low-wage industry. The same is also true of Japan. The absence of data on large low-wage firms in Japan, however, makes this conclusion a little less strong than it would be otherwise.

Unionization and Collective Bargaining in the United States

Since it does not appear that exploitation of low-wage labor has produced high profits, is it possible that because the low-wage sector is not so fully organized by American unions as the remainder of manufacturing, employers have merely been lazy in the absence of the never-ending demands of organized labor? The average degree of organization for all manufacturing was 46 percent in 1968. The median for 21 industries was 49 percent. The range of organization among the seven low-wage industries was from 19.3 percent in textiles to 62 percent in apparel. The median was 44 percent. The range for the remainder of the industries was from 13.5 percent in instruments to 65.5 percent in transportation equipment, with a median of 49.1 percent.

The organized portion of the low-wage sector has not, except perhaps in the last year or two, secured wage gains comparable with those obtained by unions in the remainder of manufacturing industries. Since 1950 the Bureau of National Affairs has prepared data on median negotiated union wage settlements.[14] Prior to 1958 the industry coverage of the reports was not very complete, and the increases were grouped in ranges rather than being presented as medians for each industry. Since 1958 the median negotiated increases in cents per hour for the low-wage industries has ranged from a low of 5.5 cents in 1961 to a high of 16.5 cents per hour per year in 1969. For the rest of manufacturing, medians lay between 1964's low of 6.4 cents and 1969's high of 20.9 cents. For the period 1958-64 the average increase for the low-wage industries was 6.9 cents per year, while for the remainder it was 7.2 cents per year. Between 1965 and 1969 the median low-wage gain was 12 cents an hour, compared with 13.9 cents for the rest of manufacturing.

Even though negotiated settlements in the low-wage sector are smaller than those for all of manufacturing, it is possible that if suitable adjustments were made for their lower wage level, one could conclude that negotiated settlements in the low-wage sector were keeping pace relatively with those in the rest of manufacturing. This conclusion must be tempered somewhat, because it excludes negotiated welfare settlements, which in recent years have loomed rather large in certain negotiations and industries.

While it was not possible to look at median fringe benefit settlements by industry, it was possible to look at the percentage of payroll which various manufacturing industries devoted to these facets of employee compensation in 1962.[15]

The average percentage of straight-time payroll given over to paid leave was 6.2 percent, and an additional 6.0 percent was used to finance private welfare programs. Among the seven low-wage industries the median used for paid leave was 4.8 percent (mean 4.7 percent), and 3.2 percent was invested in private welfare. For the 11 remaining industries (ordnance, chemicals, and petroleum were not shown separately) the median figures were 6.8 percent (mean 6.6 percent) for paid leave and 5.5 percent for private welfare. There was little change either in the percentages or in the relative positions over the four years 1959-62. Considering the importance of paid leave and private welfare clauses to union negotiators in recent years, it is not surprising to find that there were differences in fringe benefits depending upon whether the majority of the workers in a firm were organized or not.[16]

Low-wage firms organized by unions devoted about the same percentage of their payroll to paid leave as did unorganized firms which were not in the low-wage sector. Unionism may be part of the explanation, but size of firm may also play a role, for unions are more completely represented among larger firms than they are among the smaller establishments. Without data which are cross-classified by union and firm size, it is difficult to determine the independent effects of both variables. There was, however, a marked difference in the proportion of payroll allocated to paid leave by firms of different sizes. Among the low-wage industries, the median proportion was 3.7 percent for firms with fewer than 100 employees, 4.1 percent for those employing more than 100 but fewer than 499, and 5.7 percent for those employing 500 or more. Among the higher-wage industries the medians for the same size classes were 5.1 percent, 6.2 percent, and 7.6 percent. The ratios of the median proportions of low-wage and nonlow-wage industries were essentially equal, though there was a slightly greater difference in the 100 to 499 class.

Unions and Collective Bargaining in Japan

Union membership is in part a function of the size of the establishment. In 1960 67.7 percent and in 1969 63 percent of all employees in firms employing 500 or more employees were unionized, but only 17.7 percent and 33.5 percent in firms of 100-499, and a mere 1 percent and 4.9 percent in firms of less than 30 employees. From the above should come the expectation that unions are less well organized among the low-wage sector industries than among other manufacturing industries. The expectation is correct. In 1969 the percentage of union members in manufacturing was 37.6 percent. Among most of the high-wage industries the organization rate was between 20 percent and 70 percent, with a median of 59 percent, but in the typical low-wage industry it was between 10 percent and 60 percent, with a median of about 22 percent. The proportion of union members covered by contracts was also lower among the low-wage industries. The all-industry average was 84 percent in 1965 and 90.3 percent in 1968. In 1965 the median for the low-wage group was 75.3 percent, and that of the nonlow-wage industries was 85.4 percent. During the period 1958-65 there was a large absolute growth in union membership, from 6.9 million to 10 million members. During the same years the proportion of members covered by contracts in manufacturing increased by 5.2 percent. In the last four years the growth rate for union members has slowed by about two-thirds, but the extension of contract coverage has continued. The medians of proportions of members covered by contracts for low- and nonlow-wage sectors rose about 16 percent between 1958 and 1968, the former from 65.5 percent to 82 percent and the latter from 74.7 to 91.1 percent. What basically characterized the differences between the two groups was the very high degree of contracts in a little over half of the nonlow-wage sector. Thus the highest degree of contract achievement in the low-wage group, 93.1 percent, was 2.0 percentage points above the median for the nonlow-wage group, yet the three lowest industries are all in the low-wage class. We conclude, then, that while unions in the low-wage group are less effectively organized, in recent years the degree of lag has not increased.

Unions in both countries are less well organized in the low-wage sector than in the rest of industry, and their most likely role can probably be seen in connection with the arguments advanced in Chapters 3 and 4. There it was suggested that unions help to transmit wage gains in the key sectors to the rest of industry and that they tend to protect the internal wage structure from too much competition from the external labor market. It is possible that these two factors, taken jointly, may partially explain the tie between low wages and low rates of unionization. Yet it must be remembered that in both countries the low-wage industries of today were largely the low-wage industries at the turn of the century, an era which predated union growth in both countries.

Product Market Competition in the United States

The characteristics of the low-wage sector of manufacturing presented above suggest the following generalization: Structural attributes of the sector cause the absolute productivity of the employees to be significantly lower than that obtained in the rest of manufacturing. This in turn results in lower wages. Furthermore, these attributes appear quite stable, for (1) there appears to be little movement into or out of the sector and (2) the relative wage position is fairly stable, although the position of the low-wage sector has worsened slightly. This has happened despite improvement in output per man-hour relative to the high-wage industries.

There are several attributes which may give rise to this situation. One is the character of product demand. A second is the type and extent of product and labor market competition. A third is the extent of capital utilized by each worker. The character of product demand may lead to low productivity, as in industries where the volatility of tastes and styles leads to a "sick" industry with too many firms and too little mechanization. A degree of competition in the low-wage sector which is greater than in the rest of manufacturing may mean that the higher-wage industries are able to restrict output legally and set prices at levels which allow them to pay higher wages, either for reasons of their own or because of union pressure. The possible importance of capital per worker as an explanatory variable raises an interesting point. In some labor markets it is certainly not important, a point illustrated by the fact that barbers' wages have increased with the general wage level even though the capital per worker in that industry has probably not changed in 30 years. In other cases of highly skilled crafts, it may be that human capital is the determining factor.

An examination of the extent and type of competition among industries is difficult, for reasons that are well known. It requires that appropriate geographical markets be distinguished and that some estimates be made of the role of substitute products. Since these steps are generally not possible, a common approach is to look at the degree of employer concentration in the various markets. This is usually measured by the percentage of total output of a product produced by the four largest firms within an industry. In 1954 there were 1,132 five-digit product classes in manufacturing.[17] For 23 percent of these product classes, the four largest producers made 60 percent or more of the product. Among the seven low-wage two-digit manufacturing industries, the industry median percentage of product class where the four largest firms produced 60 percent or more was 9 percent (mean 11.5 percent). In the remainder of the 20 industries the median percentage was 31 (mean 32.5 percent). The use of alternative measures or years yields similar results.

In 1958 the use of four-digit rather than five-digit product classes and a 40 percent rather than a 60 percent level of output for the four largest firms yielded a median for the 20 industries of 19.5 percent, while the median for the low-wage group was 8 percent and, for the remaining 13 industries, 25 percent. Similar results are obtained if 1947 data are used. Clearly, the degree of concentration among the low-wage industries is less than that for the rest of manufacturing. Relating the low degree of concentration more specifically to the low wage level is difficult. The principal problem is that correlations between wage rates and degrees of concentration in manufacturing tend to be low. Even for the nonlow-wage group, less tobacco (which is highly concentrated and has relatively low wages), there is not a meaningful correlation between concentration and wage rates by two-digit industry.[18]

It may be that industries which have low indexes of concentration tend to be those within which firms serve local markets because of convenience, transportation, or other reasons. Also, they may tend to be composed of smaller firms for similar reasons.

Just because an industry has a low concentration ratio, of course, that does not mean that firms within the industry may not have substantial monopoly power in some markets. They may even have considerable monopsony power in the labor markets. One example which comes to mind is the kind of industry (often a food or agricultural products processing plant) which has most firms operating in small towns in farming areas. With surplus labor (of farmers, ex-farmers, and the wives of each) firms which can offer employment "off peak" to such persons undoubtedly do have market power. In such cases the firm may be in a very competitive industry on the product market but dominate, almost as a monopsonist, the labor market. And, if wages make up a substantial part of total costs, this labor market power may be crucial to their product market survival.

This example can probably be multiplied many times over in different but similar situations. Firms may be specialized to a certain type of labor force, either by technical requirements (apparel finishing) or by seasonality. In turn, the labor force becomes specialized to them, partly by chance, partly through location, and in large measure through cultural factors and custom. (One thinks of the specialization of various immigrant groups to certain tasks around the turn of the century. Perhaps parts of the low-wage sector reflect the same underlying phenomena today.)

Another possibility is that low-wage, low-concentration-industry firms are competing in the product market with firms that for a variety of reasons can afford to be more capital-intensive. Then the survival of the low-wage firms and the jobs and (admittedly tenuous) stability they represent depends upon costs being kept down through low wages. This can even be the case where the effective product market competition force is the potential for a large firm to develop its own manufacturing facilities if small-firm suppliers cannot keep costs and prices down. But it is possible to examine the possible importance of capital stock somewhat more directly.

The Utilization of Capital in the United States

A book by George H. Hildebrand and Ta-Chung Liu, Manufacturing Production Functions in the United States, 1957, provides data which allow certain interesting calculations to be made concerning the use of capital in the low-wage sector. For the six low-wage industries for which data were presented (miscellaneous products was not given), it is possible to relate value added per production worker man-hour, production worker wages, and the capital available per production worker on a state-by-state basis. Parallel to what was found for two-digit industries in general, the correlation between value added per production worker and production worker wages across states is quite high, and all of the rank-order correlations were significant at the 1 percent level. The availability of capital may well be the chief explanation for that relationship. In four of the six industries, the extent of capital available was significantly related to the wage level. Two of the rank-order correlations were significant at the 1 percent level and two at the 5 percent level.

The importance of capital and of absolute productivity to the level of wages, and the fact that smaller firms pay even lower wages than do larger ones, raises the possibility that the size of the employing firm is important. How important, it is difficult to say. Among those industries which are not in the low-wage group, the largest-size firm pays hourly wages which are much greater than those in the lowest wage class, those employing 50 to 99 employees. The difference was 67 cents per hour, or 34 percent. For the low-wage industries the difference was not nearly so great; the medians were 30 cents an hour apart, only an 18 percent differential. A greater proportion of low-wage industry employment is in small firms than is true in the rest of manufacturing. If size of firm plays an important role, perhaps it is economies of scale that are unexploited or unexploitable in low-wage industries which make the difference. We don't know what these scale factors are, but the evidence to date suggests that they are related to the use of physical capital. In addition to the factors discussed in the preceding section, it is also possible that some people have positive preferences for working in small firms. Personal contacts with the boss and other employees, an environment which may be more within the scope of control by the individual, and other similar characteristics may be valued enough so that some people are willing to give up prospects of higher wages to enjoy them. While this line of argument is plausible, there does not seem to be any evidence suggesting how important the principle may be. Yet it would seem possible to design research studies which might shed some light on this.

The Utilization of Capital in Japan

In Table 35 it was seen that the tangible fixed assets per employee were much less in the low-wage group than in the nonlow-wage sector, and that this has not changed. This suggests that, as in the United States, the smaller absolute levels of productivity and wages per worker in the low-income industries may be associated with their modest supply of capital. Tangible fixed assets per employee in 1967 ranged between a high of 2.4 million yen in petroleum to 71 thousand yen in apparel. For establishments the high was 185,399 thousand yen in petroleum and the low of 2,339 thousand yen in apparel. Both measures--tangible fixed assets per employee and per establishment--were and are significantly correlated with cash earnings per employee. The rank-order correlations were .72 and .73 in 1963. A similar relationship also appeared to hold within industries. For two representative industries a correlation between cash earnings and tangible fixed assets by nine employment classes was calculated. In chemicals the rank-order correlation was .93, and in textiles it was .78, both significant at the 1 percent level.

Some additional insights into the capital, value added, and wage structures were obtained by calculating a composite low-wage and a nonlow-wage industry. This was done for 1963 based upon Census of Manufactures data. Certain aspects of the relationship between size of firm and low-wage industries may be of interest. While for both composite industries the magnitudes of value added, capital, and wages (all on an employee basis) rose with the increasing scale of enterprise, two differences between low-wage and nonlow-wage stand out. In smaller establishments the wages in the nonlow sector were high relative to the levels of capital and value added, whereas in large units the low-wage sector's wages were much lower than the amount of capital would lead one to predict, certainly in comparison with the nonlow-wage group pattern. To the extent that economies of scale were evident, the turning point would appear to have been at the same size class in both industries, 200 employees. Thus it must be concluded that while tangible capital is important in the explanation of low wages, certain additional factors intrude at the small-scale and large-scale levels to widen the wage differential between the two sectors.

The importance of physical capital suggested that the general role of technology may be important or, indeed, that what has been identified as low-wage may really have been the no-technology sector. One method of assessing this was to classify the industries on the basis of their proportions of technical and engineering personnel, as recorded in the 1960 census. Out of some 9.5 million manufacturing employees there were 112,900 technical and engineering personnel, about 1.2 percent. The industry ratios in manufacturing ranged between the high of 4.5 percent in petroleum to the low of .047 percent in apparel. The median for the seven low-wage industries was .21 percent, while that of the other group was 10 times larger, 2.08 percent. As a general rule, the greater the proportion of technological employees, the higher the average wage, the rank-order correlation between these two being a significant .70.

Within the nonlow-wage sector is was possible to identify a technologically oriented group. These seven industries were chemicals, petroleum, iron and nonferrous metals, machinery and ordnance (grouped together by the census), electrical machinery, transportation equipment, and precision instruments. They had a median engineer and technician ratio of 2.94 percent, compared with .88 percent for the rest of the industries, including the low-wage ones. Certain of the ratios and growth rates which had been calculated for the low-wage and nonlow-wage groups were prepared for this technological sector. The results were what might have been anticipated, since the seven industries in the technological sector were leaders in the nonlow-wage group, and no significant new insights into the low-wage problem were obtained. Thus the median value added per employee for the technological group was 1,047 thousand yen, compared with 737 thousand for the rest. The ratio of value added to wages was 2.93 for the technological group and only 2.50 for the rest of the industries, whereas the nonlow-wage and low-wage figures for the same year, 1963, were 2.60 and 2.50. Yet in terms of growth rates of value added or wages, the technological group fell behind the rest of industry in the same way that the nonlow-wage group had fallen behind the low-wage sector. Also, internal wage structures for the technological group compared with the nontechnological group were essentially the same as for the low-wage and nonlow-wage classifications.

Historical Perspective in the United States

Earlier it was noted that most three-digit manufacturing industries which were in the low-wage category in 1963 had also been low-wage industries in 1953. This raises the interesting, and perhaps disturbing, question of whether certain industries have always paid low wages. This question may be examined in two ways: by consideration of pre-World War II manufacturing censuses and by reference to studies of economic history and growth. There were 43 three-digit manufacturing industries which were included in the low-wage sector on the basis of the examinations of the 1958 Census of Manufactures and the 1963 Bureau of Labor Statistics industry wage data. With the exception of three of these industries (miscellaneous plastic products, electronic components, and tobacco stemming and redrying), it is possible to find or construct data for a roughly comparable three-digit industry from the returns of the 1939 Census of Manufactures.

To be a low-wage industry in 1939 meant that average annual wages, obtained from total wages divided by average number of wage earners, were $991 or less. This figure is 86 percent of the average for all manufacturing, the same relationship which applies to the 1963 low-wage standard and the all-manufacturing average wage. Thirty-two of the 40 1963 low-wage industries for which there were data in 1939 were low-wage industries then. Eight industries were not included: textile finishing; floor covering mills; men's and boys' suits and coats; millinery, hats, and caps; logging camps and contractors; public building furniture; watches and clocks; and office supplies. Only one of the eight, floor covering mills, reported wages above the all-manufacturing average of $1, 152. In addition to the 32 industries which were repeaters, there were six other three-digit industries which paid low wages in 1939: cigarettes, transportation equipment (not elsewhere covered), hardwood distillation, charcoal and naval stores, structural clay products, animal and vegetable oils (other than cooking), and buttons. Wage gains by the first four were sufficient to carry them beyond the poverty level by 1958. Animal and vegetable oils and buttons, while retaining their low-wage rates, were shifted into other industry groupings. Thus we find a continuation from the past of the postwar experience of a relatively stable low-wage configuration in manufacturing.

Trying to trace the pattern of low-wage industries in even earlier periods of U.S. industrial history raises a number of difficulties. These chiefly concern the quality and extent of the data, the proper matching of industries, the linking of data series from different sources, etc. Consequently it was necessary to utilize secondary source data rather than to construct original ones. One source of consistent industry information is John Kendrick's book on productivity,[19] which presents rankings of average hourly earnings for two-digit manufacturing industries for the period 1899-1953. The seven current low-wage industries had median rankings of 15 in 1889-1909, 15 in 1919-29, and 16 in 1948-53. This suggests that the relative wage positions of the various industries in manufacturing have remained almost unchanged since the turn of the century. Additional evidence of stability comes from the fact that the rank-order correlation between industry wage ranks in the earliest and latest periods is .69 (significant at the 1 percent level). The stability of the relative wage positions may also be seen in the rates of change in wages for the various industries between 1899 and 1953. Low-wage and nonlow-wage industries experienced approximately the same rate of increase in average hourly earnings for the years 1899-1929, the median increases being 368 percent for the low-wage and 363 percent for the rest. Between 1929 and 1953, however, the low-wage industries did less well. Their median rate of increase was 288 percent, compared with a rate of 323 percent for the nonlow-wage manufacturing industries.

Over this rather long period, such stability is striking.[20] Despite the uneven incidence of technological change, great shifts in demand due to population growth and urbanization, a great depression and a great war, low-wage industries managed, by and large, to keep their position. Whatever else this indicates, it certainly suggests that the forces determining their position do not seem to change rapidly.

Historical Contexts in Japan

In 1963, 29 percent of the three-digit manufacturing industries were classed as low-wage. In 1954, 56 out of 138, or 40 percent, of the three-digit industries had been low-wage. This decline from 40 percent to 29 percent suggests that there was considerable movement over the nine years, yet further analysis indicates that only about half of the improvement was real. The rest resulted from changes in the Standard Industrial Classification of industries in 1957. When the 1954 data were reclassified according to the 1957 classifications,[21] it turned out that only 50 of 143 industries, or 34 percent, were low-wage. Consequently, the improvement was only 5 percent over the nine years 1954-63. In the four years after 1963 there was a decline of an additional 3 percent. Even these movements of five and three percent, representing as they did the movement out of low wages by 19 industries and the reversion of four others, was considerably more movement than was observed in the United States. Consequently it will be of value to look more closely at those industries which shifted across the barrier. These are shown in Table 36.

All of the 11 industries which escaped between 1954 and 1963 had experienced a growth in value added which exceeded that of the average industry. Their median rate of growth was 22 percent faster. In terms of employment, there was no apparent difference. Indeed, the growth in employment of the median escaping industry was a little below that of the average. Exactly opposite results characterized the 1963-1967 escaping industries. The importance of value added in setting the limits of the low-wage sector in the postwar period can also be seen in the following: Between 1954 and 1960 the efficiency wage of the low-wage sector did not increase, but average wage gains just kept even with events in the rest of manufacturing industry, where labor cost was falling. Then, in 1960-63, when labor cost in the low-wage sector fell, the low-wage sector was able to improve its relative wage position.

Viewed at the more aggregative two-digit level and in the context of half a century of growth and development, the lack of dynamic change in the low-wage sector becomes clearer. Data for manufacturing industries has been regrouped into 19 consistent two-digit industries for key years by Watanabe Tsunehiko.[22] In 1950, six of the seven industries which here have been classed as low-wage were ranked 14-19. Only the rubber industry, which was ranked ninth in that year, avoided the lower reaches. In 1930 these seven industries again constituted six of the seven lowest industries. Furniture, at 11th, escaped and glass and cement, at 13th, would have been included. The greatest difference occurs in 1909 and 1914. In those years the current seven low-wage industries were five of the seven low-wage ones. The wood industry was just outside, at 12th position, in 1914, down from its median position five years earlier; and the furniture industry, with the sixth and seventh highest average earnings, was clearly not a low-wage industry. Included among the bottom seven at the beginning of industrialization were the paper and printing industries, which now rank among the higher-wage ones. We

TABLE 36

Three-Digit Industries Which Escaped the Low-Wage Trap, 1954-63, 1963-67

SIC Code	Growth in Value Added		Growth in Employment (year end)	(average)
	1963/1954	1967/1963	1963/1954	1967/1963
231		1.52		1.01
239	3.15		1.37	
243	2.82		2.72	
244		1.45		.80
245		1.53		.89
254	2.42		1.22	
267	3.45		.42	
294	2.36		2.22	
296	2.96		1.46	
299		1.88		.60
308	3.42		2.38	
336	2.89		1.49	
337	2.69		2.23	
342	3.06		1.70	
352		1.55		.86
353		2.46		3.18
373	2.78		2.50	
391		1.13		.85
395		1.78		.88
Median 1954-63	2.88		1.70	
" 1963-67		1.54		.89
Avg. for All 143 Industries				
1954-63	2.30		1.76	.95
1963-67	1.61			

Note: Most employment appears to have gone down because in 1963 the employment data were for firms of 10 and more employees, but in 1967 they were for those of 20 and more employees.

Source: Kōgyo Tōkei Hyō [Census of manufacturers] 1954, 1963, 1967.

can thus conclude that despite the magnitude of the changes wrought in Japanese society by half a century of rapid growth, the China incident and World War II, the structure of the low-wage sector has largely remained immune to relative change.

LOW WAGES IN TWO COUNTRIES: A COMPARISON

In low-wage industries, as in other aspects of the Japanese and American economies, there are basic similarities interspersed with some differences. At the two-digit level in both countries there has been great historical continuity in the composition of the low-wage groups. In the case of Japan, six of 1964's seven low-wage industries were among the seven lowest-paying industries in 1950. The same high proportion, six of seven, was to be found in 1930. In 1914 the consistency was somewhat less, when only five of the 1964 low-wage industries were included in the seven lowest-paying manufacturing industries. Yet the lumber industry was ranked 12th, or just one step removed from the low-wage group. The shifting industries were furniture, which was ranked sixth in 1914; printing, which in 1964 had the third highest wages but was 15th in 1914; and paper, which in 1964 was seventh but had been 16th in 1914. In the United States the seven low-wage industries in 1964 were six of the seven lowest-paying manufacturing industries. (The problems associated with tobacco and rubber, which give rise to this failure of the low-wage group to be seven of seven, have been explained earlier.) In 1947 the seven low-wage industries accounted for five of the seven low-wage industries. Rubber was then much higher, at seventh, probably reflecting the small size of the plastics industry, and food was 18th. Based upon Kendrick's data, the seven low-wage industries were five of the lowest-paying in 1948-53, four of seven in 1919-29, but five of seven in 1899-1909. Allowing for the contradictory roles of rubber and tobacco, the only difference between 1899 and 1966 in terms of low-wage industries is that the miscellaneous industry has become low-wage, and during the years 1909-37 apparel rose out of the bottom category.

Interpretation

After this review, some of the characteristics of the low-wage problem stand out in bold relief. Perhaps the most striking is the fact that some industries retain their place at the low end of the wage structure despite what would have to be called major structural changes elsewhere in the economy. In the case of occupations this could be easily understood to be rooted in the nature of the tasks involved and the small amount of skill required. For industries, however, the persistence does not seem to be so easily explainable.

There are those who would argue that the explanation lies in the emphasis upon industrial characteristics, and that if proper attention were given to personal characteristics, the paradoxes would be resolved. To quote Weiss:

> In general, employers who for any reason pay high salaries receive "superior" labor in the bargain. The general picture is one of fairly efficiently working labor markets, even where substantial monopoly may exist.[23]

Such a view must be rejected, because it is not based upon an analysis which measures the additional output associated with superior personal characteristics. It is based solely upon the fact that high-wage firms employ workers with higher skills. This is only proof of an efficient personnel department, not of an efficient labor market. The difficulties in relating personnel qualifications, such as more education, male sex, older ages, etc., to higher output which would justify the higher wages received are extensive, and to date the results are largely inconclusive.[24]

A straightforward hypothesis, which tends to be rather easily accepted by casual observers, is that the technology of low-wage industries is such that they use a large proportion of unskilled labor. But comparing such examples as automobile assembly line workers and textile mill employees can cast some doubt on this notion. Another common hypothesis is that technological change has been somehow "slower" in the low-wage industries. This impression does not find general support in data from the United States, though Japanese figures give it more support. There still remains the very difficult question of whether in fact low labor costs may be a cause of slow rates of technical progress. This could certainly be the case where, say, automation of some kind might be technically feasible, but not economical at existing relative prices.

The argument that declining industries tend to occupy the low end of the wage structure does not hold in any simple way either. For this purpose "declining" should be taken as actual declines in total employment. Rigid wages prevent short-run direct adjustments, and in the longer run those industries showing employment declines are likely to be those where technological change may change profit rates and skill requirements in such a way that (reinforced by seniority provisions or the nenkō system) they can even cause average wage rates to increase sharply. At the other end of the scale, employment in the trade and services sectors has been increasing rapidly. Yet, except for isolated segments, their wage rates tend to be those most affected by state and federal minimum wage legislation in the United States.

Only evidence of the most fragmentary kind seems to be available on the supply side of the explanation for persistently low-wage industries. The most recent evidence from Japan on the widening in inter-industry differentials in the 1920's indicates that it did not greatly affect the ranking of industries. It did, however, affect the degree of low-wageness. Looking only at the largest factories (100-500 employees) in 1909 and (1,000+) in 1964, the ratio of average wages in the 1963 low-wage to nonlow-wage groups rose from 1.11 in 1909 to 1.43 in 1964. Yet what is interesting is that if the standard of 86.5 percent of the median wage were to be independently applied to these two sets of data, in 1964 it would produce eight low-wage industries but only two in 1909. Thus, though the ranking of industries does not appear to have been affected by the great growth of differentials in the late 1920's, differentials which were reestablished after World War I, the degree of low-wageness grew perceptibly. It was not a simple case of the dispersion widening, for that increased only from .32 to .36; rather, it was as if the median moved upward through the distribution between 1909 and 1964. Thus the lower tail of the distribution moved farther away from the median, creating the low-wage group, and the upper tail moved closer to it, to maintain the dispersion.

Have there been any great shifts in the supply situation in the United States? Inter-industry differentials tended to be stable even during the period of extensive immigration. The pace of the flight from agriculture has quickened somewhat since World War II. Our data on this are as yet poor. However, it seems very likely that, especially in the South and in smaller cities, it has exerted a strong downward influence on rates in the low-wage sector. The similarly rapid postwar shift in the labor force participation rates of married women may also be an important factor. Here trade and services are likely to have been the beneficiaries of the supply pressure. Also worthy of mention is the coming of age of the babies born in the boom after the war.

In Japan there has been, except for a brief period during World War I and in a relative sense since 1960, a constant pressure from the supply side, generated both by population growth and by a movement out of agriculture and, in recent years, out of other types of self-employment. Indeed, historically it has been common to speak of agriculture[25] as being a reservoir out of which flowed the necessary labor force when times were good and into which labor flowed in times of distress, though now it is recognized that other forms of trade and services and self-employment also fill a similar role.[26]

Somewhat related to the size-of-firm effect is that of the relation between the wage level and the size of the city in which firms are located. This raises the question of real rather than money wage differences. The cost and availability of housing may be dominant influences here. So may the direct and opportunity costs of commuting. If one assumes that the value of leisure is at least as great for the small-town dweller as it is for his city cousin, a difference of one hour per day in travel time can be calculated to be "worth" about 25 cents per hour in the United States. But the problem is much more complex, involving the differences in cost and availability of income in kind and both public and private goods and services in making static comparisons. In determining pressures for mobility, all of these factors, plus uncertainty and appropriate time-discount rates, would have to be taken into account. It would seem likely that migration from agriculture has provided some downward pressure on some wage rates. The influences may be different in small towns and in big cities, but to understand them, one would need to know more about the timing, direction, and motivation of such mobility than is known now. The role of a subsistence sector, such as marginal agriculture, has been explored in the context of Japan and of underdeveloped economies. Perhaps it would be appropriate to take a similar point of view with regard to agriculture in certain parts of the United States as well as, perhaps, the armed forces and the welfare roles.

Evaluation and Policy Considerations

Of the three general propositions advanced in the introduction, the initial evidence uncovered and brought together here on the basis of this bi-national comparison suggests that the third set of causal forces is the one most consistent with the facts. Hypothesis III said that the earnings distribution depends upon endowments of abilities, tastes, and various assets. So long as these are unequal, the earnings distribution will be unequal. A relatively "low-wage" sector will then persist as a result of "natural" inequality. Consequently, all persons can achieve a minimum absolute income standard only by a system of subsidies and/or as the entire income distribution moves to higher levels. This leads to a tentative explanation of low wages in some industries. Initially the key factor is the degree of similarity in the composition of the industries in the low-wage and nonlow-wage groups. This might simply mirror the fact that Japanese technology is largely an adaptation of technology of the United States and Western Europe. Yet ranged against conformity for that reason are the vast differences in the magnitudes of many economic variables and in the institutional frameworks. The importance of the similarity of composition lies in the similarity in the nature of the structural operation of the labor aspects of the economy, as shown in Chapters 2, 3, and 4.

The second key factor is the finding in a variety of situations in both countries that wage levels are associated with the extent of available capital per worker. Normally it could be expected that the competitive operation of the labor market would drive down the wages in the high ability-to-pay sectors and that the growth of total capital would tend to lessen the difference in available capital per worker. Yet, as we have seen in Chapters 3 and 4, there are strong forces insulating high-wage workers from the full fury of the winds of competition. And in a dynamic world, the rate of invention and innovation may be rapid enough so that even a well matured economy like that of the United States may still suffer a relative capital shortage.

These two factors in turn lead to the following formulation. The technologically advanced industries will attract to them a predominance of capital, leading to the ability to pay high wages, which in turn results in their paying high wages because of union pressure, the need to attract and hold high-talent manpower, or grounds of equity.

The nontechnological group under wage and profit pressure will attempt to utilize that segment of the labor force which is willing to work for low wages. A combination of rigidity in the operation of labor and capital markets and in the accepted relative wage position between different groups, plus a continuing innovation in the technological group and relative capital shortage, tends to perpetuate the existence and to ensure the continuity of the low-wage sector. It is only when circumstances conspire to drive value added per worker rapidly upward, as they did for the 11 Japanese low-wage industries between 1954 and 1963, that an industry is able to escape from the low-wage trap.

Policy Considerations

For the immediate need to "solve" the low-wage problem there are two basic approaches. One is to increase the productivity of the workers involved; the second is to deny employers the right to utilize low-wage labor. The first can be accomplished by affecting the complementary factors of production with which these workers are employed, or by investments in the education, skill, and training of the individuals themselves. The second can be most easily accomplished by the imposition of significantly higher minimum wages. In Japan it would also require a change in the minimum wage system to allow the government to set a national minimum. The results of this chapter can perhaps be utilized to assess the likelihood of success which policies in these areas might enjoy.

A lack of education, the principal measure of employee quality available, while associated with lower than average income, does not always appear to be closely correlated with employment in a low-wage occupation or industry. Thus, while remedial programs to improve an individual's ability to perform job-related tasks may be desirable in themselves, they would not seem to warrant a major role in a policy designed to combat "low wages." Among other factors of production, the only one which appeared to have a significant relationship to low wages was a low level of physical capital per worker. Additional research into the causal relationship between limited capital and low wages would be required before intelligent policies to deal with this could be devised.

There are several reasons why a policy which denied employers the opportunity to use low-wage labor might be employed. One is to prevent employer exploitation. A second is to prod the employer into a more efficient utilization of labor. The third is to redistribute income to the low-wage sector through higher wages and prices. As indicated earlier, there is no general evidence that low-wage employers are exploiting the workers. While it is possible that the low absolute productivity of the low-wage sector might be improved by forcing employers to pay higher wages, the persistent ability of the industries which constitute this sector to remain low-wage in the face of all the economic and political changes of the last 60 years suggests that the causal forces are too deep-seated to respond to a significant increase in the minimum wage by raising productivity. This leaves redistribution as perhaps the most meaningful basis upon which to support an increase in the minimum wage. The argument is quite straightforward and consistent with the model of the formation of the low-wage sector given above. Certain individuals, whether through union action, the accidents and fortune of birth, product monopoly, etc., obtain wages which are disproportionate when compared with wages of those whose jobs are in the low-wage sector. A redistribution away from the favored toward these others can be obtained by artificially raising the prices of labor and product in the low-wage sector. To the extent that this redistribution tax is not avoided, either by a refusal to purchase or a compensating increase in incomes in the high-wage sector, such a program can succeed.

Since past experience with minimum wage legislation in the United States has not involved really significant increases when compared with the size of average hourly wage increases, there are few data from which to judge the probable success of such a redistribution tax. The data that are available do suggest, however, that increased unemployment would, at least in part, be the result, for wealth and power are not easily given up. And unlike the current restrictions on the importation of foreign agricultural laborers, the impact of the lost jobs would not fall on Mexico and Canada.

Before turning to a more positive approach, some mention should be made of those public policies which tend to encourage the payment of low wages. No attempt is made here to provide a catalog of such policies, but merely to point to their existence and provide an illustration or two. Perhaps the clearest cases are the Interstate Highway Program and the apparel industry in the United States. Since an immigrant population in New York is no longer available, certain parts of the apparel industry have shifted to rural areas, within a given number of hours by truck from New York. Therefore, the more efficient the road network, the more extensive the source of employees willing to work for low wages. Subsidized rail lines may play the same role in Japan. The example also points up a related problem: that low wages, even in the apparel industry, may seem attractive when compared with certain kinds of alternatives, like subsistence agriculture in both countries.

By implication and explicit statement, it has been suggested that certain traditional policies often proposed for use in the low-wage field are imperfect. These counterproposals are, in turn, quite modest. The internal stability of the manufacturing portion of the low-wage sector, the only one for which reasonably complete historical data are available, is impressive. This indicates both the real strength of the economic forces which maintain certain industries as low-wage ones, and the role of continued supplies of potential low-wage labor. Viewed in this way, the solution of the low-wage problem is essentially one of obtaining increases in total productivity which will be sufficient to raise the level of low wages to a satisfactory standard of living.

NOTES

1. The discussion of low-wage industries in the United States and the conceptual basis of the chapter are largely taken from "Low Wage Employment: An Inventory and an Assessment," September, 1965, a report prepared in fulfillment of Grant 91-20-06 under Title I of the Manpower Development and Training Act, United States Department of Labor. The work under this grant was done and the report written in association with Professor George E. Delehanty of Northwestern University. Views expressed here, however, should not be attributed to either Professor Delehanty or the Department of Labor.

2. See the Introduction to Wages in Japan and the United States 1966, a joint report of Japan's Ministries of Labor and International Trade and Industry, and the United States Department of Labor.

3. See also Laurie D. Cumings, "The Employed Poor: Their Characteristics and Occupations," Monthly Labor Review, LXXXVIII (July, 1965), 828-35, which utilizes a significantly lower arbitrary standard for low wages.

4. See "Seikatsu Suijun no Kokusai Hikaku" [International comparison of living standards], Kokumin Seikatsu Kenkyū [Research studies in national standards of living] (June, 1965), 1-31.

5. An alternative approach would have been to select that income which was received by the 20th percentile income group. In 1964 this would have been 27,000 yen a month. A second alternative would have been to use an income equivalent to the $3,000 level in an earlier year when the United States per capita income was closer to that of Japan. This yielded a monthly income of 38,500 yen, a figure below which 36 percent of the Japanese population were found. A third alternative was to use the ratio of $3,000 to median family income in 1963, or 48 percent. This produced a monthly wage of 23,200 yen which is too low.

6. It is traditional for the Japanese to think of low wages and small-scale undertakings as inter-related, especially within the same industry. This view is not discussed directly because I feel that the general industry characteristics are also very important. Also, the work on U.S. data centered upon industry rather than size characteristics, and there is an extensive literature on this aspect of the Japanese economy for the reader who is interested. See, for example, Tokutarō Yamanaka, ed., Small Business in Japan (Tokyo: Japan Times Co., Ltd., 1960); Taikichi Itō, "The High Growth of the Japanese Economy and the Problems of Small Enterprises," The Developing Economies, 2 (1963), 137-68; and Yoshio Sato, "Recent Trend of the Small Business Problem in Japan," Keio Business Review, III (1964), 77-94, and the literature cited therein.

7. For example, Leonard W. Weiss, "Concentration and Labor Earnings," American Economic Review, LVI (March, 1966), 96-117; Tuvia Blumenthal, "The Effect of Socio-Economic Factors on Wage Differentials in Japanese Manufacturing Industries," Economic Studies Quarterly, XVII (September, 1966), 53-67.

8. Using industry characteristics alone, the squared regression coefficients are smaller than .05, while combinations of industry and personal characteristics move the R^2's into the range .25-.35. Weiss, op. cit., pp. 104-07. Low R^2's also characterized equations for Japanese wage differentials discussed in Chapter 4.

9. The results reported here are consistent with those reported in Lloyd Ulman, "Labor Mobility and the Industrial Wage Structure in the Post-War U.S.," Quarterly Journal of

Economics, LXXIX (February, 1965), 73-97. Ulman found correlations of .16 between changes in hourly earnings and changes in employment for 57 industries between 1948 and 1960 and of -.11 between 1957 and 1960.

10. Tsunehiko Watanabe, "Technological Progress and Economic Growth," Kyoto University Institute for Economic Studies Discussion Paper No. 6608 (June, 1966).

11. George J. Stigler, Capital and Rates of Return in Manufacturing Industries (Princeton: Princeton University Press, 1963).

12. U.S. Federal Trade Commission and Securities and Exchange Commission, Quarterly Financial Report for Manufacturing Corporations.

13. Data are from the Bank of Japan's Chū shō Kigyō Keiei Bunseki [Analysis of the management of small and medium-size firms]. The years 1957-59 are modest exceptions to the trend, for the ratios were only 2.0 to 2.6.

14. Bureau of National Affairs, Collective Bargaining Negotiations and Contract Facts for Bargaining and Labor Relations Yearbook.

15. Employer Expenditures for Selected Supplementary Compensation Practices for Production and Related Workers, Bureau of Labor Statistics, Bulletin No. 1428 (April, 1965).

16. Organized firms in low-wage industries had a median percentage of payroll applied to paid leave of 5.8 percent, unchanged from 1959, while their unorganized counterparts had a median of 3.1 percent, down .1 percent since 1959. Similar differences are observable in the remainder of the industries. There the medians for paid leave were 7.2 percent, up by .3 percent since 1959 for the organized firms, and 5.4 percent, up .3 percent since 1959.

17. Betty Bock, Concentration Patterns in Manufacturing, National Industrial Conference Board Studies in Business Economics, No. 65 (1959).

18. The role of concentration in the determination of industry wage levels has recently been investigated, using data

from the 1/1000 sample of the 1960 population census. The author concluded that the degrees of concentration and union organization were important in the determination of individual earnings, though the introduction of personal characteristics into the statistical analysis tended to reduce the significance of industry variables. Weiss, op. cit., pp. 114-16.

19. John W. Kendrick, Productivity Trends in the United States (Princeton: Princeton University Press, 1961).

20. Similar results were reported by Donald E. Cullen, "The Inter-industry Wage Structure, 1899-1950," American Economic Review, XLVI (June, 1956), 353-69; and Sumner H. Slichter, "Notes on the Structure of Wages," Review of Economics and Statistics, XXXII (February, 1950), 88-89.

21. See the 1957 ed. of Nihon Hyōjun Sangyō Bunrui [Japanese standard industrial classification] for details of the changes

22. Tsunehiko Watanabe, "Industrialization, Technological Progress and Dual Structure," a paper given at the International Conference on Economic Growth at the Japan Economic Research Center, Tokyo, September, 1966, p. 31.

23. Weiss, op. cit., p. 116.

24. Using low-wage criteria consistent with those employed here would result in classifying 26 of the 112 operative suboccupations of the 1960 census as low-wage occupations. The median educational level of 12 of these was within .6 year of the overall operative median of 9.6 years. The median educational levels for the other 14 occupations ranged from 9 to 7.9 years, but these 14 occupations constituted only 36 percent of the operative suboccupations which had median educational levels of nine or fewer years. Such a result is not consistent with the idea that the labor market pays better-educated persons more because they produce more. A similar situation exists in Japan. In 1958 a 30-34-year-old male white-collar worker with a prewar middle school education and employed in an establishment of 10-99 persons earned 17.4 thousand yen a month in the lumber industry and 24.4 thousand yen in iron and steel.

A rationale similar to the above also explains why no mention has been made of the proportion of women employed as a factor in low wages, though it is known in both Japan and the United States that women are disproportionately employed in low-wage industries. Such a fact is germane only if the productivity of women is lower than that of men or if they have a taste for a particular type of work. Neither of these would seem to be relevant in a discussion of factory employment.

25. Okōchi Kazuo, Reimeiki no Nihon Rodō Undō [The Japanese labor movement in its dawning period], Shinsho Series, 115 (Tokyo: Iwanami, 1952), pp. 4-5.

26. See the discussion in Miyohei Shinohara, "Formation and Transition of the Dual Economy in Japan," Hitotsubashi Journal of Economics, VIII (February, 1968), 28-31.

CHAPTER 6

SUMMARY AND CONCLUSIONS

In the opening section of Chapter 1 various forces were suggested as the basic ones whose operation in America and Japan could be expected to shape the respective labor economies. In the subsequent chapters the characteristics of particular facets of the countries' labor economies were presented and analyzed. On the whole, the data and the analyses suggested a basic similarity between the two countries, but a similarity which was interlaced with differences. The differences were shown to be related to a variety of factors. Some were historical, as in the case of the locus of union power. Others were cultural, as in the nature of the employment relationship. The later commencement of economic growth was found to be the major underlying cause of differences in the ratio of primary to tertiary employment. In general the differences were most pronounced when the discussion centered upon structural or institutional aspects of the economies, while the similarities were most pronounced in discussions of functional relationships. An example of the latter would be the importance of profits and key bargains in the determination of aggregate wages.

This chapter will try to draw some of these differences and similarities into coherent conclusions using the framework outlined in Chapter 1.

The basic conclusions of the earlier chapters can be divided into two groups: those which involve a basic similarity in the two economies, and those which involve differences. The areas of similarity are the following: (1) Institutionally, aggregate wage patterns are set by key industries and followed by other industries, while the level of increase for both leading and following industries depends upon some combination of institutional and market forces. The exact mixture of influences under various conditions is still an unsettled question in both economies. (2) Occupational wage differentials in the United States and age and size-of-firm wage differentials in Japan are determined primarily by the needs and characteristics of internal labor markets. (3) The nature and character of low-wage industries are governed largely by their technology and the levels of capital available to each worker. (4) The basic orientation of the principal union organizations, national unions in the United States and enterprise unions in Japan, is toward economic gains for their members--in other words, business unionism. (5) The attitude of the government has been transformed from the historical one of hostility through a brief period of encouragement to the current one of neutrality or indifference. (6) High levels of marginal employment and of unemployment are concentrated among those workers whose qualifications also tend to be marginal.

The areas of difference are the following: (1) The locus of union power in Japan resides in the enterprize (plant or company) union, but in the United States much more of it generally resides in the national union, especially when dealing with large firms. (2) Job mobility levels are much higher, by a factor of several times, in the United States than in Japan. (3) The concept of the employment relationship is familial in Japan, but contractual in the United States. (4) Labor force participation rates for women have been declining in Japan, but rising in the United States. (5) The proportion of the work force engaged in primary and manufacturing industries and occupations is higher in Japan than in the United States, while those employed in broadly defined service industries and occupations is smaller in Japan than in the United States.

Explanations for these principal differences and similarities, as well as other minor and allied ones, were suggested in the individual chapters. Most of the explanatory mechanisms may be identified as belonging to one of three broad classes of factors: technology, history and culture, and the stage of economic development. The association of the characteristics of the economies with the causal factors may be seen in the following.

TECHNOLOGY

Within the United States and Japan a few industries have, by virtue of their size, the apparent economies of scale which have tended to make a small number of individual firms within these industries large employers of labor and the principal supplies of its products, and their advanced technology, become the profit and ideological leaders of the manufacturing sector. As a result of their preeminent position, they have become leaders in the establishment of employment conditions. In the 1920's, when unions were weak or nonexistent, the emulation of their employment conditions was the result of management decisions. However, it is probable that employee knowledge of advances in the employment conditions in major firms was a not insignificant factor in other companies' management decisions to be followers. With the development in the post-war years of an extensive union movement, the union developed into a convenient institutional mechanism through which the system of key pattern setters and follower companies came to be regularized.

Technology also played a decisive role in the establishment of the internal labor market and the subsequent elevation of that market to a primary role in the determination of wage differentials. In Japan the process was originally associated with the heterogeneity of capital equipment available to the early Japanese firms. It was aided by the group orientation of Japanese society, which easily adapted to the use of the nenkō system. In the United States the increasing specialization of capital used in various industries and the consequent need for on-the-job training led to the reduction in the number of entry ports into the average industrial wage structure. The addition of union insistence upon seniority as the principal measure of promotion and the need for union approval for basic rearrangements of internal wages tended to fix even more firmly the limitation on ports of entry and length of service as the key to higher wages. In Japan the rise of the union in a period of privation, uncertainty, and redundant employees at the end of the war gave new life and meaning to the nenkō system, which before 1940 had applied to only a small portion of the kōin (blue-collar workers). It has also been technology which in recent years has dictated a movement away from pure nenkō factors (age, education, length of service) in wage determination. Yet the movement toward mixed factors including shokunōkyū (ability wages) has not changed the reliance upon factors internal to the firm in setting the wage level, largely because it has not changed the emphasis upon long-term employment. Thus, it is clear that the logic of technology and the swift rise of unionism, though by somewhat different routes in Japan and the United States, enshrined internal labor market forces as the basis for establishing wage differentials.

The uniformity with which the same industries are the ones which pay low wages in both countries and the association between low levels of physical capital per worker and low wages is highly suggestive that technology is the basic factor in the determination of which industries will pay low wages. This is especially true in Japan. Prior to 1912 the distribution of wages in manufacturing was narrower than it was to become in the 1920's. The number of relatively low-wage industries was also fewer. Since the widening of manufacturing industry wage differentials in the 1920's was the result of changes in technology and yielded an increased number of low-wage industries, additional credence is given to the technological explanation of low wages.

There is still the nagging question of why the highly machine-paced and simplified work of the auto worker should command high wages while the equally machine-paced and simplified work of the textile worker yields relatively low wages. There appear to be two answers. The higher profits, market power, and greater dollar value of capital per worker utilized in automobiles give rise to pressures within the internal labor market to maintain high levels of wages. The conversion of textile employment early in its existence from a largely male to a largely female occupation also appears to have played an important role, since it allowed the industry access to a low-wage labor supply.

This leads to two additional observations. Where the technology of operations is most suitable for women, the probability of their employment will be greatest. Then, to the extent that the supply curve of women lies below that of men, these industries will tend to be low-wage ones--not because of the women, but because of the complementarity between the industries' technology and the ease of employing women. The second observation is that where internal labor markets have historically included promotion along given job ladders and some of the jobs on those ladders require the use of men, there will be a strong tendency to employ men in all the jobs, even though only a few employees will ever be promoted. The difficulty of women is obtaining jobs in American management and the difficulties of blacks in upgrading themselves are consistent with these observations.

HISTORY AND CULTURE

The business orientation (their primary concern with their own members' working conditions) of American unions lies largely in the three-quarters of a century (1820-90) series of failures by humanitarian and social welfare-oriented unions, such as the Knights of Labor, to achieve either their broadly conceived goals and aims or viability. Therefore the skilled craft unions, which came together to form the AFL in the 1880's, believed that if they concentrated their energies upon the situation in the work place, there was the hope of success. This hope, for them, was largely fulfilled. The relative success of business unionism, at least to the mid-1920's, only reinforced the lesson which had been learned in the 1880's. It is true that there was a wider social concern among some who founded the CIO in the midst of the depression, yet the very depressed conditions which persisted until the war provided a powerful stimulus to the newly organized, both AFL and CIO, unions to place their main energies in business unionism.

In Japan business unionism is not so readily apparent because of the close association between national labor groups and left-oriented political parties. Careful examination of the record strongly suggests that the unions' principal efforts have been divided into two parts, political activities at the level of the national labor groups (Sōhyō, Dōmei, etc.) and economic activities at the level of the enterprise union and the company confederations. These economic activities have been devoted to the needs of the job situation, long-term tenure, higher wages, opposition to rationalization (reductions in the size of the work force in conjunction with technological change), etc. The decision to place an emphasis in these areas was never accorded the dignity of an ideology and has been largely masked by the rhetoric of the highest union officers. The political and economic division stems largely from the failure in the early 1920's of more idealistically oriented unions and the supression by the Occupation authorities of radical political activities by the unions while allowing more traditional economic demands to be advanced.

The logic of business unionism in Japan and the United States may also be phrased more theoretically.[1] In periods of labor surplus, a union can hope to succeed only if it can either (1) organize a sufficient number of workers so that managers and capitalists cannot play one group of workmen against another or (2) organize a strategic minority which, on the principle of exclusion, may exercise some control over the conditions of their own employment. Minority exclusionist unions will of necessity be firm-, skill-, or industry-based. This, in conjunction with the concept of exclusion, leads naturally to business unionism. In the United States the two key periods of union formation, the 1880's and the 1930's, were both periods of excess labor. Japan's two key periods, the 1920's and 1946-48, were likewise periods of surplus labor. In the United States, it was initially the skilled craft union which was established and then, in the 1930's, the single-employer industrial union. Both of these excluded from their concerns those who were not members. In Japan the exclusionist principle was applied upon the basis of those who were regular employees as against all categories of temporary, day, and subcontract laborers. Thus it may be concluded that historical situations of surplus labor during those key periods of union development in both countries played a decisive role in the establishment of an ideology of business unionism. The ideology was formally adopted in the United States, but its adoption in Japan has been largely on a de facto basis.

The locus of unemployment is largely a product of culture and history. As a simple first approximation, it is rational for employers initially to offer employment to the most skilled and most trustworthy members of the labor force. This leads to the expectation that unemployment will tend to be concentrated among members of those classes with the least skill and responsibility. Since with rare exceptions no members of the labor force are literally unemployable, employer policy merely means that the incidence and number of weeks of unemployment are concentrated among these groups. In societies with equality of opportunity, such a situation means that the least qualified of each generation would carry the brunt of the unemployment, but that the burden would not tend to become fixed upon any one class. Where opportunity is not equal, unemployment will tend to become centered upon the lower classes, either because of discrimination, as in the case of the American black or the Japanese burakumin (eta, or outcast), or because these groups have not had the opportunity to develop the kinds of skills or responsibility which firms with the most desirable employment seek.

In recent U.S. experience, unemployment has tended to center upon two types of groups. One consists of the natural minority groups--first-generation immigrants, blacks, etc.--and the other consists of skill or age groups least in demand by employers, currently laborers and the young who lack work experience.

In Japan the major difference has been that Koreans and burakumin have been too few to bear the complete burdens of surplus labor, so much of it has had to fall upon ordinary Japanese. The principal method of judging the potential skill and responsibility, and thereby allocating the burden of unemployment, has been through judgments concerning schools attended and associations made. Those who were deemed most highly qualified in terms of skill and responsibility, on the basis of their education and associations, obtained the opportunity for employment among the better-paying firms and government agencies. Those who did not were forced to wander forever among the ranks of the temporary employees, workers in small companies, and in self-employment or unpaid family service. Academic ability and low tuition rates did allow some talented lower-class Japanese to improve their positions by gaining admission to the better schools. Even then the better job opportunities were probably closed to them because they would still largely lack the appropriate contacts and persons, except for their professors, to speak in their favor. This tended to make the system less equalitarian.

It can be concluded that hiring systems based upon education, skill, and responsibility in both countries largely determine those who have access to the better employment opportunities and those who must wander among the U.S. unemployed and Japan's marginal jobs. Over time there are equalitarian aspects, but they have been reduced in Japan by the group orientation of the society and in the United States by the large group of individuals against whom it is easy to discriminate.

Culture and history are also the basis of one major difference between the labor economies. This relates to the group orientation of much of Japanese society, as against a more individualistic orientation of the American workingman.[2] In Chapters 1 and 4 it was pointed out that group orientation has been a major factor in the Japanese emphasis upon internal labor markets, lifetime employment systems, and low rates of mobility among employees of the better employers. The more individualistic orientation of the employment relationship in the United States has encouraged inter-firm mobility, at least among younger employees. At older ages, especially after the age of 35, it appears that, as in Japan, the demands of the internal labor market have drastically reduced the levels of mobility.

THE PACE OF ECONOMIC DEVELOPMENT

Japan's lower level of economic development and her much later start along the road to economic growth and development have given rise to a number of structural differences between the labor economies. In general, however, these structural differences should be considered to represent lags rather than fundamental differences. Japan has not yet completed her movement through the secondary or manufacturing stage of development, whereas in the United States this stage was essentially completed in the mid-1940's and the country then entered the tertiary, or service and white-collar, stage of development. Given that the distribution of occupations varies across industries, with increased proportions of professional, service, and governmental employees in a tertiary as opposed to a secondary economy, it would appear that the differences in industrial and occupational distributions of employment are largely the result of these different stages of growth.

Stages of growth differences are probably also reflected in the divergent patterns of labor force participation of women. The two primary determinants of participation are family income and wages offered to women. Higher family income acts to draw married women out of the labor force, and job opportunities act to draw them into the labor force. Normally the higher levels of income available in the more developed economies would, other things being equal, tend to depress the participation of women. If, however, as has been the situation in the United States, the process of economic growth also creates a movement in job creation which opens up increased opportunities for female employment, it is not possible to predict in which direction married women's labor force participation will move. The direction will depend entirely upon the relative strength of the two opposing forces: rising income and increasing job opportunities.

During periods of rapid increase in the labor force participation of women in the United States, 1942-46 and the early 1950's, women served as a source of relatively low-wage labor when otherwise labor costs were rising and labor markets were generally tight. This suggests that as the labor shortage in Japan deepens and real wages rise, employers may move to enlarge their potential labor supply by encouraging the reentry of married women into the labor markets. To a small degree this has already happened, but it should increase with time.[3] Here too, then, the structural difference in labor force participation reflects the different development stages rather than more fundamental differences.

There is one aspect of the stage of growth which may well reflect a difference in structure rather than merely a lag. The rapid growth of real output in Japan, which averaged 10.6 percent for years 1957-58 to 1967-68,[4] was achieved within an economic structure which fostered high rates of capital formation, placed an emphasis upon industrial output as opposed to public service output, encouraged corporate mergers, gave favorable tax treatment to corporate income, etc.[5] Thus the industrial structure within which the Japanese economy has operated has been much more favorable to business than has been true in the United States. The impact of this different structure upon the labor aspects of the economy are more difficult to ascertain. It might have been expected that wages would have risen more rapidly in the favored sector, mainly large firms in manufacturing, than in others. There is evidence to suggest that this did occur until about 1960, but of late has been reduced (see Table 23.)[6] In the last decade what seems to have occurred is that significant real wage gains in the larger firms have been more than paid for by improved productivity, but that the relative labor shortage, which was one by-product of the rapid growth, has pushed up wages among medium-size and small enterprises, which in turn has led to the recent rapid increase in the consumer price index.[7] The tie between government policies and price inflation would seem reasonably evident, but the connection to the labor economy would seem to be more diffuse. The economic growth pattern of Japan seems heavily influenced by government policy. Once the influences of growth upon the labor aspects of the economy are accounted for, additional direct or indirect governmental influence upon the labor economy is much less evident.

SUMMARY

On the basis of the foregoing discussion, several conclusions may be drawn. The first is that the twin factors of technology and the level of economic development are basic in the determination of the structure and functions of the labor economy. Secondly, the primary role of the historical and cultural dimensions has been partly to mold institutions into a particular character and, more generally, to color the external way in which certain aspects of the labor economy are seen.

The clearest example of these is probably in the area of the firm's internal labor market. In both economies the separation of these markets from the external economies stems largely from the same factors: questions of equity and the importance of technology-induced on-the-job training for increased productivity. In both economies the practical imports of the internal labor market are rising wages with age and a reduced level of mobility. In Japan the institutions of the internal labor market make these wage and mobility patterns quite evident. In the United States the importance of these forces tends to be masked by the emphasis upon occupational wages and very high mobility rates among the younger age groups.

Another example is in the area of pattern bargaining. The United States, with its national unions concentrated in particular industries, seems to be a natural candidate for a pattern bargaining type of aggregate wage determination. Japan, with its enterprise unions, would appear less favorable to the development of such bargaining. Yet in the form of Shuntō (spring wage offensive) the Japanese have a clear-cut and dynamic institution of pattern bargaining. This last suggests that strong economic and political forces are capable of converting a variety of institutional forms into the instruments through which they exert their influence.

Taken together, these two suggest that in an inter-country analysis of labor economies, it will be possible to utilize the same sort of theoretical approach in both economies, but that care must be taken to understand the true meaning of what may appear at first to be completely divergent structural forms. This has been done with respect to Japan and the United States. It was found that functionally the economies are very similar, though there are some differences in institutions and structure. However, the relationships of institutions to the various functional requirements are quite similar.

Our tale is now told: difference and similarity, similarity and difference, change and growth, growth and change--but underlying all a basic similarity between the labor economies of Japan and the United States which implies that there are lessons to be learned in each country which are applicable to the other.

NOTES

1. This formulation is drawn from Adolf Sturmthal, "Industrialization and the Labor Movement," in Japan Institute of Labor, Labor Relations in the Asian Countries (Tokyo, 1967), pp. 51-62.

2. Arthur M. Whitehill, Jr., and Shin-ichi Takezawa, The Other Worker (Honolulu: East-West Center Press, 1968), pp. 98, 101, 343.

3. A different conclusion concerning future labor force participation is reached in Nihon Keizai Chōsa Kyogikai [Committee on Japanese economic surveys] Shōwa 40 Nendai no Koyō Mondai [Current employment problems] (Tokyo: Kaikyō Purinta, 1967), I, 64-65.

4. Data are from Keizai Kikakucho [Economic planning agency], Kokumin Shotoku Hakusho [White paper on national income] (1963), p. 176; and Kokumin Shotoku Tōkei [Statistics on national income] (1968), pp. 78-79.

5. For a description of these policies, see Kozo Yamamura, Economic Policy in Postwar Japan (Berkeley: University of California Press, 1967), Chapters 6, 8, and 9; and Eleanor M. Hadley, Antitrust in Japan (Princeton: Princeton University Press, 1970), Chapters 14-17.

6. This is discussed in some detail in Yamamura, op. cit., Chapter 9.

7. See, for example, the brief discussion "The Price Problem," Japan Quarterly, XXXVII (January-March, 1970), 6-10.

BIBLIOGRAPHY

Abegglen, James C. The Japanese Factory. Glencoe, Ill.: The Free Press, 1958.

Akamatsu, Tadashi Hanami. "Women Workers and Retirement After Marriage," Japan Labor Bulletin, VIII (May, 1969), 6-8.

Allen, G. C. Japan's Economic Expansion. London: Oxford University Press, 1965.

Anderson, Paul S., Michael L. Wachter, Adrian W. Throop, and George L. Perry. "Wages and the Guideposts: Comments and Reply," American Economic Review, LIX (June, 1969), 351-70.

Ayusawa, Iwao F. A History of Labor in Modern Japan. Honolulu: East-West Center Press, 1966.

Baba, Masao. "Economic Growth, Labor Unions, and Income Distribution." Postwar Economic Growth in Japan. Edited by Ryūtaro Komiya. Berkeley, Calif.: University of California Press, 1966.

Ballon, Robert J., Makuto Sakurabayashi, and Ichiro Tsunekawa. Wage Survey of Male Blue Collar Workers. Sophia University Socio-Economic Institute, Industrial Relations Section, Bulletin 14 (April, 1967).

Behman, Sara. "Wage-Determination Process in United States Manufacturing," Quarterly Journal of Economics, LXXXII (February, 1968), 117-42.

__________. "Wage Changes and Relative Factor Prices in Manufacturing," Review of Economics and Statistics, LI (August, 1969), 227-38.

Bernstein, Irving. The Lean Years. Baltimore, Maryland: Penguin Books, 1966.

Blackmore, Donald J. "Occupational Wage Relationships in Metropolitan Areas, 1961-1962," Monthly Labor Review, LXXXVI (December, 1963), 1426-31.

Blau, Peter M., and Otis D. Duncan. The American Occupational Structure. New York: John Wiley and Sons, 1967.

Blumenthal, Tuvia. "The Effect of Socio-Economic Factors on Wage Differentials in Japanese Manufacturing Industries," Economic Studies Quarterly, XVII (September, 1966), 53-67.

__________. "Scarcity of Labor and Wage Differentials in the Japanese Economy, 1958-1964," Economic Development and Cultural Change, XVII (October, 1968), 15-32.

Brody, David. Steelworkers in America. Cambridge, Massachusetts: Harvard University Press, 1960.

Bock, Betty. Concentration Patterns in Manufacturing. National Industrial Conference Board Studies in Business Economics, No. 65 (1959).

Cain, Glen G. Married Women in the Labor Force. Chicago: University of Chicago Press, 1966.

Cook, Alice H. Japanese Trade Unionism. Ithaca, New York: Cornell University Press, 1966.

Cullen, Donald E. "The Inter-industry Wage Structure, 1899-1950," American Economic Review, XLVI (June, 1956), 353-69.

Cumings, Laurie D. "The Employed Poor: Their Characteristics and Occupations," Monthly Labor Review, LXXXVIII (July, 1965), 828-35.

Dore, Ronald P. "Mobility, Equality and Individualism in Modern Japan." Aspects of Social Change in Modern Japan. Edited by Ronald P. Dore. Princeton: Princeton University Press, 1967.

Dunlop, John T. "The Task of Contemporary Wage Theory." New Concepts in Wage Determination. Edited by George W. Taylor and Frank C. Pierson. New York: McGraw Hill, 1957.

Eckstein, Otto, and Thomas A. Wilson. "The Determination of Money Wages in American Industry," Quarterly Journal of Economics, LXXVI (August, 1962), 379-414.

Economic Planning Agency, Economic Survey of Japan, 1967-68. Tokyo: Japan Times Ltd., 1968.

Evans, Robert, Jr. "Wage Differentials, Excess Demand for Labor, and Inflation: A Note," The Review of Economics and Statistics, XLV (February, 1963), 95-98.

________. "Shuntō Japanese Labor's Spring Wage Offensive," Monthly Labor Review, XC (October, 1967), 23-28.

Gordon, Robert A. "Unemployment Patterns with Full Employment," Industrial Relations, VIII (October, 1968), 46-72.

Grob, Gerald E. "Knights of Labor and the Trade Unions, 1878-1886," Journal of Economic History, XVIII (June, 1958), 176-92.

Grossman, Jonathan. William Sylvis, Pioneer of American Labor. New York: Columbia University Press, 1945.

Hazama, Hiroshi. "Fukuri Kokka ni okeru Keiei" [Prosperity and management], Chūō Kōron [Public opinion review] (March, 1962), pp. 274-83.

________. Nihonteki Keiei no Keifu [A genealogy of the Japanese system of management]. Tokyo: Nihon Noritsu Kyōkai, 1963.

Hildebrand, George H., and George E. Delehanty. "Wage Levels and Differentials." Prosperity and Unemployment. Edited by Robert A. Gordon and Margaret S. Gordon. New York: John Wiley and Sons, 1966.

Hotani, Rokuro, and Takashi Hayashi, "The Evolution of Wage Structure in Japan," Industrial and Labor Relations Review, XV (October, 1961), 52-66.

Isao, Kamata, et al. "Kaihyō Kigyō no Shoshin sei Kaku" [Promotion policies in representative companies], Chūō Kōron [Public opinion review] (September, 1966), pp. 306-25.

Itō, Taikichi. "The High Growth of the Japanese Economy and the Problems of Small Enterprises," The Developing Economies, 2 (1963), 137-68.

Japan, Bank of. Chūshō Kigyō Keiei Bunseki [Analysis of the management of small and medium-size firms], semi-annual.

__________. Shuyō Kigyō Keiei Bunseki [Analysis of the management of principal firms], semiannual.

Japan. Federation of Employers Association News, quarterly.

Japan Institute of Labour. Japan Labor Statistics. Tokyo, 1967.

__________. Japan Labor Bulletin, monthly.

__________. Kokusei Chōsa ni yoru Shokugyō Jinko no Saikōsei [A reconstruction of Japanese census data on occupational employment]. Census Research Series 70, 1965.

Japan, Ministry of International Trade and Industry. Kōgyō Tōkeihyo [Census of manufacturers], annual.

Japan, Ministry of Labor. Chingin Kōzō Kihon Tōkei Chōsa [Basic survey of wage structure], annual.

__________. Rōdō Kumiai Kihon Chōsa [Basic survey of trade unions], annual.

__________. Rōdō Sōgi Tokei Chōsa Nen Hōkoku [Yearbook of labor dispute statistics], annual.

__________. Rōdō Tōkei Nenpō [Yearbook of labor statistics], annual.

__________. "Sangyō betsu in mita gijutsu kakushin to Chingin Seido no Dākō" [Trends in technical changes and the wage system]. 1967. (Unpublished.)

__________. Shoninkyū Chōsa [Census of initial salaries], annual.

Karsh, Bernard. "The Exportability of Trade Union Movements: The Japan-U.S. Trade Union 'Cultural Exchange

Program,'" *The Changing Patterns of Industrial Relations.* Tokyo: Japan Institute of Labor, 1965.

——— and Robert E. Cole. "Industrialization and the Convergence Hypothesis: Some Aspects of Contemporary Japan," *Journal of Social Issues,* XXIV, (1968), 45-63.

Katakami, Akira. "Types of Joint Consultation and Their Relations to Collective Bargaining in the Industrial Relations of Japan," *Bulletin of University of Osaka Prefecture,* Series D, 10 (1966), 52-64.

Kawada, Hisashi. "Continuity and Discontinuity: An Approach to Industrial Relations Systems." *The Changing Patterns of Industrial Relations.* Tokyo: Japan Institute of Labor, 1965.

Kazuo, Noda. "Traditionalism in Japanese Management," *Rikkyō Diagaku Shakaigakubu Ken Kyū Kiyō, ōyō shakai Kenkyū Dai Rokushū Bessatsu* [Rikkyō University Faculty of Social Science research bulletin, applied social science research], 6 (March, 1963).

Kerr, Clark, John T. Dunlap, Frederick H. Harbison, and Charles A. Myers. *Industrialism and Industrial Man.* Cambridge, Massachusetts: Harvard University Press, 1960.

Kindleberger, Charles P. *Europe's Postwar Growth.* Cambridge, Massachusetts: Harvard University Press, 1967.

Kishimoto, Eitaro. "The Characteristics of Labour-Management Relations in Japan and Their Historical Formation," *Kyoto University Economic Review,* XXXV (October, 1965), 33-55, and XXXVI (April, 1966), 17-38.

Kono, Shigemi, and Mitsuru Shio. *Inter-Prefectural Migration in Japan, 1956 and 1961: Migration Stream Analysis.* New York: Asia Publishing House, 1965.

Koshiro, Kazutoshi. "Industrial Relations in the Japanese Iron and Steel Industry, II," *Japan Labor Bulletin,* V (July, 1966), 4-8.

Levine, Solomon B. *Industrial Relations in Postwar Japan.* Urbana, Illinois: University of Illinois Press, 1958.

__________. "Labor Markets and Collective Bargaining in Japan." The State and Economic Enterprise in Japan. Edited by William W. Lockwood. Princeton: Princeton University Press, 1965.

__________. "Postwar Trade Unionism, Collective Bargaining, and Japanese Social Structure." Aspects of Social Change in Modern Japan. Edited by R. P. Dore. Princeton: Princeton University Press, 1967.

Levinson, Harold M. "Pattern Bargaining: A Case Study of the Automobile Workers," The Quarterly Journal of Economics, LXXIV (May, 1960), 296-317.

Lewis, H. Gregg. Unionism and Relative Wages in the United States. Chicago: University of Chicago Press, 1963.

Maher, John E. "The Wage Pattern in the United States, 1946-1957," Industrial and Labor Relations Review, XV (October, 1961), 3-20.

Matsuda, Yasuhiko. "Government Employees in Japan," Japan Labor Bulletin, V (October, 1966), 4-8, and V (November, 1966), 4-8.

McGuire, Timothy W., and Leonard A. Rapping. "The Role of Market Variables and Key Bargains in the Manufacturing Wage Determination Process," Journal of Political Economy, LXXVI (September-October, 1968), 1015-36.

Nakamura, Atsushi. "Rōdō shijō Chingin Kōshō to Chingin Kattei" [The labor market and wage negotiations and decisions]. Kōza Nihon Keizai [Japanese economic lectures]. Tokyo: Nihon Hyōronsha, 1965.

Nakamura, James I. Agricultural Production and the Economic Development of Japan, 1873-1922. New York: Columbia University Press, 1966.

Nihon Keizai Chōsa Kyogikai [Committee on Japanese economic surveys]. Shōwa 40 Nendai no Koyō Mondai [Current employment problems]. Two volumes. Tokyo: Daikyō Purinta, 1967.

Nishikawa, Shunsaku. "Domestic Labor Migration in Japan," Keio Business Review, I (1962), 79-99.

Odaka, Konosuke. "The Structure of Japanese Labor Markets," Riron Keizai Gaku [The economic studies quarterly], XVIII (June, 1967), 25-42.

__________. "Historical Developments in the Wage Differential Structure." (July, 1967). Unpublished.

__________. "A History of Money Wages in the Northern Kyūshū Industrial Area, 1898-1939," Hitotsubashi Journal of Economics, VIII (February, 1968), 71-100.

__________. "Rōdō Shijō no Jukyū Chōsei Kinō to Chingin Kōzoku" [Toward a Theory of Wage Differential Structure], Keizai Kenkyū [Economic review], XIX (April, 1968), 168-72.

__________. "A Study of Employment and Wage-Differential Structure in Japan." Unpublished Ph. D. dissertation. University of California, University Microfilms, 1969.

Odaka, Kunio. "Implications of Dual Allegiance in the Modernization of Industrial Relations in Japan." The Changing Patterns of Industrial Relations. Tokyo: Japan Institute of Labor, 1965.

Ohkawa, Kazushi. The Growth Rate of the Japanese Economy. Tokyo: Kinokunya, 1957.

__________, and Henry Rosovsky. "Postwar Japanese Growth in Historical Perspective: A Second Look." Economic Growth: The Japanese Experience Since the Meiji Era. Edited by Lawrence Klein and Kazushi Ohkawa. Homewood, Illinois: Richard D. Irwin, 1968.

Okamoto, Hideaki. "Enterprises in Japan: A Sociological Perspective," Japan Labor Bulletin, VI (July, 1967), 4-8.

Ōkochi, Kazuo. Labor in Modern Japan. Science Council of Japan, Economic Series 18. Tokyo, 1958.

Patrick, Hugh T. "Some Aspects of the Interwar Economy." A paper presented to the Sixth Seminar Conference on Modern Japan, San Juan, Puerto Rico, January 2-7, 1968.

Pelling, Henry. American Labor. Chicago: University of Chicago Press, 1960.

Perlman, Richard. Labor Theory. New York: John Wiley and Sons, Inc., 1969.

Perry, George L. Unemployment, Money Wage Rates, and Inflation. Cambridge, Massachusetts: M.I.T. Press, 1966.

__________. "Wages and Guideposts," American Economic Review, LVII (September, 1967), 75-82.

Ripley, Frank C. "An Analysis of the Eckstein-Wilson Wage Determination Model," Quarterly Journal of Economics, LXXX (February, 1966), 121-36.

Reder, Melvin W. "The Theory of Occupational Wage Differentials," American Economic Review, XLV (December, 1955), 833-52.

__________. "Wage Structure Theory and Measurement." Universities National Bureau Committee for Economic Research. Aspects of Labor Economics. Princeton: Princeton University Press, 1962.

Sakurabayashi, Makoto, and Robert J. Ballon. "Labor-Management Relations in Modern Japan: A Historical Survey of Personnel Administration." Studies in Japanese Culture. Edited by Joseph Roggendorf. Tokyo: Sophia University, 1963.

Sano, Yōko. Chingin Kettei no Keiryō Bunseki [The Measurement and Analysis of Wage Determination]. Tokyo: Tōyō Keizai Shinhōkai, 1969.

__________. Dainiji Taisenzen niokeru Kibobetsu Chingin Kukusa Shiryō [Data on wage differentials by size of firm before World War Two], Keio University Institute of Management and Labor Studies Series, 25 (1961-62).

__________. "An Analysis of Industrial Wage Differentials," Keio Economic Studies, IV (1966-67), 29-43.

__________. "Waga Kuni no Shuntō Soba no Bunseki to Yoseki" [An analysis and prediction of the shuntō settlement in

Japan], Rōsei Jihō [Labor review] No. 1876 (January 6, 1967).

__________. "Waga Kuni Chingin Kittei Kōzō no Keiryō Bunseki (=)" [A quantitative analysis of wage determination in Japan (2)], Mita Gakkai Zasshi [Mita journal of economics] (May, 1968), pp. 51-80.

__________, Koike Kazuo, Ishido Hideo, Izeki Toshiaki, and Shimeda Haruo. "Chingin Hakyū no Kōzō to Mekanizumu" [The structure of wage spill-over], Sangyō Kenkyū [Review of industry and labor], VI (December, 1968), 1-163.

__________ and Toshiaki Izeki. "Labor and Product Markets as Wage Determiners: A Local Market Study," Keio University Institute of Management and Labor Studies, XVIII (September, 1966).

Sato, Yoshio. "Recent Trend of the Small Business Problem in Japan," Keio Business Review, III (1964), 77-94.

"Seikatsu Suijun no Kokusai Hikaku" [International comparison of living standards], Kokumin Seikatsu Kenkyū [Research studies in national standards of living], IV (June, 1965), 1-31.

Seltzer, George. "Pattern Bargaining and the United Steel Workers," Journal of Political Economy, LIX (August, 1951), 319-31.

__________. "The United Steel Workers and Nationwide Bargaining," Monthly Labor Review, LXXXIV (February, 1961), 129-36.

Shōwa Dojinkai, ed. Wagakuni Chingin Kōzō no Shiteki Kōsatsu [Japanese wage structure]. Tokyo: Shiseido, 1960.

Shimada, Haruo. "Waga Kuni Chingin Kettei Kizō no Keiryō Bunseki" [A quantitative analysis of wage determination in Japan I], Mita Gakkai Zasshi [Mita journal of economics], LXI (May, 1969), 541-70.

__________. "A Quantitative Analysis of Negotiated Wage Settlements in Japan." (December, 1968). Unpublished.

Shinohara, Miyohei. "Formation and Transition of the Dual Economy in Japan," Hitotsubashi Journal of Economics, VIII (February, 1968), 1-38.

Shirai, Taishiro. "The Changing Pattern of Collective Bargaining in Japan," British Journal of Industrial Relations, III (July, 1965), 201-09.

Simler, N. J., and Alfred Tella. "Labor Reserves and the Phillips Curve," Review of Economics and Statistics, L (February, 1968), 32-49.

Stigler, George J. Capital and Rates of Return in Manufacturing Industries. Princeton: Princeton University Press, 1963.

Sturmthal, Adolph. "Industrialization and the Labor Movement." Labor Relations in the Asian Countries. Tokyo: Japan Institute of Labor, 1967.

Sumiya, Mikio. Social Impact of Industrialization in Japan. Tokyo: Japanese National Commission for UNESCO, 1963.

Taira, Koji. The Dynamics of Japanese Wage Differentials, 1881-1959. Unpublished Ph. D. dissertation. Department of Economics, Stanford University, 1961.

__________. "The Labor Market in Japanese Development," British Journal of Industrial Relations, II (July, 1964), 209-27.

Tominaga, Kenichi. "Shokugyō Idō no Yukue" [The state of occupational mobility], Chūō Kōron [Public opinion review] (March, 1962), pp. 322-38.

Totten, George O., III. The Social Democratic Movement in Prewar Japan. New Haven: Yale University Press, 1966.

__________. "Collective Bargaining and Works Councils as Innovations in Industrial Relations in Japan During the 1920's." Aspects of Social Change in Modern Japan. Edited by Ronald P. Dore. Princeton: Princeton University Press, 1967.

Trauber, Irene B. The Population of Japan. Princeton: Princeton University Press, 1958.

Tsuda, Masumi. The Basic Structure of Japanese Labor Relations. Tokyo: Musashi University, 1965.

__________. "Nenkō Joretsu Chingin to Nenkō Seido" [Age and service Based Wages and the Wage System] Nihon-gata Chingin Kōzō no Kenkyū [Research on the structure of Japanese Wages]. Edited by Shinohara Miyohai and Funehasihi Noamichi. Tokyo: Rōdō Hōgaku Ken Kyū Sho, 1962.

Ulman, Lloyd. "American Trade Unionism-Past and Present." American Economic History. Edited by Seymour E. Harris. New York: McGraw Hill, 1961.

Umemura, Mataji. Sengo Nihon no Rōdō Ryoku [The postwar Japanese labor force]. Tokyo: Iwanami Shoten, 1964.

__________. "Nenkō Chingin ni suite" [Some notes on wage structure], Keizei Kenkyū [Economic review], XVIII (April, 1967), 160-63.

United States Department of Labor, Bureau of Labor Statistics. Handbook of Labor Statistics, 1968, 1969.

United States Department of Labor. Wages in Japan and the United States, 1966.

Ware, Norman J. The Labor Movement in the United States, 1860-1890. New York: Vintage Books, 1964.

Watanabe, Tsunehiko. "Price Changes and the Rate of Change of Money Wage Earnings in Japan, 1955-1962," Quarterly Journal of Economics, LXXX (February, 1966), 31-47.

__________. "Industrialization, Technological Progress and Dual Structure." Economic Growth: The Japanese Experience Since the Meiji Era. Edited by Lawrence C. Klein and Kazushi Ohkawa. Homewood, Illinois: Richard D. Irwin, Inc., 1968.

Weiss, Leonard W. "Concentration and Labor Earnings," American Economic Review, LVI (March, 1966), 96-117.

Whitehill, Arthur M., Jr., and Shin-ichi Takezawa. The Other Worker. Honolulu: East-West Center Press, 1968.

Yamamura, Kozo. "Wage Structure and Economic Growth in Postwar Japan," Industrial and Labor Relations Review, XIX (October, 1965), 58-69.

__________. Economic Policy in Postwar Japan. Berkeley: University of California Press, 1967.

Yamanaki, Tokutarō, ed. Small Business in Japan. Tokyo: Japan Times Co., Ltd., 1960.

ABOUT THE AUTHOR

Robert Evans, Jr., Associate Professor and Chairman of the Economics Department at Brandeis University, has long been active in the study of the labor economics and industrial relations of Japan and the United States. He is a member and current Secretary of the Japan Economic Seminar. His research interests have been broad. He is the author of papers on subjects as diverse as slavery, clipper ships, and labor law. In the latter area, he is the author of Public Policy Toward Labor (1965). Most recently, in addition to Japan, he has been concerned with criminal justice and prisons.

Professor Evans was formerly a member of the Industrial Relations Section of the Massachusetts Institute of Technology and spent 1966-67 as a visiting Professor at the Sangyō Kenkyū Sho (Institute of Management and Labor Studies) of Keio University in Tokyo. He has also performed research for and been a consultant to the governments of Massachusetts, Canada, and the United States.

Mr. Evans received a degree in economics and chemical engineering from the Massachusetts Institute of Technology and was awarded a Ph. D. in economics from the University of Chicago. He lives in Acton, Massachusetts, with his wife and six children.